The Roger Caras Dog Book

ROGER CARAS

The Roger Caras Dog Book

SECOND EDITION

Photographs by
ALTON ANDERSON

M. EVANS & COMPANY, INC.
New York

For
Yankee, Penny, "T", Nel, Jeremy, Oomiac, Bridgette, Tigger,
Ludo, Libby, Winnie, Peter, Tutu,
and lots of other friends standing square on four legs.

Copyright © 1980, 1992 by Roger Caras
Photographs © 1980, 1992 by Alton Anderson
New Breeds photographed by Jane B. Donahue, Welesly,
Mass. (Portuguese Water Dog, Tibetan Spaniel), and Bette
Isacoff (Finnish Spitz).

Library of Congress Cataloging-in-Publication Data
Caras, Roger A.
      [Dog book]
      The Roger Caras dog book / Roger Caras ; photographs by Alton
   Anderson. — 2nd ed.
         p.   cm.
      Includes index.
      ISBN 0-87131-706-0 : $12.95
      1. Dog breeds.   I. Anderson, Alton.   II. Title.   III. Title: Dog
   book.
   SF426.C34   1992
   636.7′1—dc20   92-10175
                                                            CIP

M. Evans and Company, Inc.
216 East 49th Street
New York, New York 10017

Manufactured in the United States of America

9 8 7 6 5 4 3 2 1

Contents

Author's Note

The descriptions that follow have been written to help potential but relatively inexperienced dog owners make breed selections best suited to their own life-styles. All the information in this book should be viewed in that light.

There are very few absolutes in this world, at least in my experience, and much of what follows is admittedly opinion. It is not my opinion alone, however. There has been input from dog handlers, judges, and breeders. John Mandeville, assistant to the president of the American Kennel Club, has read the manuscript and made valuable suggestions. Violent disagreements, though, should be directed to me alone. The final choice of language and each individual statement or assessment was mine alone to make.

Check the scaled characteristics. They are relative, of course, but again they are opinion *after* consultation. They suggest the amount of exercise and coat care a breed is likely to require and how well suited it is likely to be to an urban environment. Inevitably there will be readers whose personal experience with a representative of a breed will differ from that suggested by the scale. This is the old problem with absolutes again. The scales indicate the general rule one is likely to encounter when dealing with a breed.

A popularity ranking is listed for each breed. This number is derived from the population of dogs of that breed registered with the American Kennel Club in 1989. Again, it is not necessarily an absolute, but it is indicative.

A point of clarification: the word *dog* is used indiscriminately, both in these opening remarks and in other places in this book. In true canine parlance *dog* means male alone and *bitch* means female, just as *drake* is the male and *duck* is the female of the species. As used here, though, the generic *dog* means canine friend of either sex.

The superb photographs in this book are largely the work of one man, Alton Anderson. He has been called the Karsh of Canines. I rather think of Karsh as the Anderson of People. His work is representative of some of the finest dog photography ever done, and I am honored to share this volume with him. Unfortunately, Alton died before this new edition appeared. He is missed.

The use of *Ch* before a dog's name means that he or she was a champion when the photograph was taken. If no *Ch* appears, the dog was probably on the way to becoming a champion. A champion is a dog who has won fifteen points in recognized shows. There are also stipulations about major shows—a major show is one in which a given minimum number does vary from breed to breed, and a show may well be a major for one breed but not for another.

Under most breeds there will be entered a breed club with an address. This address is almost invariably the home of an officer of the club and it can change as elections are held. You can check with the American Kennel Club at 51 Madison Avenue, New York City, NY 10038 for an update on a club's address.

Well over half the homes in the country have dogs as members of the family. Man has been keeping dogs for over twenty-five centuries, since well back into the time of the cave dwellers. There must be something to the idea, to the dog itself, and what it does to our hearts and our sense of belonging. My family owns nine dogs at the moment, and although I expect few of my readers to be mad enough to try that many companion animals at one time, I do hope many of you will find the help you need in the pages that follow, enough to select the one or two or three dogs best suited to you and best able to share a life-style with you. Happy reading but, above all, happy dog.

Introduction:
Owning a Dog

The most important aspect of dog ownership is original selection. Everything starts with your choice—all that is good and all that might turn out badly.

What then are the considerations? What is important for the prospective dog owner to know? Given an individual or a family on the one hand and the whole vast world of dogs on the other, the only way to proceed is by process of elimination. Let's see what you should consider, and how you should honestly assess your answers.

Point One: Should you own a dog at all?   Not everyone should own a dog. Not even everyone who thinks they should! Dogs are meant for certain kinds of people. Before committing yourself, make certain you are one of them.

This is not to suggest that people who aren't right for dogs are themselves bad or deficient. It is essentially a matter of life-style. Does your lifestyle allow you to accept the responsibility for another very dependent life? Dogs, unlike children, are never independent. From the day a dog enters your life until the day he leaves (and that can be fifteen years or even longer), he will be wholly dependent on you for all the essentials of canine life: food, water, shelter, exercise, coat care, veterinary prophylaxis, and treatment. As one who has owned not one but several dogs all his life, I do not see these matters as problems. They all are attended to without a second thought. But that is not necessarily the way it will be for everyone.

This is a book on dog selection, not a book on dog care or training. We must, though, touch on those matters briefly in this discussion of whether *you* as an individual should consider adding a dog to your life. Are you active physically? If you are, then there is an endless variety of dogs for you to select from—*if* you are willing to share your active physical time with your pet. If you are sedentary by nature or restricted in your activities, then you are either not a dog-owning candidate or a person who should choose from a smaller range of breeds.

Do you travel a great deal? If you do, who will care for your pet while you are away? Is your home empty all day and sometimes into the evening? Who will be a companion for your pet during those long hours? A dog is not a fixture, he is a companion, and only with companionship will your dog keep the promise of his breeding.

Are you the kind of person who will control your temper when a puppy breaks rules? For all puppies do break all rules. They wet and mess in the house, they chew shoes, and they cry in the middle of the night. None of this need be a problem for the dog lover, because the dog can be trained away from each bad habit as it is revealed, just as children are trained. But as it is with children, you must be gentle and understanding, though firm. Is that you?

New dogs must be licensed and must get shots. All dogs must be fed every day (some more often than once). They must have clean water at all times, they must be given heartworm medicine during the mosquito season, they must be wormed periodically. They must also be checked for ticks in the summer, be exercised under control, have coats seen to, and be loved. Is all of that your thing?

I purposely have tried to stress the negatives here because to understate them would be a disservice to the people who are thinking of getting their first dog, and to the dog they might buy or adopt. None of these things need be problems or hardships when seen in the balance of pro and con, but they can be of considerable importance to some people.

What of that balance? What are the positive elements of dog ownership? Love and companionship head the list. Your dog will give you both without limit or qualification. No dog ever accused his owner of doing something wrong, of forgetting something, or complained of his mood. A dog just loves, no questions asked. In a world full of pressures, that is worth a great deal.

Dogs help children grow up into healthy adults. Dogs teach children a kind of love and responsibility that they can get nowhere else. We learn all kinds of love in this world from all kinds of sources: siblings, parents, grandparents, teachers, friends, playthings—and pets. Dogs have a brand of love all their own, and demonstrably children benefit from it.

Dogs are objects of pride. People talk about their dogs and show them off. You have seen that yourself, surely. Pride is worth something in hours of doubt. Your dog can be an "up" factor when everything else is "down."

I have known people so roughly treated by time and fate that a dog was all they had left in the world. I remember a very old man, a widower whose only child was either deceased or living on the other side of the world, I have forgotten which. The man was restricted in his physical activities by poor health. His seventeen-year-old Boston Terrier was literally all that was left to him on this earth. The love that man knew for and from that dog was remarkable. I truly believe he would have gone quite mad without it. When the veterinarian finally convinced the old man that his dog had aged beyond help and really had to be put to sleep, the man stuffed papers under the kitchen door, turned on the gas from his range, and sat down with his friend in his arms. They went to sleep together.

I know a certain home for severely alienated alcoholics of the skid-row type. At the time these men (and sometimes boys) are admitted, they rarely are able to talk to each other, much less anyone who doesn't share their bitterness. They have hit bottom. As an initial phase of their treatment, they are given Labrador Retrievers to care for. It has been found that the dogs enable the men to bridge over into normal give-and-take relationships that they otherwise might find impossible to achieve. One man in that home told me that *his* dog was the first responsibility he ever had been able to accept without panicking. He also pointed out that *his* dog never asked him why he was a drunk and a "bum."

I visited a school for PINS (people in need of supervision). We used to call them juvenile delinquents. The boys live in cottages, twenty-four to a unit, and each unit raises a breed of dog. The boys do a fine job of it and learn not only how to trust something that loves them but how to accept the responsibility for caring for something that needs their love in return. The authorities at this school believe that the program has helped immeasurably in the effort to save boys on their way to permanent trouble.

There are scores of stories like these, all examples of how man can benefit from owning a dog. On the other side of the ledger stand such nuisances as housebreaking, rabies shots, and chewed shoes. Now you decide whether you should have a dog. At this point, the choice is a matter of human consideration. Only later will it involve a dog.

Point Two: Do you want a purebred or a random-bred dog? There has been so much nonsense written on this subject that some clarification is needed. All dogs, purebred and random-bred (I prefer *random-bred* to *mongrel*, *mutt*, or *mixed breed*), are members of one species. It may seem hard to believe that the Chihuahua, the Saint Bernard, and the Old English Sheepdog are all one species along with the nondescript random-bred in the local pound, yet it is true. Purebred dogs, all former random-breds themselves, have been refined by continuous breeding in order to obtain certain characteristics. By breeding generation after generation with a goal in mind, a dog is evolved that "breeds true." As long as he is henceforth bred to his own kind, he will produce his own kind. At some point (and that point for many breeds has been vague, indeed), the dog is said to be purebred.

Because all dogs belong to one species, they all have approximately the same needs. It is simply not true that a random-bred dog makes a better pet or is more intelligent than a purebred dog. A single random-bred dog *may* be more intelligent than some individual purebreds, but he almost certainly will be less intelligent than others. Certain breeds have been bred for intelligence, but we will get to that matter shortly.

Well, then, what is it to be—purebred or random-bred? There are pluses in obtaining a random-bred dog from a pound or humane shelter. The cost is negligible, and you will have the satisfaction of saving that dog from the gas chamber or worse. But there are also decided advantages to the purebred dog. You will have some idea of what you are getting. By knowing the breed and its characteristics, you at least can make a reasonable assessment of your puppy as a mature animal. That is rarely true with a random-bred pup. You can show a purebred dog, while you cannot show a random-bred. And some people just like the feeling of having a superb example of anything around them. Although either kind of dog can make a loving pet, some people just like that added feeling of style and perfection. I feel my family has the solution. We always have both around, and we love them equally.

If you do opt for a random-bred dog, there are two things you must remember. He will require exactly the same food, veterinary care, and love that the finest purebred dog would need, and you *must* have the females spayed and the males altered. *No random-bred dog should ever be permitted to reproduce.* Millions must be destroyed every year for the want of homes.

Point Three: Should you choose a dog or a bitch?　Which makes the best pet? There is no definite answer. Bitches do *tend* to be a little softer, and this is more true of some breeds than others. Even there, though, it is a matter of opinion and experience. I honestly can't say which is best, and in our house we always have both.

Are there any clear-cut advantages or disadvantages? Some. It is more expensive to spay a bitch than it is to alter a male. (Spayed and altered dogs cannot be shown, but if dogs are not intended for the show-ring, then your life and theirs will be much improved by a little surgery.) Bitches that have not been spayed can be messy when they come into heat twice a year, and they tend to attract a lot of stray males to your front yard.

Many people will disagree with my next statement, but I think it is easier to find a splendid male example of most breeds than it is to find a superb female. Many females tend to have a "bitchy look," and that is often less attractive than the broader, heavier, "doggy" or masculine, look. That is *not* a rule, however, and some of the most magnificent show dogs seen every year are bitches. You may have to look a little longer, that's all.

Males tend to wander and fight more than females, but that is a tendency, not an inevitable fact of life. There is also the fact that mature males lift their legs, and if you have a lot of expensive shrubs in your yard, that can be bad. Dog urine can burn and eventually kill even hardy evergreens. Bitches do not have this problem, and since they generally don't go around marking territory as dogs do, they can be taught to use a special place in the corner of the yard.

Once again, when it comes to male versus female, it is a matter of personal choice. Of course, if you are getting a superlative example of a breed and you wish to do further breeding, it is the bitch that has the puppies—an incontrovertible fact of life.

Point Four: What age should the puppy be?   Only under the most extraordinary circumstances should you consider a puppy under ten weeks of age. A puppy needs that time with his mother and to some extent with his litter mates. After the age of ten to twelve weeks, though, it becomes a matter of options that have more to do with your ambitions than with the dog himself. A young pup will be *likely* (not certain) to settle into a new home and become imprinted with his new family quickly. Older dogs may be slower to do so, but often that is not the case.

If you are seeking an example of the breed for showing or breeding (more likely, both), you will do well to wait a little longer than three months, because the older the pup gets, the more you will be able to tell what he will be like at maturity.

These factors must be weighed in each individual case, and no declarations of absolute certainty can be made. I have seen four- and five-year-old dogs come into a household, settle down immediately, and be the best of all possible pets, and I have seen young puppies simply not make it at all. I have owned two Poodles in my life. The first one was obtained as a puppy of twelve weeks. After biting everything and everybody in sight from the beginning, he had to be given up on. He was the only dog I have ever failed with. The other Poodle came to us at the age of four and was probably the nicest little dog I have ever known. She came from a home where there were no children and no other pets into a new home literally exploding with kids and animals. She adapted instantly.

Point Five: Should you get a coated or noncoated dog?   Whether you have settled on a purebred or a random-bred dog, you can pretty well divide either field into dogs with coats that need care and dogs with coats that do not. Eventually, whatever else you do by way of selection, you will have to choose between the two. With purebred dogs it can be more important because there is a standard you are trying to maintain, although coated random-bred dogs also should be kept neat and clean and free from nasty mats and tangles.

As to which you select, it is a very personal choice. Do you want to fuss? No one knows but you. In the breed descriptions that constitute the bulk of this book, the amount of coat care each breed needs is indicated. The rest is a matter of taste and how much time or money you want to invest. You do have that choice—if you don't like caring for a dog's coat or if you haven't the time, you can have it done by a service, which will even pick up and deliver. All you have to do is pay. But do not select a coated breed unless you are going to see to the job one way or the other. A coated dog is a commitment, but as the descriptions that follow show, it is a matter of degree.

Point Six: Do you want a large or small dog? If you have, let us say, decided on a purebred dog and have chosen between a male and a female (although you should not do that until you find what the breeder has available) and between a coated and a noncoated dog, you have gone a long way toward eliminating a fair percentage of the dog world. The next major determination should be size. How big a dog should you get?

The factors here are many and often complicated because they involve you and your life-style, your immediate neighbors, the place where you live, and not least of all, the welfare of the dog you select.

Large dogs produce more fecal matter than small dogs and are messier to that degree. Large dogs, generally, are more intimidating and make people who are not dog fanciers uncomfortable in elevators and apartment-house lobbies. A very large dog who is not obedience-trained or is ill-behaved in any way is more of a menace than a small dog in direct proportion to the size difference. Also, of course, a large dog who tends to be nervous or even hostile with strangers is a very heavy responsibility.

Throughout the breed descriptions in this book it will be noted that I generally am opposed to large dogs in the urban setting, as well as in some suburban settings. It is not just that large dogs need a great deal of exercise, and they do; it is the life-style in a crowded environment that militates against them. Many small dogs require even more exercise than some large breeds, so exercise isn't so much the problem as how your neighbors will react to your dog. That must be taken into account if future unpleasantness is to be avoided. Few spectacles are as disheartening as fights and lawsuits between neighbors because one of them has gotten the wrong dog or has failed to train him properly. It is a bad situation, and often the dog is the victim. Either he is poisoned or shot by someone whose senses have left him altogether, or he is passed along from home to home. It is much wiser to get the right dog in the first place.

There are easy-to-train and very difficult-to-train large and small dogs, so the division cannot be made along those lines. There are lethargic and very active large and small dogs, so the division does not lie there either. The main factors governing size are: How much house room do you have, assuming your dog will be an inside animal? Will you or your guests be constantly tripping over your pet, and will you have to drive him from room to room because his size is oppressive? How much outside room do you have? Will your dog get regular exercise? Remember, the shorter a dog's legs are, the less ground he has to cover to be exercised. A Corgi walking one mile is like a Great Dane walking five or six. Big dogs need big areas at least part of the time. How close are you to your neighbors? Will you be going through an apartment-house lobby, or up and down in a public elevator? Will your neighbors react to a Bull Mastiff or a Rottweiler the way they will to a Corgi or a Boston Terrier? That, surely, must be taken into account.

Some people favor large dogs in any setting because they are afraid of intruders and see their pet as a deterrent. There is no doubt that some people with criminal potential will to a degree be deterred by a large, formidable dog, and there is no doubt whatsoever that some dogs make better watchdogs than others (this is all discussed in the breed sections that follow). But deterrence is not reason enough. There are some things you should know about so-called guard and attack dogs before making any decision based on safety precautions.

Professional criminals rarely are bothered by guard dogs. Any dog who is close enough to bite is close enough to be put out of action. A man with a gun can shoot a dog as easily as he can shoot you. A professional "casing" a home or business can easily poison a dog in advance. Poisoned bait tossed into a yard or pen or slipped through a mail slot or window that has been jimmied open an inch or two is all that is needed. A five-dollar tear-gas pen or a can of Mace ordered through the mail will also wipe out any dog for several minutes at least. Anyone wanting to enter a fenced yard simply has to climb the fence and wait for the infuriated guard dog to start leaping up at him. A cinder block dropped from six or eight feet settles things down very quickly. It is not the professional criminal who gets hurt; it is the innocent bystander or the crazy kid who decides on impulse to break in. The punishment for teen-age burglary and vandalism in this country is not death, and that should be taken into account when considering the need for guard or attack dogs.

Five out of the six breeds now in the Caras household are large dogs. We have Bloodhounds, a Golden Retriever, a Siberian Husky, an English Bulldog, a random-bred something-or-other Shepherd, a Yorkshire Terrier, and a Papillon. Past dogs have included the two Poodles, a Pug, and other random-breds; as a boy I had an English Cocker Spaniel, a Collie, a Wire-haired Fox Terrier, a Boston Terrier, and other assorted canines of less than clear-cut origin. I point this all out to show that I am not personally prejudiced. We have nine dogs today, five of them large, because we live in a country house and have land and our own beach, a large fenced area, and enough people always on hand to care for our pets. We also have five cats, a horse, and other sundry creatures. I have no prejudices against any animal, but I have a great many against a person who will buy the wrong animal for the wrong reason in the wrong place. Not only will that animal suffer, but discontentment grows and feeds upon itself. In time, poorly chosen animals brought into urban and suburban settings result in ever stricter rules and regulations affecting all pet owners. The wise choice of a pet is the most important step any pet owner ever takes.

Point Seven: Where do you get your pet? The obvious answer is that you get your pet wherever you can find a fine, healthy puppy who is what you want him to be. A friend may give him to you; you may discover perfectly fine, pet-quality, purebred as well as random-bred pups in pounds and shelters waiting for adoption; or you may buy through an ad in the local newspaper. There are some *best* places, however.

If you are looking for a random-bred pup, then you should adopt him. There are hundreds of pounds and shelters in this country and they all have puppies, all the time. You gain a double blessing when you adopt a pet from them. You gain your friend and companion, and you save a life. Millions of these animals are destroyed every year for the want of a home.

If you are seeking a purebred dog, however, you should seek the specialty breeder. Perhaps a point of clarification is in order here. By definition, anyone who breeds a dog is a breeder. Simple as that. If I take two dogs of any kind and put them together and they mate and have puppies, I am a breeder. The differences among *kinds* of breeders, however, are profound and should be of interest to every prospective dog owner.

In the American Midwest principally, but in other parts of the country as well, a number of people (many of whom seem to be hog farmers) supplement their income by mass-producing puppies for the pet trade. The wholesale trade journals carry ads, and one farmer advertises that he has sixty-four breeds of dogs in stock!

A professional breeder who devotes his or her life to perfecting a line of one breed (rarely two) finds it a full-time occupation. One does not develop outstanding examples of Cocker Spaniels, or Basset Hounds, by tossing two similar dogs in a pen. It is a long, arduous job that takes years of development and consultation, heartbreak, investment, and ultimately triumph. No hog farmer can do that properly with sixty-four breeds in his spare time.

Repeatedly, these backyard breeding operations are raided by local law enforcement authorities and humane organizations, and the conditions they find in many cases are appalling. I have gone through the files of the Humane Society of the United States in Washington, D.C., and the photographs in those files defy description. I have personally visited a number of "puppy-mill" breeders in Kansas and Missouri. It is hog-farm operations like these that produce many of the puppies we see in pet shops. Other sources of "puppy-mill" dogs are incidental local breeders, regular breeders who want to dispose of what they consider substandard puppies, and anyone else, really, who walks off the street with a basket of salable puppies. Most, I would venture to say, come from the mass-producers.

You are not going to get a show-quality puppy from a mass-producer or a pet shop except by accident. You may not even get the full-blooded dog you are paying for.

There is no possible way that the American Kennel Club, the principal dog-registration agency in the United States, can check on the hundreds of thousands of dogs that are registered every year. Let us say that I own a registered Beagle dog and a registered Beagle bitch. I breed them, register the litter, and ship the puppies to a pet shop along with copies of their pedigree. Fair enough. Then either my bitch or my dog dies or grows too old to breed. I happen to have a Foxhound or even a mixed-blood Beagle that looks pretty good. The A.K.C. has no way of knowing that my dog has died or that he or she is no longer breeding, and so I produce another litter using the mixed-blood Beagle or the Foxhound and record the same sire and dam names I did on the previous registration and in the previous pedigree. Only I know the true facts, and the pet shops and their customers cannot be the wiser. There is no way that this can be controlled, and a pedigree and registration papers are only as good as the honesty of the people who file them. The pet shop and the pet-shop customer never really know who these people are, much less can they vouch for their honesty. Such practices go on all the time.

The biggest problem in buying from a puppy mill is the fact that they deal in puppies and not dogs. You, as an inexperienced customer, see some puppies playing on shredded newspaper in the shop window, or you walk in and have a puppy thrust at you, and you are overwhelmed. All puppies are undeniably cute. You don't happen to know much about this breed, and you ask a few questions. The clerk, who is likely to be a high school or college kid working part time, gives you all the usual assurances. You do not know anything about that particular puppy's background, and the clerk may never even have seen a mature specimen of the breed, much less handled or attempted to train one. But you make your purchase. Many thousands of times a year the result is total disenchantment.

As a rule of thumb, "Never buy the puppy." Buy the dog the puppy one day will be. That means, simply, look ahead. Know all you have to know about the breed, and about the background of the puppy you are taking under consideration.

The best way to go about selecting and buying a purebred dog is hardly a mystery. It does require that you do your homework, however. Here are the steps in logical sequence:

Step 1: Go to one or more all-breed dog shows. You may think you know the breed you want, but take a last look around. Spend a pleasant day or two with your family at a couple of shows. Watch the judging, wander around the bench or exercise areas, and talk to people. Ask them about their dogs. Meet mature specimens of the breeds that seem to interest you. Get to know some people and some dogs. Then, when you find yourself homing in on one or more breeds, start doing your real spadework.

Step 2: Read. Carefully check the breeds that interest you in the breed descriptions in this book. Then check with Howell Book House (845 Third Avenue, New York, NY 10022). They publish many fine breed books, and very likely they have a book on the individual breed that is of interest to you. Read about your breed. You may want to consult a veterinarian for an opinion. Check with a dog trainer at an obedience school, and by all means go back to a dog show and get to know some breeders of that breed. Get involved with it, ask a lot of questions, and know what you are thinking of getting into for the next ten to fifteen years. A dog should be a carefully considered addition to your family, not an impulse purchase.

Step 3: Visit the breeders you have gotten to know. Meet the adult dogs they are using for parent stock if you have not already done so and then, and only then, make your purchase.

The satisfaction you are likely to gain over the years may be directly proportionate to the amount of care you take at the beginning. Surely, if you want a show dog, this is the way to go about it. When you do visit a dog show, keep in mind that those superb examples you see of each breed generally were obtained with at least this much care and caution. They were not impulse purchases except in the rarest of circumstances.

Point Eight: What do you pay for your puppy?   Here, clearly, there is no single answer. Larger, rarer breeds usually cost more than common breeds and very often cost more than smaller breeds. That rule flies into a cocked hat, however, once you start dealing with fine examples of any breed. Irish Wolfhounds and Scottish Deerhounds, for instance, may generally be more expensive than Beagles or Cocker Spaniels. But then a superb Beagle or Cocker, as an individual animal, may cost many times what even a very good Irish Wolfhound might command. It depends on the individual animal, his lineage, and most of all his potential.

Many breeds start at between $75 and $100 for pet-quality animals. For that price you are not going to get a show specimen. Difficult-to-breed and extremely small toys are going to start at a much higher figure (from $250 or $300 and up), and so will the larger, rarer breeds. Show-quality animals of any breed are going to start at $400 and go straight up from there. We once paid $600 for a five-month-old show-quality dog, and by the time he was a year old and a champion, he was worth $3,500 had we been willing to sell him, which we most certainly were not.

The selection of a breed and the selection of an individual puppy are both personal and involve taste, living style, ambition, and self-image (and not just that of one person, very often, but that of an entire family). Pure-bred dogs are best purchased only after great care and consideration and then only from breeders who can be met face to face and whose dogs also can be met and known. As for the random-bred dogs, they make super pets in millions of homes (there are over forty-seven million dogs in American homes today), and they are free and literally dying for love and care. It is my own opinion that every dog-owning home should have both if possible.

Errata

Since this book was readied for press four additional breeds have been admitted to the roster of the American Kennel Club. None of the breeds is new, but each has finally developed enough of a following in this country to warrant a stud-book and to have a place in American's dog show arenas.

Two breeds were shown at The Westminster Kennel Club Dog Show at Madison Square Garden in New York, an all-champion show, for the first time in February, 1992:

The Petit Basset Griffon Vendeen—in the Hound Group. A breed developed in France about 400 years ago and long popular in France and Denmark. A basset-like hound with a terrier coat and demeanor. Destined for great popularity in America.

The Chinese Crested—in the Toy Group. Of Chinese origin but first discovered by Spanish explorers in Mexico, Central and South America. Two types—hairless and coated. The latter referred to as a powderpuff. Coat is very silky in the latter.

In addition, *the Chinese Shar-Pei* is being shown in the Non-Sporting Group. It comes from southern China and is said to have once been a fighting dog.

The Miniature Bull Terrier, which, as its name implies, is a miniature version of England's great gladiator, the bull terrier (which is not to be confused with the so-called "pit bull").

The Sporting Dogs

Pointer
German Shorthaired Pointer
German Wirehaired Pointer
Chesapeake Bay Retriever
Curly-Coated Retriever
Flat-Coated Retriever
Golden Retriever
Labrador Retriever
English Setter
Gordon Setter
Irish Setter
American Water Spaniel

Brittany Spaniel
Clumber Spaniel
Cocker Spaniel
English Cocker Spaniel
English Springer Spaniel
Field Spaniel
Irish Water Spaniel
Sussex Spaniel
Welsh Springer Spaniel
Vizsla
Weimaraner
Wirehaired Pointing Griffon

The Pointer was developed in Europe during the Middle Ages, but no one is certain just where. One hears, from various supposed authorities, that France, Belgium, Germany, Spain, and Portugal were all the original home of this breed. We simply aren't sure, but we do know that from the mid-1600s on, England is where this breed flourished. ¶ Originally Pointers were used in conjunction with Greyhounds. The Pointer found the hare, and the Greyhound ran it to ground. Later, when ballistics made wing-shooting possible, the Pointer became exclusively a bird dog. He is considered to be the ultimate dog in this field today. ¶ Pointers are pow-

Pointer

Land of origin: MAINLAND EUROPE, then ENGLAND

Original purpose: Pointing hare and later wing shooting

Recent popularity ranking by A.K.C. registration: 93rd

American Pointer Club, Inc.
Mrs. Joyce Skrob, Secretary
Route 1, Box 76
Morriston, FL 32668

HEIGHT: Dogs to 28 inches   Bitches to 26 inches

WEIGHT: Dogs to 75 pounds   Bitches to 65 pounds

COAT
Smooth and short but dense and with a very definite sheen.

COLOR
Liver, lemon, black, or orange—solid colored or any one in combination with white.
Great variety seen.

Amount of care coat requires: 1 2 3 4 5 6 7 8 9 10

Amount of exercise required: 1 2 3 4 5 6 7 8 9 10

Suitability for urban/apartment life: 1 2 3 4 5 6 7 8 9 10
WHOLLY UNSUITED

erful, durable, clean-lined dogs of great poise and character. They do well in bench shows and excel in field trials. They are better suited to kennel life than are most large sporting dogs, for they require somewhat less human attention. Pointers will work well for a stranger more readily than will most other field dogs. The Pointer has one thing on his mind: Find that bird. ¶This breed is packed with nervous energy and requires an enormous amount of exercise. A Pointer that is cooped up is ready to explode when finally brought out into the open. There are exceptions, of course, but the Pointer is generally not as ideal a pet as are some of the other large sporting dogs. Pointers have quick tempers and really would rather be working than wasting their time on other things. Some have made excellent pets, but usually with a family that works the dog in the field. How good they are in the average household is questionable. For a nonsporting family, one that cannot build a bond with the dog in the area the dog knows and loves best—field work—the Pointer may be less than ideal. ¶Pointer owners are, of course, devoted to their splendid breed. Because Pointers are so energetic and intent on their profession, they are not good city dogs—certainly not apartment dogs. It has taken hundreds of years to perfect this masterpiece of upland wing shooting, and it is a rare Pointer indeed who will respond well to any other life-style. None of this is to say that the Pointer is not an affectionate pet. He can be, but he is best suited to a master of a special type.

German Shorthaired Pointer

Land of origin: GERMANY

Original purpose: All-purpose hunting

Recent popularity ranking by A.K.C. registration: 32nd

German Shorthaired Pointer Club of
America, Inc.
Ms. Geraldine A. Irwin, Secretary
110 West Quincy
Englewood, CO 80110

HEIGHT: Dogs to 25 inches   Bitches to 23 inches

WEIGHT: Dogs to 70 pounds   Bitches to 60 pounds

COAT
Short and thick, tough and hard.

COLOR
Important: solid liver or liver and white (gray) only.

Amount of care coat requires: 1 2 3 4 5 6 7 8 9 10

Amount of exercise required: 1 2 3 4 5 6 7 8 9 10

Suitability for urban/apartment life: 1 2 3 4 5 6 7 8 9 10
                                              UNSUITED

The handsome German Shorthaired Pointer carries a number of bloodlines, only a few of which we know about with certainty. An old German bird dog is there, a Spanish Pointer and a scent hound, perhaps even the great Bloodhound himself. There is terrier there, too. The Germans who bred this animal up from obscurity, drawing on dogs from all over Europe, outdid themselves. This is one of the better pets among the heavy field dogs. ¶The German Shorthaired Pointer is a supremely active animal and generally is unsuited to apartment or city life. He is full of energy and always ready to go—and *go* does not mean simply to the curb and back. This is an animal that has to move! ¶The German Shorthaired Pointer is a loving companion and constant friend.

He is not petty or mean, ill-tempered or moody, and he gets along with his master's family. If cooped up, however, his whole manner can change; in the city he can become crazed and act beyond control. He becomes yappy and foolish and seems to lose his intelligence along with his dignity. The German Shorthaired should always be dignified—and will be if trained and worked. You certainly don't have to be a hunter to use this combination upland-lowland dog—this trailer, pointer, and retriever in one package—but you have to like long walks in the clean, crisp air. Don't expect a German Shorthaired Pointer to display all of his original characteristics and quality on hard pavement and in crowded living conditions.

When the Germans decided they wanted the perfect all-purpose hunting dog, they took their justifiably famous Shorthaired Pointer and combined him with Terrier, Poodle, and other blood-lines to evolve the striking German Wire-haired Pointer, one of the finest hunting dogs in the world today. ¶The German Wirehaired Pointer is everything you could desire in a field dog—a flawless retriever, a pointer, a steady, solid, and determined friend and companion animal. His coat, one of the breed's most striking and impor-tant features, provides protection against all weather; it is virtually water-repellent, so there need be no hesitation about using

German Wirehaired Pointer

Land of origin: GERMANY

Original purpose: Rugged, all-purpose hunting

Recent popularity ranking by A.K.C. registration: 68th

German Wirehaired Pointer Club of America, Inc.
Laurie McCarty, Secretary
2506 Ann Arborn Lane
Blowie, MD 20716

HEIGHT: Dogs to 26 inches   Bitches to 24 inches

WEIGHT: Dogs to 70 pounds   Bitches to 60 pounds

COAT
Extremely important feature: protective undercoat full and dense in winter and all but invisible in summer. Outer coat straight, harsh, wiry, rather close lying; 1½ to 2 inches in length.

COLOR
Liver or liver and white. Nose dark brown. Head brown, occasionally with white blaze. Ears brown. Any black is a serious fault.

Amount of care coat requires: 1 2 3 4 5 6 7 8 9 10
                                       •••

Amount of exercise required: 1 2 3 4 5 6 7 8 9 10
                                   •••••••••••••••••••

Suitability for urban/apartment life: 1 2 3 4 5 6 7 8 9 10
                                               UNSUITED

the dog to retrieve in icy waters. The coat also protects against briers and thorns in the roughest terrain. There is even a bushy mass to protect the eyes. In winter the coat is thick, but it thins considerably by summer. It is easy to care for and naturally clean—the dog shakes dirt off the way he does water. Coat condition is obviously an important factor and is carefully considered by all judges. ¶ The German Wirehaired Pointer is one of those dogs really not at all suited to city life. He was bred for the field, and only in the open will he display his exceptional qualities. ¶ This breed makes almost ideal companion animals for their owners, though cross or ill-tempered examples should not be tolerated. While not unfriendly or aggressive, the dog is aloof and slow to accept strangers. ¶ The German Wirehaired is an exceptional breed when living in special, planned-for circumstances. In other situations—if forced to fit into an inappropriate lifestyle—the good qualities he is known for may vanish. Some people try to take outstanding working or sporting dogs and remold them. It usually does not work, and only rarely will the family be satisfied. In a country setting, of course, dogs like the German Wirehaired Pointer make fine family pets. ¶ This special and highly developed breed should never be obtained from anyone but a specialty breeder who can show you not only the parents' conformation show ribbons but their field-trial awards as well. Although handsome, rugged, and even noble in his canine way, the German Wirehaired Pointer was made to perform, and that should be clearly evident when you examine a prospective puppy's background.

The Chesapeake Bay Retriever is descended from two dogs rescued from a sinking British brig off the coast of Maryland in 1807. The dogs are believed to have been Newfoundland puppies named Sailor and Canton, and there are many guesses as to what was bred to these two dogs, or possibly to their offspring. Approximately eighty years later a definite type emerged—the dog we today call the Chesapeake Bay Retriever. ¶ The Chesapeake is by all standards a superior dog. He is one of the greatest of all water retrievers and one of the hardiest. No weather will deter this dog from doing what he was born to do: go into the water and retrieve fallen game. Not

Chesapeake Bay Retriever

Land of origin: UNITED STATES

Original purpose: Water retrieving

Recent popularity ranking by A.K.C. registration: 42nd

American Chesapeake Club, Inc.
Mrs. Andre L. Havens, Secretary
25720 W. Lehmann Blvd.
Lake Villa, IL 60046

HEIGHT: Dogs to 26 inches   Bitches to 24 inches

WEIGHT: Dogs to 80 pounds   Bitches to 70 pounds

COAT
Thick and short, up to 1½ inches long only, with a fine, dense, and woolly undercoat. Coat is wavy in places but never curly.

COLOR
From dark brown to "deadgrass." Solid color preferred, but very small white spots on chest and/or toes allowed.

Amount of care coat requires: 1 2 3 4 5 6 7 8 9 10

Amount of exercise required: 1 2 3 4 5 6 7 8 9 10

Suitability for urban/apartment life: 1 2 3 4 5 6 7 8 9 10

only is he peerless with waterfowl, he is also a consummate companion. ¶The Chesapeake is a good watchdog and a responsive pet. He is fine when obedience-trained, since he is one of the most intelligent dogs and one of the most willing. Put him to any task and he will do it. Disposition is an extremely important factor in judging, for this is one breed of dog that is expected to be even-tempered, sensible, and nonaggressive. Anything less than that is considered unworthy. ¶All of this is not to say that the Chesapeake is wishy-washy or without strong character. Just the opposite. This is a dog of great purpose and highly developed skill. He is aloof to yapping nonsense but fine with other animals who show an appropriate amount of respect. ¶The Chesapeake Bay Retriever, one of the few American breeds, has been used successfully as a guide dog for the blind. He can survive in an apartment as long as he is surrounded by people who care about him and as long as he gets sufficient exercise. It is not fair nor is it even humane to have an active sporting dog like this living the life of a toy. The Chesapeake thrives on work, on being needed for a tough and demanding job. Above all, the Chesapeake wants and needs open water. If one of these splendid dogs is kept in the city, it should be by people who will exercise him every day and from time to time get him out to some river, lake, or shoreline where he can retrieve sticks and display his real nature.

The arguments among dog people as to the real origin of the Curly-Coated Retriever will go on as long as there are dog people to argue. It usually is stated that the breed comes down from the English Water Spaniel popular in the 1500s. To that line is said to have been added a form of setting retriever. The Irish Water Spaniel is also said to be a foundation breed to which everything from Poodle to Newfoundland is supposed to have been added. However it may have come about, several hundred years ago the base was laid down, and by 1803 a breed could be described. Its first appearance in shows came in 1859. ¶The Curly-Coated Retriever is a special-pur-

Curly-Coated Retriever

Land of origin: ENGLAND

Original purpose: Water retrieving

Recent popularity ranking by A.K.C. registration: 119th

Curly-Coated Retriever Club of America
Sue Tokolics, Corres. Secretary
303 South Concord Road
West Chester, PA 19382

HEIGHT: Dogs to 24 inches   Bitches to 23 inches

WEIGHT: Dogs to 70 pounds   Bitches to 65 pounds

COAT
Crisp curls all over the body, the tighter the better. Saddle or area of uncurled coat seriously faulted in judging.

COLOR
Black or liver; sparse white hairs on chest allowed.

Amount of care coat requires: 1 2 3 4 5 6 7 8 9 10

Amount of exercise required: 1 2 3 4 5 6 7 8 9 10

Suitability for urban/apartment life: 1 2 3 4 5 6 7 8 9 10
                                                UNSUITED

pose dog with incredible stamina and skill. As a water retriever he is surpassed by few breeds. Popular with duck hunters in Australia and New Zealand, the breed hardly is known here. Most people have never seen an example, and he can be confused with the Irish Water Spaniel by those who have seen only one or two of that breed. The Irish Water Spaniel has a distinctly ratlike tail, while the breed we're discussing has a tail covered with ringlets. Actually there is little difference in popularity—the Irish dog rates 106th in this country and the Curly-Coated 117th. ¶The Curly-Coated Retriever is not suited to apartment or urban life. He is an action dog for foul weather and water. He needs and wants to swim, to know the wind and the feel of freshly forming ice on salty marshes under a gray and threatening sky. It is not easy to re-create those conditions in the living room. People who try to take this breed into an apartment and reshape the dog will be dissatisfied. Walks along city streets simply are not enough. The Curly-Coated is a good companion for his owner and even for his family, but demands should not be made upon him by strangers. They should be quite satisfied with him when he is aloof. ¶Training should start early with this breed and continue over a long period of time. It is a serious matter for dog and master. This dog is smart, very smart, and will take over if allowed. Because he is a big animal, such assertiveness is intolerable, and snapping should be severely curtailed. Like many other really fine hunting breeds, the Curly-Coated Retriever can be stubborn, or, rather, single-minded. Without that quality he would not be the great field performer he is. ¶You will not find it easy to locate an outstanding specimen of this breed.

It is ironic that the Flat-Coated Retriever should rank down near the very bottom of the popularity poll in America. Not only is he an exceptional dog, but also he is one of the few truly American breeds. He was derived from the Newfoundland and the Labrador Retriever. His main development, however, took place in England dur-ing the reign of Queen Victoria. ¶The solid, sturdy, and well-muscled Flat-Coated Retriever is a field dog first and foremost, but he also can be an ideal family pet. Marvelous with children, he is loving and gentle with the whole family. He holds his peace with strangers, though he wants to know a lot about someone coming

Flat-Coated Retriever

Land of origin: AMERICA

Original purpose: Water and upland retrieving

Recent popularity ranking by A.K.C. registration: 94th

Flat-Coated Retriever Society of America, Inc.
Margot Hallet, Corres. Secretary
Eastbrook Rd.
Hampton, CT 06247

HEIGHT: Dogs to 23 inches   Bitches to 22 inches

WEIGHT: Dogs to 70 pounds   Bitches to 65 pounds

COAT
Dense, fine, and flat.

COLOR
Black or liver.

Amount of care coat requires: 1 2 3 4 5 6 7 8 9 10

Amount of exercise required: 1 2 3 4 5 6 7 8 9 10

Suitability for urban/apartment life: 1 2 3 4 5 6 7 8 9 10
UNSUITED

---

through the door before he offers friendship. Once one of these fine dogs does offer it, the arrangement is permanent. They are loyal and outgoing, stable and intelligent. ¶ The Flat-Coated Retriever lives for his master and takes training very well. He wants to learn and to please, and he loves being congratulated and rewarded. In this he is like a child, once his interest in a project is aroused. More cheerful than some of the other gundogs of his general size and configuration, he resembles the Golden Retriever and Labrador Retriever in his attitude toward human beings. Though not exactly a jolly clown, he is a pet and he does need attention. ¶ A Flat-Coated Retriever should be taken regularly to an open area where he can run and retrieve. He is particularly fond of water and should be allowed to swim—in any weather. His coat is easy to maintain, and he is easily kept. ¶ Considering the popularity that the Golden and Labrador Retrievers enjoy, it just might be that the Flat-Coated Retriever will have his day. The breed is now obviously only on the first rung of the popularity ladder. For comparison it should be noted that in 1974 the American Kennel Club reported registering 36,689 new Labradors and 20,933 Goldens; the number of Flat-Coated Retrievers registered was a mere 90. ¶ People wanting a dog of the retriever style, but also wanting something different, might think about starting the long, hard hunt to find a really good example of this rare breed. They could be getting in on the start of a whole new thing.

It was in early nineteenth-century England that the retrievers first came into prominence. Four main types were developed almost simultaneously—the Curly-Coated, the Flat-Coated, the Labrador, and the Golden. Setters, water spaniels, and other sporting dogs were crossed with a light retrieving dog known as St. John's Newfoundland to achieve these ends. ¶From the beginning the extraordinary qualities of the Golden Retriever were recognized. He is a truly superior hunting dog with a soft mouth and great intelligence. The Golden is hardy and can thrive in almost any weather. He will never shy from leaping into icy water to please his master

Golden Retriever

Land of origin: ENGLAND

Original purpose: Water retrieving

Recent popularity ranking by A.K.C. registration: 4th

Golden Retriever Club of Amreica
Mrs. Linda Atwell, Corres. Secretary
6516 Esther NE
Albuquerque, NM 87109

HEIGHT: Dogs to 24 inches   Bitches to 22½ inches

WEIGHT: Dogs to 75 pounds   Bitches to 70 pounds

COAT
Dense and water-repellent. Good undercoat. Flat against body with some wave.

COLOR
Lustrous gold of different shades. Solid. No white markings allowed.

Amount of care coat requires: 1 2 3 4 5 6 7 8 9 10

Amount of exercise required: 1 2 3 4 5 6 7 8 9 10

*Suitability for urban/apartment life:** 1 2 3 4 5 6 7 8 9 10

*But *only* if exercised, or at least walked, no less than two hours every day in all kinds of weather.

and do the job he was bred to do. He is hurt and seemingly embarrassed when denied the opportunity to help, to carry, to bring you something in order to show his affection. His need to retrieve is legendary—he is never as happy as when he is fetching and carrying. ¶The Golden is never mean or petty. He naturally loves children and other animals, cats and kittens included. He is loyal, almost unbelievably affectionate, and so intelligent that he is becoming one of the most popular of all guide dogs for the blind. All these qualities make him an ideal family dog and pet. ¶It is difficult to discuss this breed without allowing a distinct prejudice to creep in. The author believes that the Golden Retriever comes very close to being the greatest of all breeds. Although other people may have different favorite breeds, almost no one has anything bad to say about this one. ¶The Golden Retriever is so much the perfect companion and family dog that there is very naturally a tendency to think of him as perfect for every set of circumstances. This is not quite true. The Golden Retriever is an outdoor animal, and although he will adapt to city life (he will adapt to *anything* as long as he has his family nearby), he requires exercise—lots and lots of exercise. No one should think of owning a Golden unless he is willing to walk the dog at least two hours every day, no matter what the weather. It isn't fair to treat this superb dog otherwise. He also should have frequent opportunities to retrieve, especially from water. He loves to swim all year round. The Golden isn't a terribly expensive dog to buy; $250 should fetch a good example of the breed. Since retrievers are prone to a congenital malformation known as hip dysplasia, they should be obtained only from reputable breeders. Animals that show any signs of dysplasia should not be bred, for there is a 65 percent heritability factor.

It is no accident that the Labrador Retriever has become one of the most popular dogs in America, now consistently ranked among the top ten. He is a peerless pet as well as a superlative performer in the field, under the gun or in field trials. He can be used as a guide dog for the blind or as a general watchdog. There are people who insist that the Labrador Retriever is the most even-tempered of all dog breeds. ¶ The Labrador can be owned under almost any circumstances because he is so sensible, so steady, and so adaptable. It is up to the owner, however, to be fair and give the dog a chance to be himself. There is no doubt that this splendid animal needs exer-

Labrador Retriever

Land of origin: NEWFOUNDLAND and ENGLAND

Original purpose: Water retrieving

Recent popularity ranking by A.K.C. registration: 2nd

Labrador Retriever Club, Inc.
Dr. Bernard W. Ziessow, Secretary
32695 Redfern
Franklin, MI 48025

HEIGHT: Dogs to 24½ inches   Bitches to 23½ inches

WEIGHT: Dogs to 75 pounds   Bitches to 70 pounds

COAT
Short, very dense, and not wavy. Feels hard to the hand, and there are no feathers.

COLOR
All black, yellow, or chocolate. Very small white spot on chest allowed. Eyes black to pale yellow; brown or hazel generally preferred.

Amount of care coat requires: 1 2 3 4 5 6 7 8 9 10

Amount of exercise required: 1 2 3 4 5 6 7 8 9 10

Suitability for urban/apartment life:* 1 2 3 4 5 6 7 8 9 10

---

*But *only* if given a great deal of exercise every day plus opportunities for periodic workouts in the open.

---

cise, and it is unkind to keep one locked away all day and night without an opportunity to get out and go. It is also less than kind to maintain a Labrador in a city apartment or a suburban house without a place to swim. Labradors were made for the water, and diving in after a stick is their greatest joy—whatever the weather. The coat does not require a lot of care, but daily brushing for a few minutes will help keep it glistening and healthy. ¶ Labrador Retrievers are legendary with children as responsible baby-sitters and faithful guards. They are fine with strangers who do not appear dangerous to the household, and they are perfect with other animals. ¶ Labradors will fight, of course, but only if pressed into it. They are never petty or mean, rarely sulky or moody. They are not as demonstrative or openly affectionate as Golden Retrievers, but their love of master, family, and home is quite genuine. The very slight reserve does not suggest less love or less reliability. The Golden and Labrador Retrievers stand side by side as two of the most desirable dogs in the world. ¶ Because "Labs" are so popular, it is extremely important that they be obtained only from the best professional specialty breeders. There has been too much mass production, which is to be discouraged. ¶ Because the Labrador Retriever can be trained to do anything, or *almost* anything, that any other dog can do, some have been trained as attack dogs. This is nothing less than criminal, and a dog so trained should not be looked upon as a Labrador Retriever at all. He is no more reliable than any other potential killer. The prospective owner concerned about the safety of his or her home should not think an attack-trained Labrador is safer around a family than any other dog in that lamentable condition.

Very few dog fanciers would disagree with the claim that the English Setter not only is one of the handsomest dogs but also has one of the sweetest dispositions of all dogs and is a splendid performer in the field. No wonder that he has always had a loyal following. ¶No one knows all the steps that had to be taken to create the English Setter, but we believe he was derived several hundred years ago from Spanish land dogs—dogs that came to be called *spaniels* after their place of origin. The English Setter has done nothing but improve, until today his beauty and dignity symbolize the striving for perfection in the dog world. ¶English Setters have few peers as

English Setter

Land of origin: SPAIN and ENGLAND

Original purpose: Hunting

Recent popularity ranking by A.K.C. registration: 76th

English Setter Association of America, Inc.
Mrs. Dawn S. Ronyak, Secretary
114 So. Burlington Oval Drive
Chardon, OH 44024

HEIGHT: Dogs to 25 inches   Bitches to 24 inches

WEIGHT: Dogs to 70 pounds   Bitches to 60 pounds

COAT
Flat, without curl, not soft or woolly, and of medium length. Thin, regular feathers on legs and tail.

COLOR
Black, white, and tan; black and white; blue belton; lemon and white; lemon belton; orange and white; orange belton; liver and white; liver belton; or solid white. Heavy patches of color not as desirable as flecking all over.

Amount of care coat requires: 1 2 3 4 5 6 7 8 9 10

Amount of exercise required: 1 2 3 4 5 6 7 8 9 10

Suitability for urban/apartment life: 1 2 3 4 5 6 7 8 9 10
UNSUITED

---

family dogs. They are affectionate and loyal and are exceptional all-around companions. They love children and demand a great deal of affection in return. They are fine, smooth-working bird dogs that work and play well with other animals. ¶The Setter's coat requires some brushing every day to keep its fine appearance; this is an easy task and need not take more than a few minutes. It is shameful to let the coat go, since it is such an important element of the dog's appearance. English Setters are hams when it comes to showing, and when they set up they are breathtaking. For this reason, and because they are so easy to manage, they have long been favorites in the show-ring. Few dogs have been painted as often or by so many different artists. ¶There is one catch that the prospective owner should take into account. The English Setter needs an enormous amount of exercise, and he does not thrive in the city. He really should be exercised or allowed to exercise for hours every day, and that is usually not practical in an urban setting. Even the mild, sweet disposition of the Setter can fray and show signs of going sour if he is held in the city and denied his true nature. This should be considered very seriously, because a lot of people do find Setters stylish, and some pet shops will sell them with the assurance that they are ideal apartment dogs. They distinctly are not.

This exceptionally handsome field dog dates from the early 1600s in Scotland, but it wasn't until the fourth Duke of Gordon took the breed under his guidance a century and a half later that it really came into prominence. It has been admired and praised by dog fanciers ever since. Daniel Webster was the first American to import examples of the breed into the United States. ¶ It is hard to tell why the English and Irish Setters have been more popular in this country than the Gordon, unless it is because they are both a little faster in the open. That is the only advantage they have over the Gordon though, for this is a nearly perfect companion animal for the man afield. ¶ A Gordon in good condition is one of the handsomest of dogs, silky and shiny with the distinctive pattern of black and red that sets it apart from all other sporting breeds. This breed tends to be more stable than the Irish Setter—rather more like the English Setter in temperament. ¶ There is a saying that no one ever knew a Gordon Setter who would bite a child, and that is a lot closer to fact than fiction. Although ac-

Gordon Setter

Land of origin: SCOTLAND

Original purpose: As upland game gundog

Recent popularity ranking by A.K.C. registration: 61st

Gordon Setter Club of America, Inc.
Mrs. Jane C. Matteson, Secretary
632 W. El Morado Court
Ontario, CA 91762

HEIGHT: Dogs to 27 inches   Bitches to 26 inches

WEIGHT: Dogs to 80 pounds   Bitches to 70 pounds

COAT
Shiny, soft, slightly waved or straight, but not curly. Long hair on ears, under the stomach, and on chest, tail, and legs.

COLOR
Black with tan to red mahogany or chestnut markings. There may be black "pencil lines" on the toes. Lighter markings are important; they should appear over the eyes, on the muzzle and throat, on the chest and inside of the hind legs, under the tail, and on the feet. No red or tan hairs should be mixed in with the black. A *little* white is allowed on the chest.

Amount of care coat requires: 1 2 3 4 5 6 7 8 9 10
•••••••••

Amount of exercise required: 1 2 3 4 5 6 7 8 9 10
••••••••••••••••••

Suitability for urban/apartment life: 1 2 3 4 5 6 7 8 9 10
UNSUITED

tive, Gordons are sensible, even-tempered, and affectionate. They don't usually throw themselves at strangers and are happier with their own human family. They demand a great deal of attention, which can be a problem when there is more than one dog. Gordons can be jealous; this is often the cause of dogfights in which the Gordon participates. In fact, Gordons apparently would like it very much if all other dogs and people just vanished and left them alone with their immediate family, which is not to say that Gordons are unfriendly or quarrelsome, just that they have a preferred way of living: privately and stage center within their household. ¶Because of the breed's high style, some people do make city dogs out of Gordons. The dog can adapt because of his great affection for people, but the city Gordon Setter just isn't the same animal as the country Gordon. City life can make him tense, silly, and sometimes hard to control. The smooth, natural world of open field and cool, clean air is the ideal setting for an animal who wants to please, responds easily to training, and provides nearly perfect canine companionship. The dog held in the city will require intensive obedience training and a great deal of walking. The Gordon Setter is not a dog just to be led from apartment door to curb and back; less than two miles a day may not be cruel, but it certainly is unkind. This is an animal who was bred to move, and only in movement can one appreciate the bold, strong driving quality of his gait and character.

Once a red and white dog (and still seen that way in England), the Irish Setter is now a rich red mahogany animal of great and enduring beauty. Certainly one of the handsomest of dogs, the red Irishman may have been in part undone by his splendor. He was originally a field dog, a bird dog, and there was none better. But in recent years, at least in the United States, he has been a show animal, and many people familiar with the breed think this is a sad waste of talent. ¶ We are not sure where the Irish Setter came from. It seems certain that some spaniel and English Setter, perhaps some Gordon Setter and some Pointer were involved. Any trace of black

Irish Setter

Land of origin: IRELAND

Original purpose: As bird dog

Recent popularity ranking by A.K.C. registration: 51st

Irish Setter Club of America, Inc.
Ms. Marion J. Pahy, Corres. Secretary
16717 Ledge Falls
San Antonio, TX 78232

HEIGHT: Dogs to 27 inches   Bitches to 25 inches

WEIGHT: Dogs to 70 pounds   Bitches to 60 pounds

COAT
Of moderate length and flat. Feathering long and silky on ears and forelegs. Ideal is free from wave or curl.

COLOR
Mahogany or rich chestnut red. *Any* trace of black is a serious fault. Very small amount of white allowed on chest, throat, or toes.

Amount of care coat requires: 1 2 3 4 5 6 7 8 9 10

Amount of exercise required: 1 2 3 4 5 6 7 8 9 10

Suitability for urban/apartment life: 1 2 3 4 5 6 7 8 9 10
UNSUITED

today (which would go back to the Gordon) is considered a grievous fault. ¶ Wherever he came from and however he is used, the Irish Setter is a stunning animal and a terrible clown. A pet dog through and through, he is affectionate and extremely demonstrative. But he can be a first-class pain when he is not obedience-trained. He is capable of taking over a household where there is not a firm and knowing hand, but he is equally capable of learning anything that reasonably can be expected of an upland dog. He is one or the other, a model of decorum, or a dunce and a nuisance—it will depend on the owner. ¶ There is a difference of opinion as to where and how the Irish Setter is best maintained. In my own opinion, the red Setter, although adaptable and loving under any circumstances, is far too active for apartment life. He needs an enormous amount of exercise,

and he needs it every day. In an apartment there is no way in which this can be achieved. A walk is not the same as a run. I have seen some perfectly splendid examples of the breed as "flaky" as a dog can be from overconfinement. It is sad to see one of these splendid field dogs leaping and lunging in an apartment-house elevator for want of proper exercise. ¶ Irish Setters tend to stray, and in the suburban setting they should be carefully supervised. They are also terrible thieves, so don't be surprised if you wake up some morning to find that your Irish Setter has brought home an Oriental carpet or a family Bible. They are also born clowns and will never leave you short of stories to tell. Endearingly beautiful, active, and affectionate, in the right setting and in the hands of the right owner, the Irish Setter cannot be beat.

This hunting dog originated in the American Midwest, but not much more is known about its early history. The Irish Water Spaniel, the Curly-Coated Retriever, and the old English Water Spaniel are all suggested forebears, and other spaniel blood may have figured in as well. It is not a matter that is likely to be settled.

¶ From whatever stock he came, the American Water Spaniel is a splendid hunter. He is a superb water retriever, serves as well on land, and has an excellent nose. No weather or water temperature will deter this dog, and he will work upland game as readily as he will seek out injured waterfowl. Although not a pointer, he is hard to

American Water Spaniel

Land of origin: UNITED STATES

Original purpose: Water retrieving and other hunting

Recent popularity ranking by A.K.C. registration: 99th

American Spaniel Club, Inc.
Mrs. Margaret M. Ciezkowski, Secretary
12 Wood Lane South'
Woodmere, NY 11598-2298

HEIGHT: Dogs to 18 inches   Bitches to 18 inches

WEIGHT: Dogs to 45 pounds   Bitches to 40 pounds

COAT
Closely curled or with marcel effect. Dense enough to protect against water and weather. Not straight, kinked, soft, or fine.

COLOR
Solid liver or dark chocolate. No white except on toes and chest; as little as possible is desired.

Amount of care coat requires: 1 2 3 4 5 6 7 8 9 10

Amount of exercise required: 1 2 3 4 5 6 7 8 9 10

Suitability for urban/apartment life:*   1 2 3 4 5 6 7 8 9 10

*If exercised properly every day without fail.

beat in any other category of field sport. ¶ Except for the fact that he is not quite as lovely to look at as some of the other spaniels, the curly American Water Spaniel is almost everything anyone could want in a dog. He is, in most respects, an easy dog to keep. Unlike a good many other sporting breeds, he is a good, solid watchdog; although not testy with strangers, he will let you know when one approaches. This is an intelligent dog who is very willing to learn. He is extremely affectionate, something not necessarily true of all sporting dogs. He should be handled with care, for he thrives on praise and takes scolding to heart. He is splendid in the family setting and seems especially drawn to children. He is sensible and will fit in with other family pets. His disposition is flawless, and he takes to training as well as he does to water. He is not strenuous to deal with or difficult in any way. ¶ This is one sporting breed that will adapt to a city apartment; as a matter of fact, this dog will adjust to virtually any situation as long as his family is nearby. It is not fair to keep this loving animal purely as a kennel dog. If kept in the suburbs, he should not be allowed to roam, for he just might be enticed to wander off too far. When kept in the suburbs or the city, he should be given a great deal of exercise on a regular basis. It is only right to give him a workout in the water as often as possible. Retrieving a stick from the water is fine exercise and will allow him to fulfill his natural original mission. ¶ Not very well known in most parts of the country, the American Water Spaniel is one of those special treats awaiting the potential dog owner willing to do a little research.

The Brittany is actually too leggy to be called a spaniel, or at least he is one of the least spaniel-like of all spaniels. He is as high in the withers as he is long. He comes from ancient Spanish stock carried across Europe so long ago we can't even fix the period. While most spaniels developed in the British Isles, this breed was developed in France and has been known to European sportsmen for centuries. He shares common ancestry with all the other spaniels, the setters, and the pointers. In size and appearance he may be close to those ancestral dogs from which all three groups arose. ¶The Brittany is never shown with a tail substantially longer than four inches. The

Brittany Spaniel

Land of origin: FRANCE, from ancient Spanish stock

Original purpose: Hunting

Recent popularity ranking by A.K.C. registration: 26th

American Brittany Club, Inc.
Ms. Bettye Wells, Secretary
HCR Box 3950
Benson, AZ 85602

HEIGHT: Dogs to 20½ inches   Bitches to 19½ inches

WEIGHT: Dogs to 40 pounds   Bitches to 37 pounds

COAT
Dense and flat, wavy but not curly. Skin loose but not so loose as to form pouches.

COLOR
Dark, rich orange and white or liver and white. Never to be tricolored or to show any black at all. Colors should be strong and not faded.

Amount of care coat requires: 1 2 3 4 5 6 7 8 9 10

Amount of exercise required: 1 2 3 4 5 6 7 8 9 10

Suitability for urban/apartment life:*   1 2 3 4 5 6 7 8 9 10

---

*But *only* if properly exercised on a regular basis.

---

tail is sometimes docked, but many Brittanies are born with mere stubs, and some are born without tails at all. The first tailless specimens we know of appeared about a century ago in the Douron Valley in France. ¶The Brittany is an excellent field dog, and as such his true qualities show best. The breed is by nature aggressive and loyal. Since Brittanies are not keen on strangers, they are natural watchdogs and are quite fearless. They should, though, be watched around strangers, for they can become a little too tough and may be quite intimidating. They tend to be one-personish but will live with a family most amicably. They can be raised with other animals. ¶The Brittany is not as elegant as some of the other spaniels, although he has a certain keenness about him that is attractive. His coat can be handsome although it is not as fine as those of other spaniels.

Brittanies are sturdy, well boned, strong, and driving. Never clumsy or awkward, they move fast, their long legs serving them well. They have minimum feathering and their ears are not long, so coat care is less than for the other spaniels. ¶The Brittany needs a great deal of exercise, and if one is brought into a confined suburban home or a city dwelling, that should be kept in mind. All the wonderful drive and energy that make this breed so desirable in the field *can* degenerate into plain silliness and hyperactivity. The splendid field dog improperly cared for can become a pest. If you keep a Brittany, long walks on a regular basis are a must. ¶Beware of poor breeders and mass-producers. There are a lot of Brittanies around. You should know the original source well, and buy only after careful consideration. The range in looks, and especially in behavior, is great.

One of the least spaniel-like of all spaniels, the Clumber has a mysterious background. The long, low, and rather heavyset body suggests Basset Hound blood (and many people insist this is true), and the heavy, Saint Bernard-like head suggests an old Alpine spaniel we may no longer know. It is a matter that will never be resolved, as is true for many breeds. Animals were bred for a need of the time, and apparently no one felt that anyone in the future would be interested in how shapes and forms were arrived at. ¶The name of this breed is derived, it is believed, from Clumber Park, the seat of the Dukes of Newcastle in Nottingham. The records in-

Clumber Spaniel

Land of origin: ENGLAND and FRANCE

Original purpose: Flushing game and retrieving

Recent popularity ranking by A.K.C. registration: 124th

Clumber Spaniel Club of America, Inc.
Edythe T. Donovan, Corres. Secretary
241 Monterey Ave.
Pelham, NY 10803

HEIGHT: Dogs to 18 inches   Bitches to 16 inches

WEIGHT: Dogs to 65 pounds   Bitches to 50 pounds

COAT
Straight, silky, very dense, but not too long. Feathers long and abundant.

COLOR
Lemon and white or orange and white. Better if there are fewer markings on body. Ideal has lemon or orange ears, even head and face markings, and ticked legs.

Amount of care coat requires: 1 2 3 4 5 6 7 8 9 10

Amount of exercise required: 1 2 3 4 5 6 7 8 9 10

Suitability for urban/apartment life: 1 2 3 4 5 6 7 8 9 10

dicate that the Duc de Noailles sent several dogs over from France in the nineteenth century, dogs of a type he had been perfecting for years. No doubt they figured heavily in the development of the breed, so the listing of England as the home of the breed may be only partly true. ¶ The Clumber is a large, slow, and very deliberate worker in the field. He has enormous strength and is hardy enough to withstand almost any weather and almost any work regimen. He is a great retriever and very willing. ¶ The Clumber is, or at least can be, devoted to his master, but once again we encounter a breed that may not be everybody's ideal pet. He prefers one master and can be temperamental—some people even say sullen—when placed in a position of working with other people or animals. He is a highly polished professional at his work and goes about it in a stolid, purposeful, no-nonsense way. He does not readily express great joy and does not want to bother with anyone but his master—that is, after his master has established his right to that position. The Clumber wants to be trained early and well, and only then will that excellence in performance be evident. ¶ People selecting a fine, steady field dog without enormous social grace may want to consider this somewhat dour character. Those wanting the excitement of a canine pal and fellow socializer may find this breed less than ideal.

The Cocker Spaniel is not only one of the handsomest dogs ever bred, he also has a long record as a fine sporting animal. He is a true gentleman of the field. Without doubt the Cocker Spaniel comes down from a Spanish dog and has the same ancestry as the setters and larger spaniels of our time. Long ago, he was reduced in size, with one branch going off into the toy spaniels—strictly companion animals— and one branch developing toward the smallest of the true sporting dogs. The Cocker as we know him got his name from "cocking" dog, being especially adept with woodcocks. ¶Over the years the great beauty of this little gem of a dog began tak-

Cocker Spaniel

Land of origin: ENGLAND

Original purpose: Hunting

Recent popularity ranking by A.K.C. registration: 1st

American Spaniel Club
Mrs. Margaret W. Ciezkowski
12 Wood Lane, Woodsburgh
Woodmere, NY 11598

HEIGHT: Dogs to 15 inches   Bitches to 14 inches

WEIGHT: Dogs to 28 pounds   Bitches to 26 pounds ·

COAT
Flat or slightly wavy but *never* curly. Silky in texture and of medium length. Good undercoating. Well feathered on ears, chest, abdomen, and legs, but never to be excessive or deny sporting-dog character of breed.

COLOR
Black, white, tan, liver, and other solids with white on chest only—no white is better on colored dogs. Parti-colors definite and primary color to be less than 90 percent. The Cocker is shown in three varieties; black, parti-and ASCOB, any-solid-color-other-(than)-black.

Amount of care coat requires: 1 2 3 4 5 6 7 8 9 10

*Amount of exercise required:** 1 2 3 4 5 6 7 8 9 10

Suitability for urban/apartment life: 1 2 3 4 5 6 7 8 9 10

*Varies greatly among animals.

ing precedence over his ability in the field. More and more he was bred for the bench, while his intelligence was ignored or subordinated. Breeders strove to outdo each other in the feathery glory of their champions. When several truly magnificent Cockers began chalking up spectacular show careers, the fad was on, and everybody on the block had to own one of these dogs. The mass-producers had their day, and the Cocker Spaniel as a field dog all but disappeared. Here is a classic example of the fate that awaits the fad dog who is turned out by the basketload. ¶Through it all, however, much of the true character of the original Cocker Spaniel has remained. It wants only for enough breeders to show enthusiasm for this breed's intelligence. It will not necessarily require breeders to sacrifice much of the animal's admitted beauty to re-sume breeding for character, sense, and intelligence. ¶Anyone availing themselves of a Cocker Spaniel today is getting a dog not only of enormous style and class but also of noble field lineage. If they intend to breed, they are also investing in an opportunity to help reconstruct one of the truly great breeds. The true Cocker Spaniel is a steady, even dog, affectionate and fine with children. He is also a dog who should be able to accept training. Unfortunately, there is a better than even chance that a careless buyer will get a snappy, yappy brat without the strength of canine character to do anything but pose, if even that. The prospective owner should buy with care and only from breeders of reputation. It is time for the Cocker Spaniel to make his comeback.

English Cocker Spaniel

Land of origin: ENGLAND

Original purpose: Hunting

Recent popularity ranking by A.K.C. registration: 65th

English Cocker Spaniel Club of America
Mrs. Kate Romanski, Secretary
P.O. Box 252
Hales Corners, WI 53130

HEIGHT: Dogs to 17 inches   Bitches to 16 inches

WEIGHT: Dogs to 34 pounds   Bitches to 32 pounds

COAT
Medium length with good undercoating. Hair flat or slightly wavy and silky in texture. Well feathered but not too profuse.

COLOR
Broken and evenly distributed—white, roan, blue, liver red, orange, lemon, black, tan, and others; should be attractive in balance and placement.

Amount of care coat requires: 1 2 3 4 5 6 7 8 9 10
                                    • • • • • • • •

Amount of exercise required: *   1 2 3 4 5 6 7 8 9 10
                                    • • • • • • • • • • •

Suitability for urban/apartment life: †   1 2 3 4 5 6 7 8 9 10
                                             • • • • • • • • • • • • • • • • • •

*Varies greatly among animals.
†Only if appropriately exercised.

T he English Cocker Spaniel is a perfectly splendid-looking dog with the same background as the American Cocker Spaniel. He is, though, a little larger. Note these comparisons:

	WEIGHT RANGE	HEIGHT RANGE
Cocker	22–28 lbs.	14–15 in.
English Cocker	26–34 lbs.	15–17 in.

It wasn't until 1892 that the Kennel Club in England recognized that the English Cocker Spaniel and the English Springer Spaniel were different breeds. Up to that time they appeared in the same litter, separated only by size. ¶ There is no doubt that the Sussex, Cocker, Field, and Springer Spaniels have been closely associated and that all manner of interbreeding occurred even after they were acknowledged as different breeds and set upon their own courses of development. Interbreeding is no longer permitted. Fanciers of these handsome breeds feel each spaniel has its own character and desirable qualities. ¶ The English Cocker Spaniel is one of the finest of the small field dogs and is both intelligent and responsive. If kept in the city or suburbs, he should be exercised regularly; the more often he is taken into the country, the better. His coat does need care, but it is not a long and arduous task if the dog receives proper attention. In show specimens we often see an exaggeration of the elaborate feathering on the legs and ears. This can be overdone, and the feathering should not be so profuse as to hide the true field-dog character of this breed.

English Springer Spaniel

Land of origin: ENGLAND

Original purpose: Hunting

Recent popularity ranking by A.K.C. registration: 22nd

English Springer Spaniel Field Trial Association, Inc.
Ms. Frances A. Nelson, Secretary
3146 Arthur Street
Minneapolis, MN 55418

HEIGHT: Dogs to 20 inches   Bitches to 19 inches

WEIGHT: Dogs to 55 pounds   Bitches to 46 pounds

COAT
Flat or wavy, medium length. Waterproof, weatherproof, and thornproof. Fine and glossy. Never rough or curly.

COLOR
Liver or black with white markings, liver or black and white with tan markings. No lemon, red, or orange.

Amount of care coat requires: 1 2 3 4 5 6 7 8 9 10

Amount of exercise required: 1 2 3 4 5 6 7 8 9 10

Suitability for urban/apartment life:*   1 2 3 4 5 6 7 8 9 10

*Must be appropriately exercised.

The English Springer Spaniel carries in him all the best qualities of the English land spaniels. As a breed, he was separated from the English Cocker Spaniel at the turn of the century and is considerably larger. ¶The English Springer by nature is affectionate and loyal. This is a wonderful breed for children. He may be slow to take up with strangers, but he is not snappy or silly about it. He just likes to be sure of his ground. He therefore can make a first-rate watchdog. ¶The English Springer Spaniel is still a splendid field dog, although he will take well to a quieter and less active life. In city and suburban settings he should be given very long walks. It is a great kindness to get him out into the country as often as possible. He loves water and loves to retrieve. Most of all he loves to belong to a family and will return affection pound for pound. ¶The Springer coat, like that of all well-furnished spaniels, must be seen to if the dog is to remain handsome and regal. That does require some care, although the task need not be difficult. It is quite different, however, if a Springer is allowed to go long periods without attention. The feathering on the ears, chest, and legs will become matted, and he becomes a case for a professional. Things should not be allowed to go that far. ¶The English Springer Spaniel is one of those dogs who is as nice in character as he looks. The standards call for him to be friendly, eager to please, quick to learn, and willing to obey. One cannot ask for much more than that in a dog who already has refined beauty going for him plus a fine tradition of service and companionship!

Field Spaniel

Land of origin: ENGLAND

Original purpose: Hunting

Recent popularity ranking by A.K.C. registration: 125th

Field Spaniel Society of America
Mrs. Becki Jo Wolkenheim, Secretary
P.O. Box 187
Wales, WI 53183

HEIGHT: Dogs to 18 inches   Bitches to 17 inches

WEIGHT: Dogs to 50 pounds   Bitches to 45 pounds

COAT
Flat or slightly wavy. Never curly. Dense, silky, glossy. Feathering setterlike.

COLOR
Usually black but also liver, golden liver, mahogany red, roan—or any of these with tan markings. Should not be so colored and marked as to resemble a Springer Spaniel.

Amount of care coat requires: 1 2 3 4 5 6 7 8 9 10

Amount of exercise required: 1 2 3 4 5 6 7 8 9 10

*Suitability for urban/apartment life:** 1 2 3 4 5 6 7 8 9 10

*If properly exercised.

The Field Spaniel, the least-known spaniel in this country, was badly hurt by some rather bizarre breeding experiments that for a long time kept this dog from being as appealing as his spaniel kin. He is thought to have been derived from the Cocker and Sussex Spaniels, with the Cocker strain being largely Welsh. Much of that may be conjecture. ¶ In an effort to improve the look of the breed, both Cocker and Springer Spaniels were bred in, and eventually the present-day Field Spaniel emerged. There are very few in this country (only thirty-nine specimens were registered with the American Kennel Club in 1978), but interest in this breed could increase. ¶ By nature the Field Spaniel is steady and determined although essentially good-natured. He is not fast and flashy, but he's reliable. He will probably never be a popular gundog in this country but will make it, if he does in fact become popular in the future, as a pet. ¶ The Field Spaniel is fine in the suburbs and even in apartments if properly exercised—he is, after all, a sporting dog designed for the field—and his coat, although rather more setter-like than exaggerated as in some Cockers, does require a reasonable amount of attention. It is not the sort of task that need be oppressive, just acknowledged and taken care of regularly. ¶ Anyone seriously interested in this potentially very fine breed of companion animal may want to think about importing specimens to combine with the finest available examples here. It would be a kind of "ground-floor" venture that could pay off in satisfaction not generally available from coming into a breed after it has already become a fad. The Field Spaniel may be a dog of the future.

The Irish Water Spaniel is not everybody's dog. This is a special-purpose breed with excellent qualities and a superb record of performance. He is so ancient that we have no real information about his origin. He may go back six thousand years to Asia Minor, he may have inhabited the Iberian Peninsula when the Romans were there, and he may have arrived in Ireland with the earliest settlers of that land. All maybe, but we do know that he reached his present state of excellence in Ireland and that even Shakespeare wrote of his outstanding characteristics. ¶The excellence of this dog lies in his devotion to his master and his tolerance of his family. The Irish

Irish Water Spaniel

Land of origin: IRELAND, but possibly far back in ancient Asia Minor

Original purpose: Water retrieving and other hunting uses

Recent popularity ranking by A.K.C. registration: 120th

Irish Water Spaniel Club of America
Ms. Susan Tapp, Secretary
434 Webster Avenue
Washington Township, NJ 07675

HEIGHT: Dogs to 24 inches   Bitches to 23 inches

WEIGHT: Dogs to 65 pounds   Bitches to 58 pounds

COAT
Extremely important point. Dense, tight ringlets without any woolliness. Longer on legs, wavy and abundant.

COLOR
Solid liver. No white markings.

Amount of care coat requires: 1 2 3 4 5 6 7 8 9 10
                         •••••••••

Amount of exercise required: 1 2 3 4 5 6 7 8 9 10
                         ••••••••••••••••••••

Suitability for urban/apartment life: 1 2 3 4 5 6 7 8 9 10
                                        UNSUITED

Water Spaniel is a great water dog of endurance and skill. He is obedient, if well trained early in life, and is a top-level performer in any field for which he is suited. He is not necessarily the best of general pets, since he is tricky with strangers. For that reason he makes a better watchdog than most sporting dogs, but he does have to be guided since his natural suspiciousness tends to be nonselective. He also must be well controlled when around other animals. He can be a scrapper. ¶None of this is to say that the Irish Water Spaniel is a vicious dog (that word does not properly apply to dogs unless they have been made that way by ill treatment or disease), but rather that he is an assertive, hardheaded animal who is not approving of people he does not know well or see regularly. This can be a problem, particularly in an urban environment. ¶The distinctive ringleted coat of the Irish Water Spaniel does not require much heavy grooming unless it is badly neglected, and there's the rub. The coat does tend to mat and retain dirt unless it is brushed every three or four days at least. Although not a long or arduous process, it is an essential one that should be infallibly performed. ¶The Irish Water Spaniel is a breed with staunch devotees. They like the look of the animal, including the distinctly ratlike tail; they like the purposeful gait and stance and fiery willingness of the animal to work, to perform, to please. This, the tallest of the spaniels, despite his somewhat clownish appearance, is a special dog for special owners. Casual dog owners who are not accomplished at the art of being a master may be disappointed. Real dog people who are attracted to the dog for his antiquity, his skill in the field, and his aloof independence will be delighted.

Sussex Spaniel

Land of origin: ENGLAND

Original purpose: Hunting

Recent popularity ranking by A.K.C. registration: 126th

Sussex Spaniel Club of America
Linda Legare, Corres. Secretary
4488 280th St. E.
Randolph, MN 55065

HEIGHT: Dogs to 16 inches   Bitches to 15 inches

WEIGHT: Dogs to 45 pounds   Bitches to 40 pounds

COAT
Abundant and either flat or slightly waved. No curl allowed. Moderate feathering on legs and stern.

COLOR
Rich golden liver.

Amount of care coat requires: 1 2 3 4 5 6 7 8 9 10

Amount of exercise required: 1 2 3 4 5 6 7 8 9 10

Suitability for urban/apartment life:*   1 2 3 4 5 6 7 8 9 10

*If properly exercised.

The Sussex Spaniel is one of the least-known dogs in this country, and during 1975 only thirty-three new specimens were registered with the American Kennel Club. The breed apparently originated—or at least was perfected—in the county of Sussex, England. When it was developed, hunting was still done on foot, and there was plenty of game around. What was needed was a slow and steady dog who was at the same time companionable. These developments all took place in an area and a period of what was called rough shooting. ¶The Sussex Spaniel is a slow, not terribly elegant animal who is intelligent and deliberate in everything he does. He has a *massive* appearance, although even a big male will be under fifty pounds. He makes a good pet and will do well in any normal family situation. He has not caught on in this country because he is not stylish looking enough to fascinate the show enthusiast, and he is really not well suited to modern American hunting needs and habits. ¶Because he is slow and steady, neither mean nor silly, and because he is loyal and eminently trainable, the Sussex Spaniel holds real promise as a companion animal in this country. It is moot as to whether the breed will ever be given an opportunity to show its worth. All it takes, really, is a few determined enthusiasts to take the breed on. ¶The Sussex Spaniel is a reasonably good watchdog; he is usually calm and gentle, has very little odor, and gets along well with other animals. ¶Anyone seriously interested in this breed will probably find it difficult to locate puppies for sale. After checking with whatever breeders can be located, the potential enthusiast might want to think about importing specimens from England. Anyone looking for a cause as well as a pet might want to think about this gentleman from Sussex. There is a lot of quality built into the breed, and a little public relations could launch it on a whole new and unexpected American career.

The Welsh Springer is not anywhere near as well known in this country as its cousin the English Springer Spaniel. They are different breeds with very similar qualities. The Welsh Springer developed in Wales over four centuries ago and has always been quite distinctive. Here are some major differences between the breeds:

	HEIGHT RANGE	WEIGHT RANGE
Welsh Springer	15½–17 in.	32–40 lbs.
English Springer	17–20 in.	35–55 lbs.

	COLORS	COAT
Welsh Springer	Red and white	Not wavy
English Springer	Liver, black, tan, white, blue, roan in many combinations	Often wavy

The main differences to the eye are color and length of back. The English is the larger dog. ¶ The Welsh Springer Spaniel is a tireless hunting dog and is easily trained for a variety of tasks. The breed is intelli-

Welsh Springer Spaniel

Land of origin: WALES

Original purpose: Hunting

Recent popularity ranking by A.K.C. registration: 98th

Welsh Springer Spaniel Club of America
Edwin Cummings III, Secretary
RD 1, Box 164
Accord, NY 12404

HEIGHT: Dogs to 17 inches   Bitches to 16½ inches

WEIGHT: Dogs to 45 pounds   Bitches to 38 pounds

COAT
Straight, flat, thick, and silky. Not wiry or wavy; curliness considered especially bad.

COLOR
Red and white; colors clear, strong, and rich.

Amount of care coat requires: 1 2 3 4 5 6 7 8 9 10

Amount of exercise required: 1 2 3 4 5 6 7 8 9 10

Suitability for urban/apartment life: * 1 2 3 4 5 6 7 8 9 10

*If very well exercised regularly.

gent, steady, and responsive to approval. It is as fine a companion as it is a hunting breed. ¶ In the home the Welsh Springer shows his other and equally desirable side. He is sensible and steady and not quarrelsome or foolish. He loves to play and will be the wise old dog or the clown, depending on age and the demands of the moment. He loves to participate in all group activities and does not take well to being left behind. He is naturally fine with children and will adjust to any reasonable family situation. He needs a lot of exercise, though, as might be expected of a sporting animal, and no one should attempt to maintain one in the suburbs or the city unless a good exercise regimen can be developed and adhered to. No weather is too tough for this Welshman, and he will not understand why you find any condition not perfect for a long walk or a romp. He needs that exercise not only for his peace of canine mind but also for body conditioning. ¶ A certain amount of brushing is required if that fine and elegant spaniel look is to be maintained. It isn't much of a chore if it is performed faithfully as part of a regular weekly schedule.

The Magyar hordes swarming into central Europe ten centuries ago brought
with them a hunting dog that was probably
already an old breed. We believe that dog
gave rise to the hunting dog of Hungary
known today as the Vizsla. This is a fast,
tensely mounted animal of boundless energy and willingness. He wants to work, he
wants to please, and he wants reward in the
form of praise. ¶ This graceful animal is an
aristocrat, not unlike a thoroughbred horse
with its neat, perfected conformation and
smooth, even power. The Vizsla is also extremely headstrong and determined to
have it out once and for all with his master.
Someone, man or dog, is going to be boss.

Vizsla

Land of origin: HUNGARY

Original purpose: All-purpose hunting

Recent popularity ranking by A.K.C. registration: 57th

Vizsla Club of America, Inc.
Ms. Jan Bouman, Corres. Secretary
14808 Williamsburg Curve
Burnsville, MN 55337

HEIGHT: Dogs to 24 inches   Bitches to 23 inches

WEIGHT: Dogs to 60 pounds   Bitches to 55 pounds

COAT
Short, dense, and smooth. Lies flat, no undercoat.

COLOR
Solid rusty gold or dark sandy yellow. Dark brown and pale yellow not desirable.

Amount of care coat requires: 1 2 3 4 5 6 7 8 9 10
                                                     •

Amount of exercise required: 1 2 3 4 5 6 7 8 9 10
                                           • • • • • • • • • • • • • • • • • • •

Suitability for urban/apartment life: 1 2 3 4 5 6 7 8 9 10
                                                               UNSUITED

Sanity with a Vizsla in the home requires that this issue be settled early on. A Vizsla who has not been properly trained for life in a home is a monumental pest. Left alone he just might decide to go sailing through a plate-glass window in order to have some fun outside. He'll keep on running your glazier's bill up, too, until the rules are outlined for him and his stay-at-home manners learned. ¶ The Vizsla can be fine with his master's family, though he may be very slow to take to strangers, and he can be aloof, to say the least. Shyness, however, would be considered a fault. ¶ As is often the case with large, smooth-coated field dogs, the Vizsla is a poor choice for urban or even suburban living and not really the dog for people who are sedentary in habit. One way or another, the Vizsla is going to get the workout he needs to stay in shape and burn up his endless energy reserve. If you don't work him in the field, then he is going to be bumptious and a nuisance. Of course, you don't have to be a hunter, but you do have to like very long walks. A Vizsla needs to run and explore and respond to cool, even, but very forceful commands. ¶ You cannot fault the Vizsla on his qualities as a field dog. He is intelligent, responsive, perfected for the job he was designed to do. The Vizsla is one of the special-purpose dogs for special kinds of committed dog owners.

The Weimaraner is an all-purpose hunting dog developed in Germany from the Bloodhound. He is a large, assertive, intelligent animal of unmistakable quality. He is also a dog who requires special qualities in his master. ¶ The Weimaraner makes a better watchdog than almost any other breed of sporting dog because he is aggressive and quite fearless. He is a dog of great character, and he spends much of his time telling everyone about it. If allowed to have the upper hand, there is no worse pest than this breed. He should not be a person's first dog. ¶ This is a breed that simply must be given a full course of obedience training at the professional level. If the owner is com-

Weimaraner

Land of origin: GERMANY

Original purpose: Big-game hunting

Recent popularity ranking by A.K.C. registration: 46th

Weimaraner Club of America
Mrs. Dorothy Derr, Corres. Secretary
P.O. Box 2452
Fargo, ND 58108-2452

HEIGHT: Dogs to 27 inches   Bitches to 25 inches

WEIGHT: Dogs to 85 pounds   Bitches to 70 pounds

COAT
Short, smooth, sleek.

COLOR
Solid—shades of mouse gray to silver gray. Small white spot on chest alone allowed. A distinctly blue or black coat is grounds for disqualification.

Amount of care coat requires: 1 2 3 4 5 6 7 8 9 10
                                     •

Amount of exercise required: 1 2 3 4 5 6 7 8 9 10
                                    • • • • • • • • • • • • • • • • • • •

Suitability for urban/apartment life: 1 2 3 4 5 6 7 8 9 10
                                          UNSUITED

petent, that is fine; if not, then the cost of taking your Weimaraner to a top obedience school should be considered a part of the acquisition price. An untrained Weimaraner is going to walk all over his owner, his family, and their friends. While not dangerous, he can be pushy and extremely unpleasant to have around. Conversely, a well-trained Weimaraner is one of the most splendid-looking and gentlemanly of all breeds, sporting or otherwise. ¶ The Germans were almost neurotic in the severity with which they governed the breeding of Weimaraners. Poor specimens were destroyed, and good specimens were only bred after the most careful consideration. Predictably, when the breed became known here around 1929, it caught on. Equally predictable was the slippage in breeding standards. Weimaraners bred in this country today range from the really ex-cellent to the utterly hopeless. Retail all-breed puppy outlets often feature these dogs, but they should never be obtained from this source. Be suspicious of the inexpensive Weimaraner: only the finest show and field-trial stock should be accepted, and only after a visit with the breeder and a chance to see and meet the puppy's parents. ¶ The only real problem with the Weimaraner as a breed is that he is often more intelligent than the person who owns him. When this happens, it is not the happiest of man dog relationships. The owner should always be smarter and should always be in command. Any person smart enough and strong willed enough to properly select, train, and manage a Weimaraner is in for an unparalleled dog-owning experience. The owner who overrates himself or underrates his Weimaraner is in for an ordeal.

This seldom-seen hunting dog began his career in Holland late in the nineteenth century. One man, really, was responsible for developing the breed from a mixture of spaniels, setters, hounds, and mixed-breed dogs. Because of a family quarrel the man, E. K. Korthals, eventually left Holland for Germany and then moved on to France. He took his dogs with him and kept up the breeding experiments for the rest of his life. In France they still refer to this dog as the Korthals Griffon. ¶The Wirehaired Pointing Griffon is a somewhat slow, very deliberate, and skillful multipurpose hunting dog. He is a pointer, as well as a retriever. His harsh,

Wirehaired Pointing Griffon

Land of origin: HOLLAND

Original purpose: All-purpose hunting

Recent popularity ranking by A.K.C. registration: 122nd

HEIGHT: Dogs to 23½ inches   Bitches to 21½ inches

WEIGHT: Dogs to 60 pounds   Bitches to 55 pounds

COAT
Unique in sporting dogs—downy undercoat and hard, dry, stiff outer coat like bristles on a wild boar.

COLOR
Steel gray, white with chestnut splashes, all chestnut, or dirty white and chestnut. Black a serious fault.

Amount of care coat requires: 1 2 3 4 5 6 7 8 9 10
                                    • • • • •

Amount of exercise required: 1 2 3 4 5 6 7 8 9 10
                                   • • • • • • • • • • • • • • • • • •

Suitability for urban/apartment life: 1 2 3 4 5 6 7 8 9 10
                                           UNSUITED

rough coat makes him an ideal dog for cold climates, miserable weather, and tough terrain like saltwater marshes. This is a steady, positive, and intelligent breed of dog. He is also a particularly pleasant companion breed. ¶The Wirehaired Pointing Griffon is loyal to his master and good with children. He is calm and reasonable with strangers, although he can be slow to offer affection or to show enthusiasm. He is detached and perhaps cautious by nature when he is unsure of newcomers. ¶The Wirehaired Pointing Griffon, a very rare dog in America, is not an apartment or city dog. Confined, he cannot be relied upon to retain his naturally calm, intelligent way of dealing with life. He needs enormous amounts of exercise to stay well and happy, and the more exposure he gets to rough ter-

rain and hard living, the happier he seems to be. People attempting to remold Korthals's many years of hard work and skillful breeding in a single generation are in for a disappointment. This is one breed that will not be recast that easily. This is a dog for an active family—perhaps ideally an active single person. He thrives on miserable weather, rough water, and long days that begin before sunrise. If you have that kind of abuse and misery to offer, you are going to have a happy dog. He will curl up by the fire at night and kick his legs in dreams that re-create the day, but he wants that day to be rough enough to try him. ¶A Wirehaired Pointing Griffon should not be difficult or ill-tempered. There is a solid, workaday look about him, a pragmatic Dutch way of going about the day's labors.

[Group 2]

The Hounds

Afghan Hound
Basenji
Basset Hound
Beagle
Black and Tan Coonhound
Bloodhound
Borzoi
Dachshund
American Foxhound
English Foxhound
Greyhound

Harrier
Ibizan Hound
Irish Wolfhound
Norwegian Elkhound
Otter Hound
Pharoah Hound
Rhodesian Ridgeback
Saluki
Scottish Deerhound
Whippet

The handsome Afghan Hound is an aristocrat. The breed goes back almost six thousand years, and he was no doubt the companion of kings. He is also a clown, for he loves to play and romp and is almost never mean or petty. ¶The Afghan Hound is one of the few large active dogs who can make it in the city. Although this dog requires a great deal of exercise and should be taken on long, fast walks several times a day, he can adapt to apartment life. Despite the "klutzy" act he puts on and the general prejudice that the coursing, or sight, hounds aren't always the brightest dogs on the block, the Afghan is a willing dog who is anxious to please. Because of the Afghan's size and his occasional good-natured bumptiousness, it is a good idea for a new owner and his dog to take obedience classes together. ¶The Afghan

Afghan Hound

Land of origin: SINAI PENINSULA, then AFGHANISTAN

Original purpose: Hunting, including leopard

Recent popularity ranking by A.K.C. registration: 55th

Afghan Hound Club of America, Inc.
Mrs. Norma Cozzoni, Corres. Secretary
2408 A, Route 31
Oswego, IL 60543

HEIGHT: Dogs to 27 inches   Bitches to 25 inches

WEIGHT: Dogs to 60 pounds   Bitches to 50 pounds

COAT
Thick, silky, very fine in texture. Not clipped or trimmed. Long hair except on back in mature dogs, where saddle is short.

COLOR
All colors are seen, but white markings, especially on the head, are not desirable.

Amount of care coat requires: 1 2 3 4 5 6 7 8 9 10

Amount of exercise required: 1 2 3 4 5 6 7 8 9 10

Suitability for urban/apartment life:*   1 2 3 4 5 6 7 8 9 10

---

*Assuming that the dog will be taken on long walks several times a day and at least occasionally be taken someplace where he will be able to run.

is a stunning-looking dog, and the coat should be well brushed to enhance the liquid motion that is so characteristic of this animal of style and beauty. Ropy or matted Afghans are unforgivable and tell one a great deal about the owners who bought a dog they were not prepared to properly keep. ¶ Afghans are fine with children, although there is the problem of small toddlers being bowled over by a great galumphing hound bounding to the door to see who is there. ¶ This ancient hound does well with other animals and usually will not fight. Of course, two mature males always can be a problem, but perhaps less so with this breed than with a good many others. ¶ There is no doubt that many people like the idea of high style in a dog, and one would have to go far to find a breed better suited to that ego need than this one. And this is not to be condemned. It is just as easy

to love a dog who gives an added aesthetic satisfaction as it is to adore one who doesn't. The potential Afghan owner should, however, be certain that it isn't *just* style he wants. This breed is sensitive, constantly in need of affection and a sense of participation; although splendid-looking in a fashion layout, the Afghan is not merely an ornament. ¶ Any dog, once purchased, becomes a long-term commitment. It is no more true of any other breed than it is of this ancient hound. He once shared the tents of sheikhs in the Sinai wilderness and later coursed the rugged mountains of Afghanistan for leopard and gazelle in blistering summer heat and bone-cracking winter cold. Despite his picturesque and seemingly delicate beauty, the Afghan remains a hunting hound—hardy, tough, and willing.

There aren't many animals from Africa on the European and American scene, and for that reason alone the Basenji began catching on almost as soon as he was first seen in America in 1937. He was a curiosity with a fascinating history. This dog was brought to Egypt for the pleasure of the pharaohs thousands of years ago. With the fall of that ancient civilization, the breed was able to hang on in its native central Africa, where it was used for hunting. ¶The Basenji is a swift, silent dog with a remarkable nose and great determination. He is an active animal and should be given a great deal of exercise every day. He has a lovely, high-stepping gait and is

Basenji

Land of origin: CENTRAL AFRICA

Original purpose: Hunting

Recent popularity ranking by A.K.C. registration: 58th

Basenji Club of America
Dr. Shirley J. Jones, Secretary
112 E. Larry Road
Shawnee, OK 74801

HEIGHT: Dogs to 17 inches   Bitches to 16 inches

WEIGHT: Dogs to 24 pounds   Bitches to 22 pounds

COAT
Short and silky. Coat very pliant.

COLOR
Chestnut red, pure black, black and tan—always with white feet, chest, and tail tip. White legs, blaze, and collar allowed as optional.

Amount of care coat requires: 1 2 3 4 5 6 7 8 9 10
                                  •

Amount of exercise required: 1 2 3 4 5 6 7 8 9 10
                               • • • • • • • • •

Suitability for urban/apartment life: 1 2 3 4 5 6 7 8 9 10
                               • • • • • • • • • • • • • •

---

great fun to watch. When happy, he bounds and leaps and is like a little deer with glistening coat. ¶ It is not true that the Basenji is mute. He does not bark like other dogs, but he does make a giggling, yodeling sound that is impossible to describe or imitate. It is a happy sound, generally reserved for close friends. ¶ The Basenji is one of the cleanest dogs. His coat needs almost no care, and he rarely if ever needs bathing—certainly not more than a couple times a year. Almost unique in the dog world is his habit of washing himself all over, just like a cat. The result is a perfect pleasure of a dog for the fastidious homeowner. ¶ Naturally well-behaved and intelligent, the Basenji will take training easily, especially if he is included within the family circle. He is a calm dog, surprisingly so for one so active. He seems to have everything under control, however, and to know instinctively how to please. ¶ Basenjis can be good with children—in almost any family situation—but they do insist on being a part of the action and are often suspicious of strangers. A Basenji who is left out, even inadvertently, is an unhappy dog. ¶ In play and pleasure, in the show-ring and on the street, the handsome, sprightly little fox-terrier-sized hound called the Basenji never fails to attract attention. One can predict with fair certainty that the breed will only increase in popularity as time passes.

The Basset Hound is an old breed developed in France and Belgium mostly from the Bloodhound, whose saintlike disposition it shares. ¶The Basset has been popular in Europe for centuries and has always been highly regarded for his many fine qualities. He is a slow trailing dog but one with tremendous stamina and deliberateness. He is said to have a nose second only to that of the Bloodhound, that grandfather of all scent hounds. The ears of the Basset, designed to swirl up stale scent particles into the ever-receptive nose, also point to the undoubted Bloodhound ancestry of the breed. Because of a naturally oily skin, he does have a pleasant, somewhat

Basset Hound

Land of origin: FRANCE

Original purpose: All-purpose hunting

Recent popularity ranking by A.K.C. registration: 21st

Basset Hound Club of America, Inc.
Mrs. Andrea Field, Secretary
6060 Oak Hill Lane
Centerville, OH 45459

HEIGHT: Dogs to 15 inches   Bitches to 14 inches

WEIGHT: Dogs to 45 pounds   Bitches to 35 pounds

COAT
Hard, smooth, short, and quite dense. Skin loose and elastic.

COLOR
Any recognized hound color. Distribution of markings of no importance in judging.

Amount of care coat requires: 1 2 3 4 5 6 7 8 9 10

Amount of exercise required: 1 2 3 4 5 6 7 8 9 10

*Suitability for urban/apartment life:**   1 2 3 4 5 6 7 8 9 10

*But plenty of exercise *is* required—preferably three or four long walks a day.

musky, "doggy" odor. ¶ The Basset is one of the most pleasant and adaptable of dogs. Almost never snappy or aggressive, he gets along well with his master (whom he adores), family, and friends (whether two- or four-legged) and he should always be included in family activities. He is peaceful, sensible, affectionate, and simply marvelous with children. As a puppy he is as engaging as an animal can be, and his cheery outlook remains with him all his life. He can be serious, of course, and when charged with a job the Basset goes about it with almost comic intensity. ¶ More agile than he appears, the Basset requires a great deal of exercise. It would be unfair to keep a Basset Hound shut in week in and week out. This is an active field animal, and he has been bred for that purpose for hundreds of canine generations. He should not be penalized just because he also happens to be almost unbelievably pleasant. The Basset Hound should be walked several times a day—long, well-paced walks—and taken to the country for an open-air run as often as possible. Because family is far more important to a Basset than anything else, he will adapt to apartment life and is quiet and reasonable when inside. ¶ Bassets are fairly long-lived, are generally strong and healthy, and can be good watchdogs. They have very loud voices. Naturally obedient and easy to train, they are good natured about taking orders. A large, fine hound of many exceptional qualities, the Basset deserves all the favor he is experiencing. Very few hounds outrank him in popularity.

The Beagle is one of the oldest of the scent hounds, probably dating back to pre-Roman times. It is believed that the breed formed in England and possibly in Wales, although we can never know for sure. Beagles have been evident all through recorded history in that part of the British Isles. ¶ The Beagle is a hunting hound who works well alone or in small groups or large packs. He has been used on rabbit and hare and other game as well. The ancestry of some packs in England is very old, and their bloodlines are jealously guarded. The breed is by nature loyal, very easily trained, and courageous. For his size this tough little dog will take almost anything that any other dog can handle. No weather bothers him, no terrain—no matter how rough and

Beagle

Land of origin: Probably WALES and ENGLAND

Original purpose: Hunting rabbits

Recent popularity ranking by A.K.C. registration: 9th

National Beagle Club
Mr. Joseph B. Wiley, Jr., Secretary
River Road
Bedminster, NJ 07921

HEIGHT: Variety 1—Dogs to 13 inches   Bitches to 13 inches
Variety 2—Dogs 13 to 15 inches   Bitches 13 to 15 inches

WEIGHT: Under 13 inches–to 18 pounds
Over 13 inches–to 20 pounds

COAT
Close, hard, typical hound; medium length.

COLOR
Any true hound color—white, tan, black in different combinations and markings.

Amount of care coat requires: 1 2 3 4 5 6 7 8 9 10

Amount of exercise required: 1 2 3 4 5 6 7 8 9 10

*Suitability for urban/apartment life:**   1 2 3 4 5 6 7 8 9 10

*But only if properly exercised.

broken—is too hard, and no amount of running will wear him down. For endurance and courage this dog is not to be beat. ¶ All of that, though, has to do with the dog in the field. Most Beagles in America today are house pets, and they excel at that assignment as well. Beagles and children are a natural mix, and the dog gets along splendidly with other animals. Beagles are often good little watchdogs, although they are fine with strangers once they have been introduced. They are affectionate and outgoing, and they have a lovely hound voice. In the city young Beagles need to be trained not to overdo the vocalizing. A Beagle loves a good howling session and may tend to do a solo when left alone. That can be a bit tiresome for the neighbors. ¶ It is no accident that the Beagle is in ninth place among American Kennel Club registra-tions today. He has been on top for years and probably always will be there. Beagles are splendid country dogs, fine in the suburban home and in the apartment as well— as long as they get exercise. They are not silly or ever ugly; they are calm, gentle, and loving. They are also clean and quite easy to train. ¶ There are so many Beagles produced in this country each year—forty-five thousand new Beagles were registered with the A.K.C. in 1975, and that is only a fraction of those born—that great care must be taken to obtain a really good example of the breed. It is wise to bypass the mass-producers and seek out the specialist. There are two distinct sizes of Beagle—up to thirteen inches and from thirteen to fifteen inches. Over fifteen inches is outsized and not to be encouraged. No sense in trying to turn a Beagle into a Foxhound.

Black and Tan Coonhound

Land of origin: UNITED STATES

Original purpose: Hunting, especially raccoon and opossum

Recent popularity ranking by A.K.C. registration: 108th

American Black & Tan Coonhound Club, Inc.
Cynthia Pantaloni, Secretary
342 Bush Street
Howell, MI 48843

HEIGHT: Dogs to 27 inches   Bitches to 25 inches

WEIGHT: Dogs to 85 pounds   Bitches to 80 pounds

COAT
Short, dense, and able to withstand rough country.

COLOR
Coal black with rich tan above eyes, on sides of muzzle, chest, legs, and breeching.
Black penciling on toes.

Amount of care coat requires: 1 2 3 4 5 6 7 8 9 10

Amount of exercise required: 1 2 3 4 5 6 7 8 9 10

Suitability for urban/apartment life: 1 2 3 4 5 6 7 8 9 10
UNSUITED

The handsome Black and Tan Coonhound apparently is descended from the English Talbot Hound, the Bloodhound, and the English Foxhound. In this country the American Foxhound was crossed in, and the breed emerged as we know it today. It shares many skills and characteristics with other Southern hound breeds not recognized by the American Kennel Club. It has been bred not only for field performance but also for its distinctive colors. ¶The Black and Tan Coonhound is a large, active, working hound. He has a magnificent voice, which he uses when he picks up a trail. He trails like a Bloodhound, seeking microscopic particles of scent material. He is all but impossible to shake off once he latches on. ¶The Black and Tan shares other characteristics with the Bloodhound: the elements of personality. Like the more ancient breed, the Black and Tan is a big, delightful slob. Although massive and powerful and without limit in his energy and endurance, he is delightful as a companion animal. There is the almost inevitable tendency to think of the Black and Tan as a ferocious dog looking for people and things to tear apart. Such is not the case at all. What the Black and Tan likes above everything else is attention, affection, and approbation. He is the near perfect dog in a give-and-take situation. Black and Tans are seldom quarrelsome with other animals, although adult males or adult females can vie with others of their own sex until a suitable pecking order has been established. In all other situations they are generally gentle and playful despite their great power and original use. ¶The Black and Tan Coonhound can be kept in the suburban home, but plenty of exercise is needed and should be an original element in the decision to own this breed. Only the most reliable specialty breeders should be consulted, and adults in the dog's line ought to be carefully examined. The Black and Tan Coonhound is a handsome, splendid breed of dog, and only breeders devoted to the maintenance of their high standards should be trusted.

The Bloodhound often is referred to as the grandfather of all scent hounds. His origins go back to ancient times, and he probably has been known in something like his present form for two thousand years. The modern scent hounds (as distinct from sight hounds such as the Greyhound and Borzoi)—the Beagles, Bassets, and Fox-hounds, for example—all carry the blood of the Bloodhound. ¶Interestingly, Bloodhounds probably got their name from the fact that in the Middle Ages in England it was only people of blue blood—aristocrats, that is—who owned this animal. To suggest that the name *Bloodhound* comes from any sanguinary propensity is just plain silly.

Bloodhound

Land of origin: Probably ancient GREECE or ROME

Original purpose: Hunting, then man trailing

Recent popularity ranking by A.K.C. registration: 63rd

American Bloodhound Club
Mr. Edward Kilby, Corres. Secretary
1914 Berry Lane
Daytona Beach, FL 32014

HEIGHT: Dogs to 27 inches   Bitches to 25 inches

WEIGHT: Dogs to 110 pounds   Bitches to 100 pounds

COAT
Short, dense, and able to withstand rough country.

COLOR
Coal black with rich tan above eyes, on sides of muzzle, chest, legs, and breeching. Black penciling on toes.

Amount of care coat requires: 1 2 3 4 5 6 7 8 9 10

Amount of exercise required: 1 2 3 4 5 6 7 8 9 10

Suitability for urban/apartment life: 1 2 3 4 5 6 7 8 9 10
UNSUITED

Bloodhounds are lovers. They do not *hunt* men; they follow trails, and that is their game. The Bloodhound's almost unimaginably keen nose enables him to follow trails no other dog could detect. When he gets to his quarry, be it a child or an escaped convict, he does not attack but wags his tail and often tries to kiss. ¶ Apart from the nonsense myth of the attacking, bloodthirsty hound, there are other nonsense tales. Bloodhounds normally are used alone, not in packs. Occasionally a brace (pair) may be used, but no more than that. They do not barrel along a trail yowling—almost all Bloodhounds trail silently. A Bloodhound is not allowed off a lead for two reasons: he would soon leave his trainer behind, and since he has absolutely no road sense, he would be liable to be hit on the first road he had to cross. ¶ The Bloodhound is a loving, gentle pet who should never be quarrelsome with people or other animals. He does not do especially well in the obedience department because his whole nature is to tell you where to go, not take directions *from* you. ¶ The Bloodhound is not a casual dog owner's dog but rather a special breed for dedicated people. Good examples do not come cheaply, and $600 is not high. Bloodhounds are suited to country living. They like to be in the company of other animals and people. Their voices are glorious, and they are more apt to "sing" in greeting to someone they love than when on a trail. Bloodhound owners should consider training their dogs to trail and registering them with the police. Many children and confused old people have been saved by hounds owned by hobbyists. The Bloodhound does require a great deal of exercise, and his feeding must be scheduled and precise, since he is particularly subject to bloat. This gastric disorder of uncertain origin can kill an otherwise healthy dog within an hour.

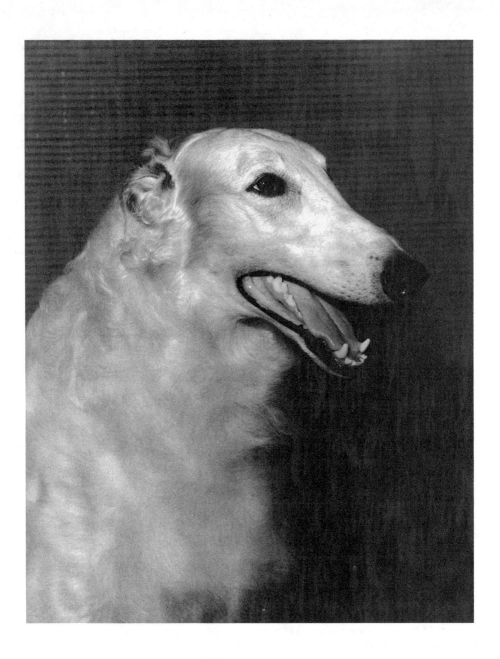

The Borzoi, originally known in the United States as the Russian Wolfhound, is one of the most aristocratic of all dogs in style, bearing, and ancestry. Arabian Greyhounds, gazelle-coursing animals of great speed, were imported into Russia by members of the royal circle. When they failed to survive the Russian weather, others were imported and crossed with a native working dog. The result, after considerable effort, was what we know as the Borzoi. ¶ Few dogs are as beautiful to behold as this magnificent hound, who is even more spectacular when seen in pairs. If a standing Borzoi is lyrical, the hound in motion is an epic poem. He floats when he gets into full stride. He is a powerful, aggressive, purposeful animal with deadly ac-

Borzoi

Land of origin: RUSSIA

Original purpose: Coursing wolves and game animals

Recent popularity ranking by A.K.C. registration: 67th

Borzoi Club of America, Inc.
Ms. Elaine Misko, Corres. Secretary
135 Dorseyville Road
Pittsburg, PA 15215

HEIGHT: Dogs to 31 inches   Bitches to 29 inches

WEIGHT: Dogs to 105 pounds   Bitches to 90 pounds

COAT
Long and silky but not at all woolly. May be flat or wavy or even somewhat curly. Neck well frilled, profuse, and curly. Feathering on hindquarters and tail, less on chest.

COLOR
Any color or combination of colors is acceptable.

Amount of care coat requires: 1 2 3 4 5 6 7 8 9 10
                                   • • • • • •

Amount of exercise required: 1 2 3 4 5 6 7 8 9 10
                                 • • • • • • • • • • • • • • • •

*Suitability for urban/apartment life:** 1 . 2 3 4 5 6 7 8 9 10
                                          • • • •

*If there is space and if exercise will be provided to suit the needs of this animal.

curacy once he is set loose. He will run a wolf to the ground and kill it, whatever its size. This should be kept in mind when other dogs are around—a Borzoi in a fight is big trouble, not only because of size and power, but also because of the breed's extraordinary speed. ¶ Any prospective owner should weigh carefully the exercise this animal must have. Since few city dwellers can provide an opportunity for the Borzoi to course, very long walks and, if there is a place where conditions are right, a chance to run are the minimal requirements. It must be remembered, though, that before a Borzoi is allowed to run, he must be thoroughly trained. He will be out of sight in seconds and well beyond a casual whistle of recall. The dogs certainly should not be allowed to molest native wildlife or other people's pets. ¶ The Borzoi makes a good pet. He is generally a calm animal, considering his purpose and design, and is affectionate with youngsters and adults. Because of the animal's lightninglike reflexes, incredible speed, agility, and great size, any sign of aggressiveness toward people must be discouraged. A puppy should be trained early, and that training should be maintained throughout the dog's life. ¶ The Borzoi is not always superb, however. There are an unfortunate number of poor examples around, animals who are too long for their height, with a disproportionate head, too short a tail, or who lack the liquid motion that so enhances the beauty of this breed; such specimens are to be avoided by knowing the parents of the animal and by not buying a puppy too young to be properly evaluated. Care in purchase is required, for relatively poor examples are found even in the show-ring. In the pet trade they can be horrendous. Beware of an inexpensive Borzoi.

Today's Dachshund is the descendant of a fiery German hunting dog of perhaps thirty-five pounds or more. He was used initially on badger, or so tradition goes (*Dachs* is the German word for "badger"), but also on a wide variety of other wildlife. He should exhibit the character and assertiveness this background suggests. ¶ The Dachshund is a wonderfully responsive and loyal dog, seemingly a hound but with many terrierlike characteristics. He is intelligent, willing to learn, and a true participant. He loves play, and he travels well. Because of his short legs, he gets more exercise per block than almost any other breed you can name. He is, then, a perfect apartment dog. ¶ The three coat styles require different degrees of care, of course, but it is never oppressive, for the naturally clean little Dachshund is never very large. The Miniature variety sports all three coats. He is a true lapdog and can be car-

Dachshund

Land of origin: GERMANY

Original purpose: Hunting, especially of badger

Recent popularity ranking by A.K.C. registration: 8th

Dachshund Club of America, Inc.
Ms. Julia W. Goulder, Secretary
7540 Silvercrest Way
Scottsdale, AZ 85253

HEIGHT: Dogs to 9 inches   Bitches to 9 inches

WEIGHT:* Dogs to 20 pounds   Bitches to 20 pounds

COAT
Smooth variety—short, thick, smooth, shiny. Not coarse or too thick.

Wirehaired variety—uniform, tight, short, thick, rough, and hard. Good undercoat. Beard on chin. Eyebrows bushy.

Longhaired variety—soft, sleek, glistening, slightly wavy, feathered.

COLOR
Red or tan, red-yellow, yellow, brindle; deep black, chocolate, gray, or blue and white. Dappled. Foregoing for smooth variety. All colors permissible in wirehaired variety. Longhaired has same range as smooth except red and black is allowed and classed as red.

Amount of care coat requires:
Smooth: 1 2 3 4 5 6 7 8 9 10

Wirehaired: 1 2 3 4 5 6 7 8 9 10

Longhaired: 1 2 3 4 5 6 7 8 9 10

Amount of exercise required: 1 2 3 4 5 6 7 8 9 10

Suitability for urban/apartment life: 1 2 3 4 5 6 7 8 9 10

*Miniature Dachshunds are bred in all three coats (see above) and are shown as a division of the open class as "under 10 pounds" when twelve months or older.

ried anywhere. ¶Dachshunds get along well with children and with other animals, although when young they are very playful and can drive other animals up the wall. They soon learn their manners, though, and settle in as fine family pets. They are, in fact, often owned in pairs because they are such fun to watch. ¶Because they do have three very distinct coat styles, a wide range of colors, and a remarkable range in size, they are able to serve a variety of tastes. This coupled with their good nature and responsiveness has kept them consistently among the most popular of all breeds in the United States. People who own Dachshunds tend to keep right on owning them all their lives. ¶Dachshunds are so extremely popular that the mass-producers have had a field day, and there are some perfectly awful specimens offered for sale every day. Stick to the best specialty breeders and make sure you have the dog you set out to own—a fine example of a truly outstanding breed.

The American Foxhound may date as far back as De Soto's landing in Florida in 1539. Some records say that he brought a hound pack with him. We do know that English hounds were imported in 1650 and that these were foundation animals for what later appeared to be an American version of the English Fox-hound. They were, in fact, better known as Virginia Hounds and were distinctly different from their English ancestors by George Washington's time. But English packs were imported in 1742 and 1770, and Washington was a subscriber to the latter importation. In 1785 Lafayette gave Washington some French hounds of similar size, and

American Foxhound

Land of origin: ENGLAND, FRANCE, and AMERICA

Original purpose: Hunting and field trials

Recent popularity ranking by A.K.C. registration: 129th

American Foxhound Club
Mrs. Jack H. Heck, Secretary
221 Oakwood Ave.
Dayton, OH 45419

HEIGHT: Dogs to 25 inches   Bitches to 24 inches

WEIGHT: Dogs to 70 pounds   Bitches to 65 pounds

COAT
Medium length, hard, close, typical of hounds.

COLOR
Any color—usually includes black, white, and/or tan.

Amount of care coat requires: 1 2 3 4 5 6 7 8 9 10

Amount of exercise required: 1 2 3 4 5 6 7 8 9 10

Suitability for urban/apartment life: 1 2 3 4 5 6 7 8 9 10
UNSUITED

---

the Virginia Hounds were improved. In 1808 more came in from England and, in 1830, another pack from Ireland. ¶ Over the intervening years more imports have helped improve the strength, durability, and versatility of what is now called the American Foxhound. He is still a little less sturdy than the English Foxhound, but he is a dog of great versatility with fine pet as well as field qualities. The American Foxhound is used today in field trials, as a trailing dog for armed fox hunters on foot, as a trailing dog in the mounted fox-hunting tradition, and as a general pack hound. Other popular hunting hounds in the South have been derived from the Foxhound, and his qualities appear among many American-developed scent hounds. ¶ This is a dog of great speed and a jealous nature. He is unbeatable when it comes to determination, and no terrain will deter him once he is on a trail. His nose is very keen, and he ignores weather completely. Because he has been a pack dog all down through history, the American Foxhound, like his English cousin, gets along with other dogs. He is loyal to master and family and can be quite protective. He may be slow in taking up with strangers—he isn't silly or snappy, just cautious. The Foxhound is a field animal with hardened muscles, a creature of the hunt and the chase. Locked up and kept from running and using his incredible nose, he can go a little "stir crazy," and the dog who is kept that way should not be expected to show all of the fine qualities that a working dog will. ¶ Many Americans split their time between the city and the country, and even people without a second residence spend long hours hiking and perhaps camping. For such owners the Foxhound is ideal. But only the very active city dweller should even consider this fine hound for a pet.

The English Foxhound's studbooks go back to the eighteenth century and have been well kept, for the breeding has been in the hands of masters of hounds. Any owner of an English Foxhound today should be able to trace that dog back to 1800 or before. ¶The well-boned, sturdy, and reliable English Foxhound on the average tends to be somewhat stouter than his American counterpart to whose origins he contributed so much. The head is large but not gross. The neck is long and clean and should extend at least ten inches from the base of the skull to the shoulder. This is not a small dog. He is symmetrical in appearance and should have a bright and ea-

English Foxhound

Land of origin: ENGLAND

Original purpose: Trailing, hunting

Recent popularity ranking by A.K.C. registration: 127th

HEIGHT: Dogs to 25 inches   Bitches to 24 inches

WEIGHT: Dogs to 70 pounds   Bitches to 62 pounds

COAT
Short, dense, glossy, and hard—typical of hounds.

COLOR
Black, white, tan, yellow; not important as long as basic hound colors are present.

Amount of care coat requires: 1 2 3 4 5 6 7 8 9 10
                                    •

Amount of exercise required: 1 2 3 4 5 6 7 8 9 10
                                  • • • • • • • • • • • • • •

Suitability for urban/apartment life: 1 2 3 4 5 6 7 8 9 10
                                          UNSUITED

ger look. Willingness is a prime characteristic of the breed. ¶ Because Foxhounds have typical hound coats, they are clean and easily kept. They do shed, but that is seldom a problem unless the animals have been allowed to develop dry coats, a condition that is easily corrected. ¶ Many of the things we have said about the American Foxhound are true of the English Foxhound as well. He is affectionate and loyal to his master and to his family. He is wary of strangers and wants to be sure of his ground before allowing too many liberties. He has a fine voice, of course, and can make a good watchdog. ¶ All the Foxhounds— American, English, and their French counterparts—are trailing field dogs and have a limited tolerance for apartment living. It isn't the apartment that matters so much as it is the life-style of urban families. The Foxhound likes to curl up in front of a fire as much as the next dog does, but that comes after a lot of time acquiring aching muscles. All weather conditions suit the Foxhound, and miles and miles of sniffing the world is what he craves. You cannot take a fine field dog, coop him up for weeks on end, and expect the classical Foxhound to show through. You will end up with a different kind of animal. ¶ City dwellers who do not spend a great deal of time hiking or jogging in the country should think twice about this breed. One other thing: scent hounds like the Foxhounds get too interested in an exciting smell for their own good. They should be kept on leads anywhere near traffic, since they will put their nose down and go. They won't stop and look when they come to the curb, and many, indeed, have come to grief as a result.

No one will ever know the exact origin of the Greyhound. This extremely ancient breed may have started in Assyria or Egypt. Carvings on ancient tombs show dogs almost identical in appearance to the Greyhound we know today, or at least dogs who were ancestral to our modern speed demon. ¶ All through recorded history the Greyhound has cropped up, always as a coursing or sporting dog. The name *Greyhound* itself is of unknown origin. It could come from *Graius*, which means "Grecian," since the ancient Greeks thought very highly of this swift animal. The name also could come from the Old English words *grech* or *greg*, meaning "dog." Grey may have been a prevailing color at one time, and that would logically

Greyhound

Land of origin: Probably ancient EGYPT or ASSYRIA

Original purpose: Almost certainly hunting, coursing game

Recent popularity ranking by A.K.C. registration: 113rd

Greyhound Club of America
Dr. Elsie S. Neustadt, Secretary
334 King Street, P.O. Box 1185
Hanover, MA 02339

HEIGHT: Dogs to 27 inches   Bitches to 26 inches

WEIGHT: Dogs to 70 pounds   Bitches to 65 pounds

COAT
Short, smooth, and very firm.

COLOR
Not counted in judging. Often gray, white, or fawn. Can be solid or marked.

Amount of care coat requires: 1 2 3 4 5 6 7 8 9 10

Amount of exercise required: 1 2 3 4 5 6 7 8 9 10

Suitability for urban/apartment life: 1 2 3 4 5 6 7 8 9 10
UNSUITED

have given the breed its present name. We are unlikely to ever know. ¶ Besides being the fastest dog in the world, the Greyhound is one of the fastest of all four-footed animals. He has been bred for thousands of years to chase other animals. All manner of quarry have been pursued, but hare was probably the natural target of this streak of canine lightning. Today, sadly, the breed is used on professional racing circuits, and the cruelties involved in that industry are too well known to list here. It is a sad fate for a superb breed of dog. When dogs on the racing circuit in America today stop winning, they generally are killed. That is a terrible loss because they make superb pets. ¶ If ever there was a breed that was capable of causing controversy, it is the Greyhound. He is a clean dog, an easy dog to maintain with just about no coat care required. On the other hand, he does require a lot of exercise, as should be perfectly obvious, and most owners are unwilling to take the time. ¶ There is a network of greyhound rescue agencies that save as many as possible of the estimated fifty thousand Greyhounds killed each year because they have stopped winning at the track. They make happy, accommodating pets, laidback and quiet. This is one breed of dog that really does seem to have a sense of humor. They are a joy to be with. They are tested before being placed in homes and are good with children and cats or the perspective owner is alerted to any suggested restrictions. ¶ Greyhounds rarely fight among themselves or with other dogs. It usually takes no more than a day or two to completely housebreak a Greyhound even if it has never been in a house before. A track Greyhound can make a near perfect "instant pet." No one should think of owning a Greyhound unless he is either active himself or blessed with at least one very athletic family member. Since before the pyramids were built the Greyhound has been bred to move, and move he should if he is to retain his original qualities.

Although records exist of Harrier packs dating back to the middle of the thirteenth century in England, no one is certain of their origin. They may have come to the British Isles with the Normans, since hounds were in common use on the Continent well before they were in England, or they may have been developed in England. All kinds of theories are on record, some seemingly well supported. Dogs *similar to* the Harrier date back to ancient Greece, but the breed is not believed to be that old. ¶ Harriers look like a bred-down version of the Foxhound, and many people believe that is exactly what they are. It would be hard to dispute that point, for

Harrier

Land of origin: Unknown; most recently (since A. D. 1260) ENGLAND.

Original purpose: Hunting, especially hares

Recent popularity ranking by A.K.C. registration: 130th

HEIGHT: Dogs to 21 inches   Bitches to 20 inches

WEIGHT: Dogs to 50 pounds   Bitches to 45 pounds

COAT
Short, dense, hard, and glossy.

COLOR
Black, tan, and white—any natural hound color pleasingly distributed. Not highly considered in judging.

Amount of care coat requires: 1 2 3 4 5 6 7 8 9 10

Amount of exercise required: 1 2 3 4 5 6 7 8 9 10

Suitability for urban/apartment life: 1 2 3 4 5 6 7 8 9 10

the Harrier does look and act exactly like a small Foxhound. It is certainly a riddle for which we will never have an answer. Hares have been run down with hounds since long before the activity was described by the historian Xenophon around 400 B. C., and since A. D. 1260 at least. Harriers have been considered highly desirable dogs for that style of hunting. ¶The Harrier is a neat, clean, well-put-together dog. He is naturally responsive and obedient, takes training well, and is friendly to man and animals alike. A well-bred and well-raised Harrier is a lovely family pet, although he is perhaps more naturally suited to country life than city dwelling. Still, if due regard is paid to the Harrier's natural desire to go, to run and sniff and feel the wind and the brush against his smooth, sleek hide, he will settle in anywhere with his master and give a flawless performance as a family dog. No one should, in all fairness, keep one of these dogs cooped up. Harriers do need long walks every day and frequent trips to the country. Families with dual residences are ideal. ¶Because the Harrier is naturally a pack animal, he gets along well with other dogs and cats and is fine for the multipet home. He is good around horses and other livestock as well, once he has been made to understand that they belong to the most important creature in a Harrier's life, his master. ¶The Harrier is nowhere near as well known as the Beagle in this country, and no doubt the Harrier and the two Foxhounds have suffered in popularity because they are so like the Beagle and possess few outstandingly different qualities that would enable them to upset one of the most popular of all breeds.

No one knows the real history of this very ancient breed. By the time of King Tutankhamen (1366 to 1357 B. C.) it already was immortalized in stone. Specimens may have been brought to Egypt from some other land long before the time of the boy king. For at least four thousand years they have survived around the periphery of the Mediterranean, but in recent years the greatest concentration has been found on the Balearic Islands off the coast of Spain. They are known by many names, but the concentration on the island of Ibiza seems to have labeled them at least as far as the English-speaking world is concerned. In Spain they are known variously

Ibizan Hound

Land of origin: Probably EGYPT, then SPAIN

Original purpose: Coursing, hunting

Recent popularity ranking by A.K.C. registration: 121st on to be given a rank

Ibizan Hound Club of the United States
Lisa Puskas, Secretary
4312 E. Nesbet Rd.
Phoenix, AZ 85032

HEIGHT: Dogs to 27½ inches   Bitches to 26 inches

WEIGHT: Dogs average 50 pounds   Bitches to 49 pounds

COAT
Short all over, shortest on head and ears—only slightly longer at back of thighs and under tail.

COLOR
White and red, white and lion, or solid white, red, or lion. Solids very desirable but rare.

Amount of care coat requires: 1 2 3 4 5 6 7 8 9 10

Amount of exercise required: 1 2 3 4 5 6 7 8 9 10

Suitability for urban/apartment life: 1 2 3 4 5 6 7 8 9 10

as Podenco Ibicenco, Ca Eivissenc, Mallorqui, Xarnelo, Mayorquais, Charnegue, and Chien de Baleares. On the island of Malta they are called Rabbit Dogs and on Sicily, Cirnecco dell'Etna. The name *Ibizan Hound* apparently has taken hold in the United States, though, and probably will not change. ¶This is one of the two most recently recognized breeds listed by the American Kennel Club. Along with the Norfolk Terrier, recognition became official on January 1, 1979. ¶People who know this breed well speak of the Ibizan Hound as being exceptionally quiet and clean. He is responsive to his human companions but is reserved with strangers. He is particularly sensitive to change and will take his time to think things through, and that includes the arrival of new people on the scene. He is not "flaky" the way some sight hounds may be. He is, rather, sensible as well as sensitive, and steady in his habits. ¶The Ibizan Hound is, like the Greyhound, the Saluki, and the Afghan Hound, a dog of grace and dignity. He is fast and sleek and particularly adept at both high and broad jumps. He is, then, above all else an athlete—and a fairly large one, too. He must have exercise, like all the true coursing hounds. It would not be proper to keep this dog in an apartment unless he was assured of very long walks and an occasional trip to a safe area where he could be allowed to run. ¶The Ibizan Hound is not a sharp breed, but he is a careful, determined friend to his master and family. It is too soon to tell how he will evolve in the United States now that his popularity is likely to rise. His mysterious and almost certainly unknowable beginnings are bound to add to his attractiveness. It is claimed that it was the Ibizan Hound (obviously known then by a different name) that was the model for the god Anubis, the guardian of Egyptian dead. He may be one of the few breeds, perhaps the only one, that was actually worshiped.

The mighty Irish Wolfhound is the tallest and one of the most powerful of all dogs. His origins are lost to us, although he was known and revered around the time of Christ. Records dating back to the third century A. D. suggest that the Celts may have brought him with them to Greece five hundred years earlier. ¶This great hound was developed for the hunt, to course wolves and even the elk of ancient Ireland. He is said to be able to run down a wolf and make the kill unaided. When coursing was the sport of kings, this regal dog was considered an appropriate gift from one king to another. There is a story of a war fought for the possession of a single specimen of the

Irish Wolfhound

Land of origin: IRELAND

Original purpose: Hunting, coursing wolves and other large game

Recent popularity ranking by A.K.C. registration: 70th

Irish Wolfhound Club of America
Mrs. Hector P. Siat, Secretary
131 Edgewood Drive
Grafton, OH 44044

HEIGHT: Dogs 32 inches and over   Bitches 30 inches and over

WEIGHT: Dogs 120 pounds and over   Bitches 105 pounds and over

COAT
Rough, hard, and wiry. Longer on face.

COLOR
Gray, brindle, red, black, white, and fawn.

Amount of care coat requires: 1 2 3 4 5 6 7 8 9 10
                                                     • • • •

Amount of exercise required: 1 2 3 4 5 6 7 8 9 10
                                         • • • • • • • • • • • •

Suitability for urban/apartment life: 1 2 3 4 5 6 7 8 9 10
                                                     UNSUITED

breed. ¶ The last of these dogs in their original form faced extinction about the time of the American Civil War. An officer in the British army—a Scot—set out to collect the few that remained in Ireland and rebuild the breed along ancient lines. He finally succeeded, and today's Irish Wolfhound closely resembles his ancestors. ¶ Despite his being bred for violent purposes, the Irish Wolfhound is a gentle and reliable animal. He is well aware of his size and power and is extremely courageous. He is also intelligent and an excellent companion. He is not suited to city life, and even a small suburban home might be crowded with an animal of this size trying to find a place to relax. This is clearly a country dog, an estate dog, or a dog for the farm. He is good with children and will take a lot of punishment without displaying bad temper. He will be a deterrent to burglars, of course, and his presence can impart a feeling of security. Because of his enormous size and strength, it would be unthinkable to train him to attack. The look of him is enough. ¶ The Irish Wolfhound is not an inexpensive dog to buy or keep. He requires a lot of food and a lot of room. A good example of the breed may cost $500 and up and should be purchased only from a reputable breeder. Like all hounds, the Irish Wolfhound does not like pulling up roots. Once he has settled into a home, he wants to stay there—for life—guarding it and sharing it with its human inhabitants. This is a splendid breed of dog for special situations only. He is for the home where there is the need and the means to own the largest dog in the world, and one of the most noble.

For the owner who envisions himself the master of a mighty wolflike beast of enormous power, the Norwegian Elkhound offers special possibilities. This great hunting dog of the North is not very large, less than half the weight of a real wolf, but he has many outstanding qualities and characteristics. ¶The Norwegian Elkhound accompanied the Vikings on their forays. He hunted with them, he herded flocks outside their villages, and he guarded man and animal alike against wolves and bears. Almost a legend now, the Norwegian Elkhound is one of the oldest and most romantic of breeds. ¶This is a northern breed, an animal well suited to

Norwegian Elkhound

Land of origin: NORWAY

Original purpose: Guarding, herding, hunting big game

Recent popularity ranking by A.K.C. registration: 47th

Norwegian Elkhound Association of America, Inc.
Ms. Bonnie Turner, Corres. Secretary
1695 Cox Road
Woodstock, GA 30188

HEIGHT: Dogs to 20½ inches   Bitches to 19½ inches

WEIGHT: Dogs to 55 pounds   Bitches to 48 pounds

COAT
Thick and hard, rather smooth lying. Longer outer coat and light, soft, woolly undercoat.

COLOR
Gray with black tips on long covering coat. Gray tones vary, but white or yellow are not desirable.

Amount of care coat requires: 1 2 3 4 5 6 7 8 9 10

Amount of exercise required: 1 2 3 4 5 6 7 8 9 10

*Suitability for urban/apartment life:** 1 2 3 4 5 6 7 8 9 10

*But only if regularly exercised to meet his demands.

rugged weather and rugged terrain. He is a bold dog, impressively powerful and packed with seemingly endless energy. He has a superb sense of smell, and his hearing is reputed to be better than that of many other breeds. He is a hunting dog and one devoted to his master. He learns quickly and takes all kinds of training well, but he is also stubborn. A Norwegian Elkhound will have no difficulty in picking out an inappropriately soft hand. A wishy-washy owner will have a bad time of it and probably will not be able to master the dog. ¶The Norwegian Elkhound can be aggressive with other animals—but this happens rarely with human beings, unless they are strangers who threaten. Because he is such a powerful and assertive animal and will march chest out into any kind of a situation, the Norwegian Elkhound requires not only early and careful training but everlasting control as well. He is not a dog to be allowed to wander through a suburban neighborhood unattended. ¶Since he is a natural guardian of all that he loves, the Elkhound makes a perfect watchdog. He should never be taught to attack, and any tendency in that direction must be discouraged, but here is the answer for those who want an aggressive-sounding, alert, and purposeful dog who will sound the alarm in the night. ¶The Elkhound is a handsome animal; he has great dignity and purpose. An ideal companion for those he knows and trusts, he tends to take life seriously. He does not take friends, devotion, insults, or intruders lightly. He was put here with a job to do, and he spends the better part of each day attempting to fulfill his mission. He should only be purchased from the best available private kennel's stock. A mass-produced Norwegian Elkhound could be dangerous, or at least unpleasant.

The Otter Hound is a dog little known in this country. Probably in use in England by the reign of King John (1199–1216), he was bred in a straight line from a mixture of several different hounds (Harrier, Bloodhound, and others) to kill otters. A somewhat coarse or rough-looking dog, he has been so perfected as a single-pur- pose animal that he has never become a popular pet. Other hounds were almost always trained to work in packs, and their precise response to commands was legendary in the last century, when otter hunting was in vogue. Those packs are now gone, as are most of the otters in England and Wales, and the breed is down almost to

Otter Hound

Land of origin: Probably ENGLAND and WALES; some argument for FRAN(

Original purpose: Hunting otter

Recent popularity ranking by A.K.C. registration: 128th

Otter Hound Club of America
Cindy Chrisos, Corres. Secretary
16306 Collins Rd.
Woodstock, IL 60098

HEIGHT: Dogs to 27 inches   Bitches to 26 inches

WEIGHT: Dogs to 115 pounds   Bitches to 100 pounds

COAT
Double; rough outer coat 3 to 6 inches long on back, shorter on legs. It must be coarse and crisp (hard). The undercoat is woolly and water-repellent. The coat is an important feature of this breed.

COLOR
Any color or combination of colors is allowed.

Amount of care coat requires: 1 2 3 4 5 6 7 8 9 10

Amount of exercise required: 1 2 3 4 5 6 7 8 9 10

Suitability for urban/apartment life: 1 2 3 4 5 6 7 8 9 10
                          UNSUITED

remnant level. The Otter Hound is one of those dogs who could vanish in the years ahead unless other qualities are accentuated. ¶ It would be a shame to lose what has taken almost ten centuries to perfect. In fact, the Otter Hound shows qualities that should not be lost and could be adapted to other life-styles. He is loyal to his master, he has a very good nose, he is amazing in the water (he has webbed feet), and he can stand any weather and any water temperature. He would probably make a fine watchdog and should adjust well to an owner's family. But he is a tough fighter, and a brawl can quickly become a savage display. He therefore needs firm handling and constant supervision. ¶ The Otter Hound is a large dog, often well over one hundred pounds, and his jaws are immensely powerful. His gait is easy and free, exhibiting great power and drive. He is a dog who never seems to tire, not letting up once he has a trail. He is out for blood and will not stop as long as he has a clue as to where the otter may be hiding. ¶ Until breeders develop those qualities in the Otter Hound that would make him attractive for today's owner, he is better suited to country life. An Otter Hound and a city apartment are not the right combination. Owners should keep in mind that if their pet can't find otters (which he probably can't), he may practice on other wildlife and a few neighborhood cats. Otter Hounds, like all powerful and headstrong animals, must be under full-time control. History has taught us that they respond well to training, so there is no excuse for an ill-behaved Otter Hound.

The Pharaoh Hound may be the oldest extant breed of dog in the world. If not it is certainly in the range of the other truly ancient breeds, the saluki and greyhound. The oldest know dog relic dates from the Stone Age and was found on the banks of the Nile. It is a disc and depicts two dogs that look very much like Pharaoh Hounds. Tomb carvings in Egypt seem to show Pharaoh Hounds as models for the dog-god Anubis. Classical antiquity is only one fac-tor recommending this breed. ¶Few dogs are more sculptured and elegant than representatives of this sleek hound with their distinctive large ears and keen, intelligent amber eyes. The overall appearance and demeanor is noble. Because they hunt by both hearing and sight they are extremely alert and very fast on their feet. Their gait is free and flowing with the head held high. Their movement appears to be effortless. ¶Pharaoh Hounds are characteristically

Pharaoh Hound

Land of origin: ANCIENT EGYPT, in all posibility, or in Middle East

Recent popularity ranking by A.K.C. registration: 122nd

Pharaoh Hound Club of America
Rita L. Sacks, Corres. Secretary
Route 209, Box 285
Stone Ridge, NY 12484

HEIGHT: Dogs 23 to 25 inches   Bitches 21 to 24 inches

WEIGHT: Not specified in standards

COAT
Short and glossy. Fine and close to slightly harsh. No feathering.

COLOR
Shades of tan to chestnut with white markings: white tip on tail highly prized. White "star" on chest, also on toes, slim white mark on center line of face allowed. White on neck, shoulders, back or sides disqualifies.

Amount of care coat requires: 1 2 3 4 5 6 7 8 9 10

Amount of exercise required: 1 2 3 4 5 6 7 8 9 10

Suitability for urban/apartment life: 1 2 3 4 5 6 7 8 9 10

friendly and affectionate. They are also very playful and are too intelligent to ignore. They want to participate in everything going on around them. It is usually far better to allow an active and alert dog to share in activities under your management than to force them to invent their own games. ¶Very sedentary people who do not really want to share their lives with a dog may do better with a less *involved* breed. The Pharaoh Hound does not take to being ignored. Decorative though they are, they need far more out of life than the opportunity to be that. What they really want is to run everybody else's life, too. ¶Like the other swift coursing dogs that are hunters by nature, Pharaoh Hounds should be conditioned before being asked to accept small animals like kittens, that are likely to race around and dart out from under things. ¶Although Pharaoh Hounds have appar-

ently been around for thousands of years, they are quite new to the West. There was little interest in them in England before the 1960's. They were given breed status there in 1968 and in Canada in 1979. The A.K.C. standard for the breed was approved in 1983. ¶The Pharaoh Hounds is an interesting "new" breed that will grow in popularity, particularly among people with space for their dogs to move. The elegance of the breed is bound to not only attract attention, but hold it. Dog fanciers who enjoy getting involved at the beginning of something exciting are sure to be drawn to this project. The fact that this is not only a handsome, gregarious pet but also one that was once the model for a god in the ancient world, is bound to bring new fans to the fold. Those with the experience say that new Pharaoh Hound adherents will never regret their decision.

This powerful guard and hunting dog of southern Africa is a cross between a number of European breeds brought there by settlers and a native dog known to us only as the Hottentot dog. That native African animal, probably little more than half wild, had a strange ridge of hair on his back that grew backward. Today's Rhodesian Ridgeback has inherited that unique characteristic, and hence the name. ¶ The Rhodesian Ridgeback was bred to care for his master and his master's family. That meant standing off all comers, including armed human beings and predatory cats. The Ridgeback does not back down easily. He is reserved with strangers and usually will not

Rhodesian Ridgeback

Land of origin: SOUTHERN AFRICA

Original purpose: As combination hunting and guard watchdog

Recent popularity ranking by A.K.C. registration: 60th

Rhodesian Ridgeback Club of the
United States, Inc.
Ms. Natalie D. Carlton, Corres. Secretary
P.O. Box 236
Cortaro, AZ 85652

HEIGHT: Dogs to 27 inches   Bitches to 26 inches

WEIGHT: Dogs to 75 pounds   Bitches to 65 pounds

COAT
Short and dense, sleek and glossy. Should never be woolly or silky.

COLOR
Light to red wheaten. Small white markings permitted.

Amount of care coat requires: 1 2 3 4 5 6 7 8 9 10

Amount of exercise required: 1 2 3 4 5 6 7 8 9 10

Suitability for urban/apartment life:* 1 2 3 4 5 6 7 8 9 10

*But not at all suitable unless given regular exercise sufficient for the individual dog's needs.

give another dog a second look. Should a dog challenge the Ridgeback, however, that is something else again. ¶ The Ridgeback can be distinctly a one-person animal, although certainly a gentleman with the rest of the family. He is a natural watchdog and can be extremely intimidating when suspicious. He takes any weather and can go for twenty-four hours without water. A combination of working and hunting dog, he will pull down fleet-footed game or flush birds, whatever is asked of him. ¶ The Ridgeback tends to be hardheaded. He will accept a balance with his master, but however much he may love him, he still will try for the upper hand. Good firm training starting early in puppyhood is required, and when it is accomplished, the reward is a good watchdog and family companion. This breed is too powerful, too bright, and too active to be anything but totally obedi-ent. A Ridgeback with bad manners is un-thinkable around other people. ¶ Some people do attempt to keep Rhodesian Ridgebacks as apartment dogs, a bad idea except in the most unusual cases. A Ridge-back locked in an apartment all day is un-likely to mature into the animal he was bred to be. In fact, some city-kept Ridgebacks become downright "flaky" and can be all but impossible to manage. Wherever the animal is raised, he should go into the best obedience class available with his master. Don't leave the training of one of these splendid animals to chance or "instinct." ¶ The Rhodesian Ridgeback has not yet hit its stride in popularity in the United States, but this is a breed on the rise. Every effort should be made to maintain quality of be-havior as well as form in this unique dog from Africa.

The exotic Saluki may be the oldest breed of purebred dog in the world. Some people insist he is the dog the Sumerians knew and used almost seven thousand years before Christ—which would make him almost nine thousand years old. Whether or not he originated in ancient Sumer, the Saluki spread throughout the Middle East and parts of Asia. Before the birth of Western civilization the breed was already known as a coursing hound. ¶ He is an incredibly fast dog, once used on gazelle and later on smaller game. He is also a dog of great stamina and endurance—no weather is too harsh and no terrain too rough. Like most coursing hounds, he has a

Saluki

Land of origin: ASIA MINOR

Original purpose: Coursing

Recent popularity ranking by A.K.C. registration: 85th

Saluki Club of America
Mrs. Marjorie Seitz, Secretary
18 Morris Avenue, P.O. Box 323
Cold Spring, NY 10516

HEIGHT: Dogs to 28 inches   Bitches to 24 inches

WEIGHT: Dogs to 60 pounds   Bitches to 55 pounds

COAT
Smooth, soft, silky, with slight feathers on the legs, at the back of the thighs, and on the ears.

COLOR
White, cream, fawn, golden, red, grizzle, and tan, tricolor (white, black, and tan), black and tan.

Amount of care coat requires: 1 2 3 4 5 6 7 8 9 10

Amount of exercise required: 1 2 3 4 5 6 7 8 9 10

Suitability for urban/apartment life:*   1 2 3 4 5 6 7 8 9 10

*But only if a great deal of exercise is regularly scheduled.

so-so nose (at least that is the reputation most often heard) but fine eyesight and almost unbelievable speed. Owners should keep in mind that, being a coursing dog, he will worry wildlife and small domestic animals if not supervised. A bolting rabbit cannot be resisted and neither, on occasion, can a cat. ¶ The Saluki never fails to attract attention, in the show-ring or on the end of a street lead. He looks the part of the exotic hound, and his grace and free-flowing movement are distinctive and most attractive. ¶ Although not demonstrative, the Saluki is a loyal friend who likes to work with and please his master. He is good with family, although small children and Salukis don't always make the happiest combination. Because there is a certain flare, there is also a flash point. Children must be taught how to behave around dogs like Salukis, and Salukis must be taught how to behave around children. ¶ The Saluki is headstrong, like any hound who has had his own head for thousands of years, so any new owner should make his position of command clear. The Saluki needs a reasonable amount of obedience training. No one wants such a good-looking dog with that kind of venerable background rolling over and playing dead or begging, but neither does one want a Saluki who bursts through screen doors and breaks loose into heavy traffic. ¶ It is questionable whether Salukis can ever get enough exercise living in an urban setting. Because of their high style and elegance, some people do keep them in the city, but they should be walked great distances and be taken regularly to a place where they can really let go. ¶ Exotic, expensive, and very handsome, the Saluki is a special dog for special owners.

The great Deerhound of Scotland is a true giant among dogs. He is in a class with the Irish Wolfhound (to which he may be related), the Borzoi, the Great Dane, and other massive breeds. Once restricted in ownership to earls and lords of higher rank, said to have been the ransom of kings and the cause of wars, the Deerhound is a part of the wild and romantic past of the Highlands. Stories about him are legion, and whether all or only partly true, they suggest a history that may be the single most noble in canine annals. ¶A dog seldom seen in America today, the Scottish Deerhound is an ideal companion. Although huge, he is even-tempered, calm, and some people say polite. He seems to understand his size and is careful not to inadvertently hurt anything smaller than himself. Not snappy, silly, or mean, he is a fine companion for children, although a toddler should be watched around an exuberant Deerhound pup. The Scottish Deerhound thrives on love and attention. As a watchdog, of course, his mere presence is enough to discourage anyone, and

Scottish Deerhound

Land of origin: SCOTLAND

Original purpose: Hunting, particularly deer

Recent popularity ranking by A.K.C. registration: 110th

Scottish Deerhound Club of America, Inc.
Ms Allyn Brewer-Babjitch, Secretary
5350 Alum Rock Avenue
San Jose, CA 95127

HEIGHT: Dogs 32 inches or more   Bitches 28 inches or more

WEIGHT: Dogs to 110 pounds   Bitches to 95 pounds

COAT
Harsh and wiry, to 4 inches long on the body and neck. Softer on head, breast, and belly.
Not woolly. Thick, close lying, ragged, crisp to touch. Some strains have silky mixed
with harsh.

COLOR
Dark bluegray is preferred. Also grays and brindles, yellow, sandy red, red fawn with black
ears and muzzle. White is considered bad, so the less the better.

Amount of care coat requires: 1 2 3 4 5 6 7 8 9 10

Amount of exercise required: 1 2 3 4 5 6 7 8 9 10

Suitability for urban/apartment life: 1 2 3 4 5 6 7 8 9 10
                                                                        UNSUITED

it need hardly be stressed that no one should ever encourage a Scottish Deerhound to be aggressive or more suspicious than he naturally is around strangers. He likes to be absolutely certain in his own mind that the incoming stranger is a welcome addition to the household. The Deerhound takes companionship and friendship seriously. ¶It should be kept in mind that the incoming stranger is a welcome addition to the household. The Deerhound takes companionship and friendship seriously. ¶It should be kept in mind that although the Scottish Deerhound is a gentle and sensible animal, he is also a hunter, and for that task he has been bred for centuries. He was designed to tear to earth animals as large as 250-pound stags. It probably would not take much to get him to assume that role again. Gentle with other pets at home, a Deerhound can play havoc on other people's cats. Though a superb companion of man, a Scottish Deerhound who misbehaves can be a gigantic pain in the neck. ¶The Scottish Deerhound obviously needs exercise. Cramped quarters without an opportunity to walk for miles and run until exhausted are not the style for this animal. One can suppose that there are huge, barnlike apartments left and imagine their owners or renters as physical people who walk miles every morning and night, so we cannot say that this breed is wholly unsuited to apartment life; Deerhounds are too loving of people and too adaptable for that. But certainly exercise should be a major consideration when thinking about this breed. The nonphysical owner cannot unmake the breeding, planning, and perfecting of centuries. The great, massive hound of Scotland will never really be a creature of pavement and traffic lights.

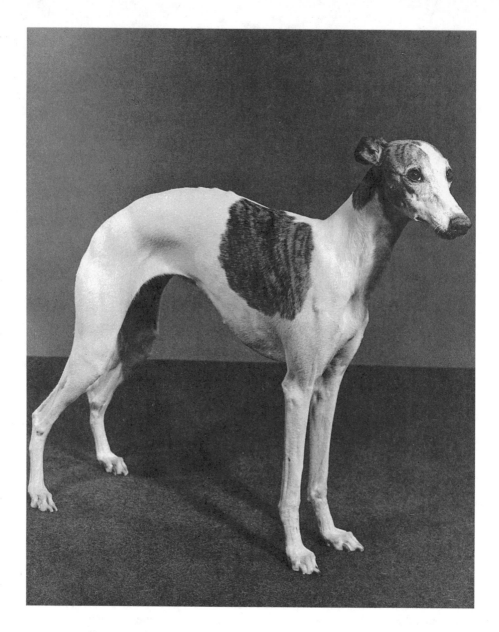

The Whippet is, in many people's opinion, one of the loveliest of all dogs. It is impossible for one of these small sight hounds, the fastest dog in the world in his weight category, to assume an awkward position. He always looks as if he just stepped out of an Aubusson tapestry or off the shelf as a piece of Sèvres porcelain. He is as elegant as any dog can be. ¶ The Whippet was developed for gaming, and for the "sport" of gambling as he raced around small enclosures killing rabbits that had no chance to escape. The more rabbits the "miniature English Greyhound" could kill or snap up (they were also called snap hounds) the better. The Whippet today has not lost that old taste for coursing, and he should be carefully watched. He can take off like an arrow and hit a stride of thirty-five miles an hour almost instantly. A dog moving at that

Whippet

Land of origin: ENGLAND

Original purpose: Rabbit coursing and racing

Recent popularity ranking by A.K.C. registration: 59th

American Whippet Club, Inc.
Ms. Harriett N. Lee, Secretary
14 Oak Circle
Charlottesville, VA 22901

HEIGHT: Dogs to 22 inches   Bitches to 21 inches

WEIGHT: Dogs to 28 pounds   Bitches to 20 pounds

COAT
Smooth, close lying, and firm. Doesn't shed.

COLOR
Given in the A.K.C. standards as "immaterial." Very often seen in grays and tans, brindles and white.

Amount of care coat requires: 1 2 3 4 5 6 7 8 9 10
                                   •

Amount of exercise required: 1 2 3 4 5 6 7 8 9 10
                                  • • • • • • • • • • • • • • • •

Suitability for urban/apartment life:*   1 2 3 4 5 6 7 8 9 10
                                            • • • • • • • • • • • • • • • • • • •

---

*Provided the animal is given sufficient exercise.

speed may be assumed to be short on road sense. When anywhere near traffic, a Whippet is best kept on a leash. ¶ There are few dogs that make better all-around family pets. Because a Whippet doesn't shed and is neat and clean, he is a pleasure to maintain; he is also easy to housebreak. For people who want to show a dog, the Whippet is grand in the ring, a born ham, and because of his small size he is easy to transport. He is, essentially, a family dog and won't really show his quality when kept in a kennel. This is a foot-of-the-bed dog for sure. He also likes to curl up in a blanket or its equivalent when he sleeps, so unless an owner wants all the beds in the house unmade, it is a good idea to leave the Whippet his own blanket. And don't step or lean on that blanket without checking—your Whippet won't make much of a lump inside it. ¶ A Whippet is fine in an apartment—he is fine

anywhere as long as the family is at hand—but he should be exercised. Long walks are needed every day, and periodically the dog should be taken to a wide open area—an abandoned beach is right—and allowed to run. You have never seen anything quite like a Whippet enjoying the power of his incredible body at full tilt. Despite what some people feel is a somewhat fragile appearance, the Whippet is hardy and durable. He is not at all keen on cold weather, however. ¶ Whippets take to children naturally and are seldom mean. They are not yappy, although they can make good watchdogs. In a home where the Whippet is allowed to be *the* child, or at least one of the kids, this dog will flourish. Whippets don't like being left out. Given his attractive looks, that is about the last thing the Whippet has to fear.

[Group 3]

The Working Dogs

Akita
Alaskan Malamute
Bernese Mountain Dog
Boxer
Bullmastiff
Doberman Pinscher
Giant Schnauzer
Great Dane
Great Pyrenees
Komondor

Kuvasz
Mastiff
Newfoundland
Portuguese Water Dog
Rottweiler
Saint Bernard
Samoyed
Siberian Husky
Standard Schnauzer

The Akita or Akita-inu is the heavy-duty work-dog of Japan. Named for the province of Akita on Honshu Island, this breed was used to hunt bear, boar, and deer and as a protector of life and limb. There are two other similar breeds in Japan—the Nippon-inu and the Shiba-inu—but they are somewhat smaller. ¶Four thousand years ago the inhabitants of Japan had a dog known to archaeologists as the *peat dog*. No doubt the Akita is a descendant of that animal. Also sometimes referred to as the Japanese Spitz, the Akita has a general Spitz-like appearance but is larger and stronger. The Akita has been likened to the Chinese Chow Chow, and it is possible

Akita

Land of origin: JAPAN

Original purpose: Heavy hunting and guard duty

Recent popularity ranking by A.K.C. registration: 37th

Akita Club of America
Barbara Hampton, Secretary
101 South Rainbow 28-96
Las Vegas, NV 89128

HEIGHT: Dogs to 28 inches   Bitches to 26 inches

WEIGHT: Dogs to 110 pounds   Bitches to 95 pounds

COAT
Double, with outer coat being somewhat on the harsh side.

COLOR
All colors permitted. White should not account for more than one-third of total.

Amount of care coat requires: 1 2 3 4 5 6 7 8 9 10
                                    • • • • •

Amount of exercise required: 1 2 3 4 5 6 7 8 9 10
                                   • • • • • • • • • • • • • •

Suitability for urban/apartment life: 1 2 3 4 5 6 7 8 9 10
                                           • • •

---

that the two have some ancestry in common, since commerce with the mainland followed the period when the peat dog was a part of every band, clan, and household. When highwaymen wandered the Japanese countryside, the Akita and his forebears no doubt played a very important role as watchdogs, a task this animal readily takes to still. ¶ We have the Akita in America today because of military personnel stationed in Japan. A number of Akitas survived the war, and American servicemen were impressed with the breed's intelligence and his adaptability as both pet and guard dog. They began bringing examples back with them, and today the Akita enjoys full breed status from the American Kennel Club. ¶ People who have come to know this new breed speak highly of his intelligence, his responsiveness to training, and his desire to please his master. Essentially a good-natured animal, this dog is still large, powerful, and assertive. There can be little doubt that an Akita who has been obedience-trained is much more desirable as a neighbor than one who has not. ¶ Every indication suggests that the Akita will grow in popularity in the United States. It is to be hoped that breeders here will be as firm in their resolve to hold to the standards as their Japanese counterparts have been for centuries. Because of their hunting background and their fearless quality, Akitas are best maintained under tight control. They can be quite aggressive toward other dogs and should only be owned by people with some prior experience with large, tough-minded dogs. The Akita is not a casual pet.

No one knows the origin of the breed we call the Alaskan Malamute. The name is derived from the Russian name for the massive northwestern-most portion of North America—*Alashak* ("Vast Country")—and from one of the tribes that were found wandering there centuries ago—the Malemiuts, who had a sled dog of great stamina and loyalty. The breed is certainly one of the northern spitz dogs, but where it first originated and how it is related to the Siberian Husky, the Samoyed, and the sled dogs of Greenland and the eastern Canadian Arctic is unknowable. ¶ Some sled dogs were bred for speed, and are indeed used in races today, but the Malamute is a freight hauler, a heavy-duty animal of great substance and endurance. Because these animals are naturally loyal to their owners, many of the examples kept as pets today are equally good watchdogs. Legend has it that every third or fourth dog generation the Innuit (the group to which the Malemiuts belong) tether their Malamute bitches out

Alaskan Malamute

Land of origin: Arctic region, usually given as ALASKA

Original purpose: As heavy-duty (freight) sled dog and camp guard

Recent popularity ranking by A.K.C. registration: 39th

Alaskan Malamute Club of America, Inc.
Mrs. Ione Zeller, Corres. Secretary
8565 Hill Road
Pickerington, OH 43147

HEIGHT: Dogs to 25 inches   Bitches to 23 inches

WEIGHT: Dogs to 85 pounds   Bitches to 75 pounds

COAT
Thick coarse guard coat, not very long and not soft. Dense undercoat 1 to 2 inches deep, oily and woolly. Guard hairs stick out, neck well maned.

COLOR
Light gray to black with white belly and white markings on feet, legs, and face. Only solid-colored dog allowed is all-white.

*Amount of care coat requires:** 1 2 3 4 5 6 7 8 9 10
• • • • • • • • • • • •

Amount of exercise required: 1 2 3 4 5 6 7 8 9 10
• • • • • • • • • • • • • • • •

Suitability for urban/apartment life:† 1 2 3 4 5 6 7 8 9 10
•

*Heavy brushing required in spring and early summer due to shedding.
†If enough exercise is given.

on the ice when they come into heat and allow wolves to service them. Whether or not that is true, the Malamute undeniably has wolflike qualities in his appearance. ¶ The Alaskan Malamute is a magnificent animal, a fine pet who is good with children. He is solid and steady and has great endurance. Loyal unto death to his family, he is usually not one-personish. He is good with strangers, although he can be aggressive with strange dogs—not always, but that is a characteristic of some specimens. Of the northern spitzlike dogs, this breed is one of the best for the average household. ¶ The harsh coat of the Malamute is best when not washed often, for washing tends to soften it and alter its desirable character. There is a coat-care consideration, though. That very dense undercoat is shed in spring and summer, and unless it is professionally stripped, it can drive the householder mad,

for its shedding is endless. ¶ The Alaskan Malamute is suited for a family with at least some active members, and in general for people who want a large, powerful, and wonderfully loyal pet. He is a heavy working dog and needs a great deal of exercise if he is to maintain condition and proper temperament. He will adapt to any living conditions as long as he is close to his human family, but confinement without proper exercise is cruel and foolish. ¶ Great care should be taken in buying a Malamute, and only when two or three generations of a line are known should a final purchase be undertaken. There is a congenital malformation known as "dwarfism" in this breed, and it can crop up in alternate generations. A puppy should be evaluated carefully before purchase, and only the truly professional Alaskan Malamute breeder should be trusted.

The Bernese is a Swiss dog descended from dogs of ancient Rome. Two thousand years ago Roman legions crossed Switzerland into northern Europe accompanied by large and probably ferocious war and guard dogs. Inevitably some of these animals fell by the way, and some of them survived. From the latter it is believed that at least four large breeds evolved in the Alpine country alone. Three of them were used to herd sheep, but one was a draft animal, and that was the dog we today call the Bernese Mountain Dog. The name comes from the canton of Berne, where the weavers kept the dogs to draw their carts to market right up until quite modern times.

Bernese Mountain Dog

Land of origin: SWITZERLAND

Original purpose: As draft animal

Recent popularity ranking by A.K.C. registration: 74th

Bernese Mountain Dog Club of America, Inc.
Ms. Lilian Ostermiller, Secretary
P.O. Box 54
Flemington, NJ 08822

HEIGHT: Dogs to 27½ inches   Bitches to 26 inches

WEIGHT: Dogs to 70 pounds or more   Bitches to 65 pounds

COAT
Soft and silky with bright, natural sheen. Slightly wavy but never with actual curl.

COLOR
Jet black with russet brown to deep tan markings on all four legs, a spot just above forelegs, each side of white chest markings, and spots over eyes. Over-eye spots are expected and required. Brown on forelegs must separate black from white.

Amount of care coat requires: 1 2 3 4 5 6 7 8 9 10

Amount of exercise required: 1 2 3 4 5 6 7 8 9 10

Suitability for urban/apartment life: 1 2 3 4 5 6 7 8 9 10

¶ The Bernese—seventy pounds and more, and almost twenty-eight inches tall—is a large animal. With his heavy coat and rugged constitution, he is an outside dog primarily and will do well in a kennel as long as he is shielded from sleet and freezing rain. He is hardy, healthy, and quite aristocratic. Adorable as a puppy, the Bernese matures into a steady, stable animal fearlessly loyal to his master. Onepersonish by nature, the Bernese will adjust to a family situation and accept family members and often-seen friends. Strangers, however, will be ignored, and are themselves better off if they ignore the dog until he is ready to attempt first overtures. The Bernese belongs to a few people and doesn't like to have his situation altered or expanded. He can be a good watchdog but should never be used for attack or other aggressive behavior. ¶ The Bernese needs a lot of exercise and is happier in colder climates than in warm ones. He is not a satisfactory apartment pet. The big city with its restrictive environment is not Bernese Mountain Dog country. ¶ The Bernese should be obedience-trained, and that training should start early and continue long. It is best if the owner takes the training sessions with the dog. In the Bernese Mountain Dog we have once again an animal too large to be tolerated as a brat. That kind of behavior may be cute and even acceptable (to a degree!) in a toy, but in a large, powerful animal like a Bernese it is quite intolerable. When it occurs, and certainly when it persists, the owner, not the dog, and certainly not the breed, is to blame.

The Boxer was derived in Germany from a number of strains common to Europe in the Middle Ages. Great Dane and English Bulldog may be included, and some of the mastiff line from Tibet is also likely. They all go back to what is called the Molossian strain, which undoubtedly came out of the Asian mountains to spread westward thousands of years ago. ¶This is a breed of enormous courage and stamina. Boxers were probably first bred for blood sports—baiting bulls and hunting boar and possibly dogfighting as well. They were bred for ferociousness, but that is gone now, and except for an occasional penchant for a good scrap, the Boxer is a gen-

Boxer

Land of origin: GERMANY

Original purpose: Probably for bullbaiting and other blood sports; later guard and companion

Recent popularity ranking by A.K.C. registration: 18th

American Boxer Club, Inc.
Mrs. Cathie Hazelwood, Corres. Secretary
55 Polk Avenue
East Northport, NY 11731

HEIGHT: Dogs to 25 inches   Bitches to 23½ inches

WEIGHT: Dogs to 75 pounds   Bitches to 70 pounds

COAT
Short, shiny, and smooth. It should lie tight to the body and never be curly, wavy, or woolly.

COLOR
Shades of fawn ranging from light tan to dark red and mahogany. Darker colors preferred generally. May also be brindled, with black standing out from fawn background. White markings often handsome, but generally not on back of torso. White face marking may replace dark mask.

Amount of care coat requires: 1 2 3 4 5 6 7 8 9 10

Amount of exercise required: 1 2 3 4 5 6 7 8 9 10

Suitability for urban/apartment life: 1 2 3 4 5 6 7 8 9 10

tleman. ¶ Alert, willing, and anxious both to participate and to please, the Boxer is an ideal family dog. He is affectionate, a fine watchdog, and good with children. He can be fine with other animals he knows and can be raised in a multianimal household. When he does fight, however, he is deadly serious. ¶ A Boxer is by nature careful with strangers, although not snappy or silly. He checks things out thoroughly, and if he decides a stranger is all right, he is open and friendly. He is not complicated and sneaky. A Boxer lets you know what he has on his mind. The agility, fearlessness, and intelligence of this breed led to its being chosen as one of the first in Germany to work with the police. Boxers also have been used to lead the blind and for guard work. There is little this dog cannot learn to do. ¶ Because they are so popular in this country, Boxers have been mass-produced, and that has been destructive to many lines. There are still so many fine examples of the breed being shown and sold as companion animals that no one need get stuck. Since a poorly bred Boxer may be ugly in disposition as well as in conformation, the prospective buyer should be willing to go far to buy from only the finest breeders. You must see the parents of a puppy and know something about them before you can properly judge the puppy itself. All Boxer puppies are adorable, but not all grow up to fulfill the breed's promise.

The Bullmastiff is not to be confused with the Mastiff. He is only 60 percent Mastiff; the rest is Bulldog. ¶ This breed is one of the few animals actually bred to attack man. Once known as the "gamekeeper's nightdog," he was used to track and knock down poachers on private English estates. He was sometimes muzzled and was not meant to maul his victims, just keep them on the ground until the gamekeeper arrived to either thrash the man or arrest him. The Mastiff was tried for this task, but he was neither fast enough nor sufficiently aggressive. That is why the old Bulldog—a bigger, rougher animal than the breed we know today—was blended in. ¶ All of that is history. Today's Bullmastiff, while not exactly a dog to challenge in open combat, is usually a gentleman. He is not a fearsome beast, as he once may have been from the

Bullmastiff

Land of origin: ENGLAND

Original purpose: Night patrol against game poachers on private estates

Recent popularity ranking by A.K.C. registration: 66th

American Bullmastiff Association, Inc.
Ms. Chris Lezotte, Secretary
28011 Old Colony
Farmington Hills, MI 48018

HEIGHT: Dogs to 27 inches   Bitches to 26 inches

WEIGHT: Dogs to 130 pounds   Bitches to 120 pounds

COAT
Short and dense, offering good protection against harsh weather.

COLOR
Red, brindle, or fawn, the latter usually with a dark face and ears. A small white spot on the chest is allowed but no other white markings. Originally darker dogs were favored because they were more difficult to see at night. Now lighter-colored animals are as highly regarded.

Amount of care coat requires: 1 2 3 4 5 6 7 8 9 10

Amount of exercise required: 1 2 3 4 5 6 7 8 9 10

Suitability for urban/apartment life: 1 2 3 4 5 6 7 8 9 10
                                                          UNSUITED

poacher's point of view. (At that time poachers had the bad habit of shooting gamekeepers, which is why the Bullmastiff came into being.) He is fine with his owner's family and generally open and willing with strangers. It might be quite another thing, though, if a Bullmastiff's family seemed threatened, for this is an alert animal. He also happens to be without fear. It is doubtful that another dog could make a Bullmastiff back down once his hackles were up. For this reason he must be trained to live with other animals. Like the Bulldog, which constitutes nearly half his bloodline, he doesn't like other animals to challenge him. ¶ There is no doubt that the sight of a Bullmastiff on the premises would be a deterrent to almost anyone, but in reality a dog is no harder than a man to disable with products like Mace and tear gas. No one should think that a Bullmastiff or any other breed will make their property

crimeproof, and for this reason the animal should never be attack-trained, nor should any aggressiveness toward people be tolerated. With giant breeds and superdogs like Bullmastiffs, this is asking for trouble. Let the sight of him alone be the prime deterrent. A professional criminal will not deliberately put himself in a position to get hurt, so it is the innocent or minor-nuisance trespasser who is likely to be seriously hurt or killed by an attack-trained dog. ¶ The Bullmastiff is a family dog, but he is hardly suited to apartment living. He is an estate dog, a dog person's dog, and a magnificent pet in the right setting. The fact that he will scare off lesser intruders is secondary. What is important is that the breed is a splendid one, represented by regal, powerful animals who are by nature devoted to their masters and without meanness or pettiness in their makeup.

The Doberman Pinscher is one breed whose history is well known. In the 1890s, Louis Dobermann of Apolda, Germany, developed the breed using old shorthaired shepherd stock mixed with Rottweiler and terrier—specifically, it is believed, the Black and Tan Terrier. The dog he was apparently trying for was the dog he got. The Doberman Pinscher has been from the beginning a superlative guard dog of noble appearance. ¶A medium-sized dog with an extremely alert bearing, the Doberman is as handsome as a dog can be. Intelligent, swift, a consummate athlete, he combines the trainability of the old shepherd stock, the inner fire of the terrier, and the positive attitude of the Rottweiler. Louis Dobermann's mixture

126 THE ROGER CARAS DOG BOOK

Doberman Pinscher

Land of origin: GERMANY

Original purpose: Guard duty

Recent popularity ranking by A.K.C. registration: 20th

Doberman Pinscher Club of America
Mr. James B. Pitzer, Corres. Secretary
55 Willow Brook Drive
St. Louis, MO 63146

HEIGHT: Dogs to 28 inches   Bitches to 26 inches

WEIGHT: Dogs to 75 pounds   Bitches to 68 pounds

COAT
Smooth, short, hard, thick, and close. There may be an invisible gray undercoat on neck.

COLOR
Black, red, blue, and fawn. Sharply defined rust markings above each eye and on muzzle, throat, chest, legs, feet, and below tail. Small white marking on chest (under ½-inch square allowed). Fawn color is known as Isabella.

Amount of care coat requires: 1 2 3 4 5 6 7 8 9 10
                                    •

Amount of exercise required: 1 2 3 4 5 6 7 8 9 10
                                  • • • • • • • • • • • • • • • • • • •

*Suitability for urban/apartment life:** 1 2 3 4 5 6 7 8 9 10
                                          • • •

*But only if proper exercise is provided!

managed to preserve the best of each type he used. ¶The Doberman Pinscher is an active dog, and long, long walks are mandatory for his health and happiness. Many Doberman Pinschers are kept in apartments, and their rise in popularity according to American Kennel Club registrations has been meteoric—from twentieth place to second in thirteen years. The reason for this great popularity lies in the fact that he is believed to be a deterrent dog. An amateur criminal probably will give wide berth to a home where a Doberman Pinscher is known to live, but a professional can incapacitate any dog on earth with a five-dollar tear-gas pen or poisoned bait. The use of Doberman Pinschers as crime deterrents by amateur owners is not to be encouraged. ¶The supremely handsome and incredibly loyal Doberman Pinscher is a controversial dog. One hears that he is a gentle, affec-

tionate, and reliable pet, and also that he is a born killer and can never be trusted. The answer lies in the middle. ¶The Doberman Pinscher is an aggressive dog. The A.K.C. standards include the following statements: "The judge shall dismiss from the ring any shy or vicious Doberman" and "An aggressive or belligerent attitude towards other dogs shall not be deemed viciousness." ¶It is true that the Doberman Pinscher is more nervous than many other breeds—not always, certainly, but often. It is also true that the breed is intelligent and will take training readily from someone who knows what he is doing. The Doberman Pinscher is far too much dog for many people, especially casual or first-time owners. For owners who can accept the responsibility, the Doberman Pinscher is one of the great breeds of the working-dog group.

M ost people do not seem to realize that the Giant, Standard, and Miniature Schnauzers are three distinct breeds, not just up-and-down versions of each other. Both the Standard and the Giant Schnauzers are working dogs. ¶The *Riesenschnauzer* or Giant is not as old a breed as the Standard (which was painted by Dürer the year Columbus sailed for the New World) but is older by a good margin than the terrier we call the Miniature Schnauzer. ¶All the Schnauzers, apparently, were developed in either Württemberg or Bavaria, and the Giant probably was developed in and around Bavaria from smaller dogs obtained from Stuttgart. He

LHASA APSO

AFGHAN

SAMOYED

BASSET HOUND

KOMONDOR

MALTESE

BULLDOG

BEAGLE

BLOODHOUND

GREAT DANE

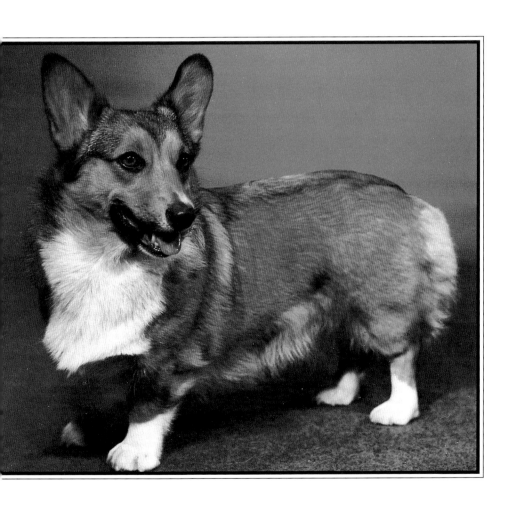

WELSH CORGI (PEMBROKE)

FOX TERRIER

DOBERMAN PINSCHER

MASTIFF

GOLDEN RETRIEVER

POMERANIAN

Giant Schnauzer

Land of origin: GERMANY

Original purpose: Cattle driving

Recent popularity ranking by A.K.C. registration: 73rd

Giant Schnauzer Club of America, Inc.
Ms. Judith DeBernardi, Secretary
2954 Driftwood Drive
San Jose, CA 95128

HEIGHT: Dogs to 27½ inches   Bitches to 25½ inches

WEIGHT: Dogs to 78 pounds   Bitches to 75 pounds

COAT
Hard, wiry, very dense; soft undercoat and harsh outer coat.

COLOR
Solid black or pepper and salt.

Amount of care coat requires: 1 2 3 4 5 6 7 8 9 10

Amount of exercise required: 1 2 3 4 5 6 7 8 9 10

*Suitability for urban/apartment life:** 1 2 3 4 5 6 7 8 9 10

*But only if suitable exercise is provided on a regular basis.

was made into a powerful drover to help get cattle to market. There is a strong belief today that the Flemish driving dog, the Bouvier des Flandres, and the black Great Dane were used with original Schnauzer stock to obtain the Giant we have today. The belief contains more than a little conjecture, however. ¶ By World War I the Giant was in use by the police, and has been ever since. His progress in this country has been slow because the German Shepherd has been so extremely popular and the two dogs do overlap in use and appeal. The Giant Schnauzer is also much tougher than the average Shepherd, much more a real dog person's dog. ¶ The Giant Schnauzer is a handsome dog of great strength and endurance. He is regal, standing very straight in a robust chest-first kind of way. He should never be shy or nervous, although he is characteristically very aggressive toward other animals. That should be kept in mind. ¶ The Giant Schnauzer has been bred from the beginning to serve man, and that means he takes training very well and is extremely loyal. He is a guard dog, a watchdog, a working dog every inch of him. He is not a dog to be taken lightly or owned casually. ¶ The Schnauzer's coat needs care. It needs pulling, trimming, and hard brushing. Only then will that splendid look be in evidence. The Giant Schnauzer is a dog that needs a great deal of exercise and should be owned by a family with at least one fairly athletic member. He can be a house dog, even an apartment dog, but long, long walks are in order every day and good runs whenever possible. Training is also mandatory, and anyone seriously considering this superior breed had better plan on some evenings at obedience school at the beginning. A well-trained Giant Schnauzer is a proud possession. One ill-trained or out of control is a lawsuit on the hoof.

The Great Dane is a true giant, one of the largest and most majestic dog breeds in the world. His history is not really known (a dozen mutually exclusive versions have appeared in print), but we do believe that his original purpose was to hunt boar. A dog of great power, courage, and endurance was needed for this dangerous sport, and that is what was bred into this German "mastiff." Actually, the dog we call the Great Dane may have been at the sport in something like his present form in the days of the pharaohs. ¶The ferociousness that must have gone into the original boar hunters is no longer apparent in the Great Dane. The dog we know is a gentleman, soft in manners, usually quiet, and very affectionate with his master and family. He is lovely with children if properly raised and not mean or petty with strangers, although he certainly is impressive as a watchdog. Needless to say, a dog of this

Great Dane

Land of origin: Ancient and unknown; GERMANY for last century or so

Original purpose: Boar hunting

Recent popularity ranking by A.K.C. registration: 33rd

Great Dane Club of America, Inc.
Mrs. Marie A. Fint, Corres. Secretary
442 Country View Lane
Garland, TX 75043

HEIGHT: Dogs to 32 inches or more   Bitches to 30 inches or more

WEIGHT: Dogs to 150 pounds   Bitches to 135 pounds

COAT
Short, thick, smooth, and glossy. It should not stand off the body or be dull.

COLOR
Great variety—brindle (golden yellow with black), fawn or clean golden yellow with black mask, steel blue, glossy black, harlequin (pure white with evenly distributed black markings).

Amount of care coat requires: 1 2 3 4 5 6 7 8 9 10

Amount of exercise required: 1 2 3 4 5 6 7 8 9 10

Suitability for urban/apartment life:*   1 2 3 4 5 6 7 8 9 10

---

*Provided that long walks will be offered several times a day. It is particularly important that the young Dane get enough exercise for condition and tone.

---

size should not be encouraged to be aggressive. ¶ Some people, of course, keep Great Danes in city apartments—presumably, in many cases, to discourage burglars. That is a foolish plan, for anyone close enough to be hurt by a dog is close enough to totally incapacitate him. ¶ The Great Dane really does need exercise. He can become stiff from improper exercise, resulting in poor muscle and bone development. Anyone keeping this giant in the city should plan on miles of walking every day, or hire someone to do it for him. No day should be skipped. ¶ The Great Dane is sociable and fine within the family circle. When young he can be a bit "klutzy," and small children can be sent flying like tenpins. That should be kept in mind. As the Great Dane matures, he does so as a well-controlled, self-possessed animal who seems aware of his giant status. Aggressive or poorly managed

Great Danes cannot be tolerated. The potential for really serious damage is far too great. ¶ Unfortunately, Great Danes are not long-lived, and nine or ten good years with their families must be considered fortunate. Since older animals are subject to heart ailments and painful joint disorders, a quiet life is in order. Contrary to a widely held belief, Great Danes do not have to have their ears cut to be attractive or to be shown. In England the practice is illegal. ¶ The Great Dane is one of the most handsome and regal of all dogs. He is a fine family pet, a good companion and protector of the home estate. He is, though, a giant; he needs room and an impressive quantity of food. He also needs obedience training, often at the professional level. A prospective owner should take all these factors into account.

The magnificent Great Pyrenees is a breed of enormous antiquity. Of the mastiff group, he probably came to the Middle East thousands of years ago from central Asia. There his ancestors existed during the Bronze Age, almost four thousand years ago, and also around the Baltic and Black seas. Examples were carried across Europe and developed to the form we know today in the Pyrenees Mountains. Great Pyrenees have a long and noble history as guard dogs, sheep dogs, and bear and wolf fighters. They were favorites of the French court and other royal strongholds. There is a lot of history in this breed, and a lot of this breed in European history.

Great Pyrenees

Land of origin: Very ancient; MIDDLE EAST and EUROPE (Pyrenees Mountains)

Original purpose: Herding and guard work

Recent popularity ranking by A.K.C. registration: 53rd

Great Pyrenees Club of America, Inc.
Mrs. Judy A. Brown, Corres. Secretary
3360 Jackson Drive
Jackson, WI 53037

HEIGHT: Dogs to 32 inches   Bitches to 29 inches

WEIGHT: Dogs to 125 pounds   Bitches to 115 pounds

COAT
Fine, heavy white undercoat; long, flat, thick outer coat with coarse hair. Straight or slightly wavy.

COLOR
All white or mainly white with badger, gray, or tan markings.

Amount of care coat requires: 1 2 3 4 5 6 7 8 9 10
                                       • • • •

Amount of exercise required: 1 2 3 4 5 6 7 8 9 10
                                  • • • • • • • • • • • • • • • • • •

Suitability for urban/apartment life: 1 2 3 4 5 6 7 8 9 10
                                        UNSUITED

¶Great Pyrenees are giant dogs with more good qualities than we can catalog. They are loyal unto death to their family; they will tackle anything that threatens them. They are very affectionate and responsive to human moods. They take to children naturally and are generally safe and reliable. They are incomparable baby-sitters. Gentle and considerate with strangers (although cautious at first), they are not usually quarrelsome. They get along with other animals and have to be driven into a fight. Once they are in combat, though, few animals can best them. In the Middle Ages they were really invincible. ¶Undeniably, the Great Pyrenees are also among the handsomest of dogs. They are especially appealing as puppies, and once grown they move with enormous purpose and self-assurance. The Great Pyrenees does require exercise and this must be kept in mind. It is unfair to confine this dog for long periods and not give him a chance to move. It is not even healthy. Any family contemplating this breed should have very active members who are devoted to long, long walks and even romps in the country. ¶This is a breed with so many special qualities one is tempted to urge restriction of ownership and breeding to people understanding and deserving enough to be granted those privileges. Unfortunately, anyone can buy a Great Pyrenees, and anyone can breed them. Like all large dogs they are subject to hip dysplasia, and poor examples are seen everywhere the breed is found. Care should be taken in buying one of these splendid dogs, and only the best of the proven specialty breeders should be trusted. Crippled, snippy dogs will not be satisfying to the owner, and should never have been brought into the world in the first place.

The Komondor has been bred in Hungary in the form we know today for over a thousand years. He probably arrived there from central Asia a thousand years before that. The Komondor (plural form is *Komondorok*) is one of the oldest breeds in Europe and probably the best guard dog of all. He was not used as a sheepherding dog, as is often stated. Smaller dogs did that work. The Komondor had the sole responsibility of driving away or killing wolves, bears, foxes, and any other animals that appeared to endanger the master's flocks. At this task the powerful and purposeful Komondor excelled. ¶ As a puppy the Komondor is playful and typical, but as he ma-

Komondor

Land of origin: HUNGARY; before that, CENTRAL ASIA

Original purpose: Guarding flocks—*not* herding

Recent popularity ranking by A.K.C. registration: 109th

Komondor Club of America
Cheri Bahrke, Secretary
12995 W. Chenango Ave.
Morrison, CO 80465

HEIGHT: Dogs to 27 inches   Bitches to 25 inches

WEIGHT: Dogs to 95 pounds   Bitches to 85 pounds

COAT
Unique. Dense, weather resistant, double. Woolly, soft, and dense undercoat with long, coarse outer coat. Outer coat tends to cord and hang in characteristic ropes.

COLOR
White only. Any other color disqualifies.

Amount of care coat requires: 1 2 3 4 5 6 7 8 9 10

Amount of exercise required: 1 2 3 4 5 6 7 8 9 10

Suitability for urban/apartment life: 1 2 3 4 5 6 7 8 9 10
UNSUITED

tures, he hardens into a guard dog with undying loyalty and resolve. He is cautious with strangers and only slowly accepts even apparent friends of the household. The one-time or first-time visitor is watched quietly but without relaxation. Anyone who seems to threaten the tranquillity of the household might expect to get a chunk taken out of him—a large chunk. ¶ The Komondor is serious but good with the family of his master. He is not especially nervous or snappy, and he is intelligent. Training is easy and should start early. It is practically impossible to call on a Komondor for more than he can deliver. His ability to learn and his determination to please and protect are apparently without limit. ¶ The Komondor lives naturally in the open, in very harsh climates, and outside quarters are a good idea for him even as a pet. There is no weather that will bother him, since he lives virtually encased in an impervious corded coat of white hair. It forms into hanging ropes, and the breed characteristically looks unkempt. That coat, though, is one of the more protective and efficient in the world of dogs. ¶ Tough, hardy, alert, the Komondor needs a lot of exercise to stay in good condition. With the fear of crime as great as it is, some people have begun to think of the Komondor as a good guard in an apartment house. That is unwise for several reasons. An apartment is not a proper setting for so large an outdoor animal, and a guard-trained or even a naturally protective Komondor is much more than the average pet owner can handle.

The handsome white Kuvasz is another great guard dog out of central Europe. He undoubtedly came to Hungary from Tibet and was known throughout the Eastern countries (including the Middle East) for many centuries. In Hungary he flourished to become the darling of kings and nobles. While the nobility plotted against each other and planned their endless intrigues and assassinations, only the great Kuvaszok (that is the plural form) could be trusted. ¶The Kuvasz is said to have an uncanny ability to detect an enemy of his master even before the master himself realizes there is danger. The breed is fiercely loyal and protective. It is said of this great

Kuvasz

Land of origin: TIBET and HUNGARY

Original purpose: Guarding, and then some herding

Recent popularity ranking by A.K.C. registration: 92nd

Kuvasz Club of America
Mayling Koval, Secretary
P.O. Box 503
Hopewell Junction, NY 12566

HEIGHT: Dogs to 30 inches   Bitches to 28 inches

WEIGHT: Dogs to 115 pounds   Bitches to 90 pounds

COAT
Rather long on neck but shorter on sides. Slightly wavy.

COLOR
Pure white only is desirable. No markings. Occasionally seen yellow saddle is serious fault.

Amount of care coat requires: 1 2 3 4 5 6 7 8 9 10

Amount of exercise required: 1 2 3 4 5 6 7 8 9 10

Suitability for urban/apartment life: 1 2 3 4 5 6 7 8 9 10
                                            UNSUITED

dog that he is either a friend or an enemy for life. In the Middle Ages the Kuvasz was undoubtedly much larger than our present standard of thirty inches. Kuvaszok must have been very intimidating to commoners, who were forbidden to own them. ¶The dogs were used in packs for hunting from the fifteenth century on. Eventually they got into the hands of the common people and were used as guards and perhaps as herders of cattle and sheep. By that time the breed had evolved to about where we know it today. ¶The Kuvasz is probably related to the Komondor, for they do have traits in common. Both are great outdoor animals, and both are extremely loyal to a very small and select core of people. People thinking of the Kuvasz as a pet might consider carefully, if this is to be their first dog, whether or not they are up to the task.

They are generally not. The Kuvasz is not a casual dog for the casual owner, nor is he a dog to be allowed to reign in the household. ¶This extremely handsome, very intelligent dog must be trained early and well and maintained that way, under constant supervision. A Kuvasz that gets the least out of hand is not only a nuisance but a potential menace. This is a dog for the firm, the strong, and the devoted among really experienced dog owners. It is a breed that is quite capable of being a little wiser than a man. There should never be any contest; the man must prevail and call all the signals. The very protective traits of the Kuvasz are things that must be kept in check, of course. No dog can be called upon to *always* know a friend from an enemy.

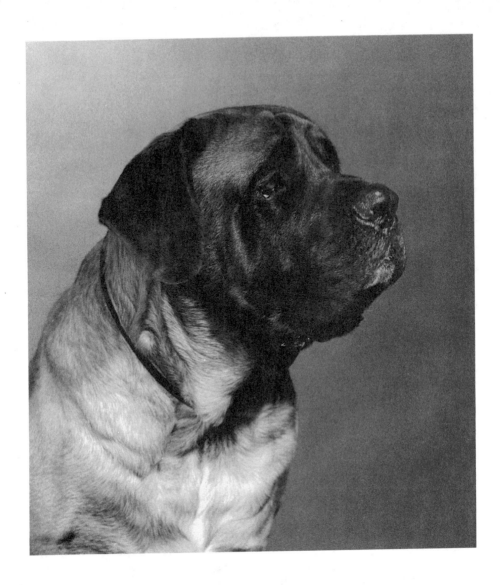

No one knows (and probably never will) where the Mastiff came from or how he was spread across the face of the world. There are lots of theories and some pretty fascinating bogus history, but it is conjecture at best. When Caesar invaded the British Isles in 55 B.C., the Mastiff was there alongside his British masters fighting against the Roman legions. As might be expected, examples of the breed were carried back to Rome. ¶The giant Mastiff (generically, the word *mastiff* implies a whole family of giant dogs) was bred for violence. He was a guard dog thousands of years ago, he was a war dog, a hunting dog for the largest game, and he was used in the pit in the most

Mastiff

Land of origin: ENGLAND for 2,000 years, before that a mystery

Original purpose: Guarding, hunting, fighting, war

Recent popularity ranking by A.K.C. registration: 54th

Mastiff Club of America, Inc,
Mr. Robert L Goldblatt, Secretary
P.O. Box 224
Talmage, CA 95481

HEIGHT: Dogs to 33 inches   Bitches to 31 inches

WEIGHT: Dogs to 185 pounds   Bitches to 175 pounds

COAT
Outer coat tends toward coarseness, with undercoat short, close lying, and dense.

COLOR
Apricot, silver fawn, or dark fawn brindle. Fawn brindle dogs to have fawn as background with brindle evenly distributed as dark stripes. Face the darker the better but always darker than body.

Amount of care coat requires: 1 2 3 4 5 6 7 8 9 10
                                          •

Amount of exercise required: 1 2 3 4 5 6 7 8 9 10
                                    • • • • • • • • • • • • • • • • •

Suitability for urban/apartment life: 1 2 3 4 5 6 7 8 9 10
                                                      UNSUITED

horrific of blood sports. It is more than a little strange that such a dog has developed into a generally docile animal. ¶ In a setting large enough for this animal (an apartment is hardly right), he is a perfect pet. He is great with children, fine with almost anyone, and usually not quarrelsome with strangers, although he may be cautious until he has assured himself that all is well. He can be protective, which presents a problem because of his size. By nature obedient and responsive, the Mastiff will take training well and will be serious about the things he is asked to do. ¶ Because he is so massive and so powerful, the Mastiff must be under control at all times. There are examples who are short with other animals, and they must be watched and, if possible, have trained out of them any sign of aggression. Other examples will be surrogate parents to the whole world and are provocation-proof. ¶ It should be noted that the Mastiff and the Bullmastiff are two different breeds. The latter is a cross between the Mastiff and the English Bulldog. In error, many people use the names interchangeably. The Mastiff is much the larger of the two. ¶ The Mastiff requires little coat care but does need exercise if he is to stay in good condition and not become stiff and lame. In situations where he must be tightly controlled, long walks are in order. He is best, of course, on a farm or a large estate, where he may exercise himself. These giants are rugged, hardy, and needless to say, very intimidating as watchdogs.

The Newfoundland is a giant of a dog, in appearance and nature every inch a "teddy bear." Named for the island off the east coast of Canada, the Newfoundland is undoubtedly descended from dogs brought there by European fishermen and later developed in England. ¶ The Newfoundland is a working dog in fact as well as in classification (this is not the case with some breeds). This was a dog who was expected to help the islanders haul their nets, pull carts, and carry loads, and he became a legend in lifesaving. The number of men, women, and children the Newfoundland is said to have pulled from icy seas is endless. How much is fact and how much romance is hard to say. It is about the same situation we have with Saint Bernards and their mountain rescue stories. Some of the lore is known to be true, some is questionable, but the whole truth does not really have to be known. ¶ The Newfoundland is a lover of a dog; he worships his master and his family. He is sensible with strangers and openly friendly once shown that his family is safe. Although not a nervous or even suspicious dog, the Newfoundland is very protective; with a dog of such size, that counts for

Newfoundland

Land of origin: NEWFOUNDLAND and ENGLAND

Original purpose: Hauling, carting, and sea rescue work

Recent popularity ranking by A.K.C. registration: 52nd

Newfoundland Club of America, Inc.
Mrs. Joan C. Bendure, Corres. Secretary
6765 West Platz Road
Fairview, PA 16415

HEIGHT: Dogs to 28 inches   Bitches to 26 inches

WEIGHT: Dogs to 150 pounds   Bitches to 120 pounds

COAT
Outer coat moderately long but not at all shaggy. Flat and usually straight, although some wave is allowed. It should not curl. The undercoat is soft and dense, and much of it is lost in the summer.

COLOR
Black, with or without a little white on chest and toes and sometimes the tip of tail. Also bronze and shades of brown. White and black dogs are called Landseers.* Beauty in color and marking is highly rated in judging.

Amount of care coat requires: 1 2 3 4 5 6 7 8 9 10
                                   • • • • • • • •

Amount of exercise required: 1 2 3 4 5 6 7 8 9 10
                                 • • • • • • • • • • • • • • • • • •

Suitability for urban/apartment life: 1 2 3 4 5 6 7 8 9 10
                                                    UNSUITED

*Dogs with the small white details on chest, toes, and tail tip are still considered black. The rare Landseers are truly pintolike.

something. ¶ Fortunately, the Newfoundland is easygoing with other animals and, indeed, seems to want to have another dog or two around. He is in fact social and sensible in all matters and therefore ideal in a family situation. ¶ Despite his heavy coat, the care of a Newfoundland is not a problem. A good work-over once a week will keep the coat from matting. If it is neglected, though, it can be a mess to straighten out. ¶ The Newfoundland was built for water. He is a powerful swimmer and certainly more than strong enough to drag a man from the sea. No weather and no water temperature will bother this great dog, who seems to flourish in the worst possible weather. In fact, about all that fazes this dog is disapproval or lack of human response. ¶ Because he is such a supreme gentleman, the Newfoundland will settle down anywhere his family wants him to. The city apartment isn't the best place, though, because most families simply can't supply enough walking time to satisfy the driving power of the Newfoundland's run and make up for the chance to break through heavy water in high wind. He is a breed that is much better in the open, much better out on the land or near the water than in an urban cave. If the family situation is right, and if there are frequent trips to the country, suburban life is fine. ¶ The Newfoundland in spirit and size is one of the all-time great breeds. Owners remain owned and seldom will allow themselves to be without the companionship, sense of security, and feeling of style, taste, and pure unabashed love this dog provides.

Photo by Moments by Jane, Jane B. Donahue

It is probable that what we know as the Working Group's Portuguese Water Dog originated as a herding dog along the border between China and Russia almost a thousand years before Christ. There are a number of theories as to how this dog got to Portugal, but none of them will ever be proven. Whether they were carried westward by barbaric German tribes across Europe, or moved across North Africa by the equally savage Berbers, they did eventually reach the Iberian Peninsula and apparently flourished there in isolated communities of fisherfolk along the coast. ¶In

Portuguese Water Dog

Land of origin: Portugal for centuries, but probably Asia way back.

Recent popularity ranking by A.K.C. registration: 95th

Portuguese Water Dog Club of America
Beverly Dees Rafferty, Corres. Secretary
13765 New Discovery Rd.
Colorado Springs, CO 80908

HEIGHT: Dogs 20 to 23 inches   Bitches 17 to 21 inches

WEIGHT: Dogs 42 to 60 pounds   Bitches 35 to 50 pounds

COAT
Profuse but no undercoat or mane. Two varieties: wavy which is rather loose with some sheen and curly with compact cylindrical curls. The latter is lusterless. Non-allergenic, non-shedding.

COLOR
Black, white, various tones of brown and black or brown combinations with white.

Amount of care coat requires: 1 2 3 4 5 6 7 8 9 10

Amount of exercise required: 1 2 3 4 5 6 7 8 9 10

Suitability for urban/apartment life: 1 2 3 4 5 6 7 8 9 10

*But only if properly exercised.

its time the Portuguese Water Dog has been a herding dog, a sporting dog, i.e. retriever, and a working dog. The last designation was the most recent, and thus the dog is legitimately classified today. The breed probably came from the same ancestral, genetic stock that gave us the Tibetan Terrier, the Poodle and the Puli, and it is a likely ancestor of both the American and Irish Water Spaniels. It is a dog with a great deal of history built into it even if much of that is lost to us. ¶In Portugal this breed was evolved to go to sea. It pulled nets and swam ashore or between boats with messages. It is an extremely rugged dog with enormous stamina. It can tolerate just about any weather and work a terribly punishing schedule and still be cheerful about its lot in life. ¶The Portuguese Water Dog is marked for its great intelligence (remember it is probably related to the poodle) and its willingness to put itself to the service of man. It is an easy dog to train for anyone able to outwit it, and a happy companion best suited to live and work with people who are at least its match. To be blunt, this is not a *whimp's* dog. ¶Many people in a number of places over a span of at least three thousand years have had a stake in this historical breed, but it is out of the village now and off the boat and the farm and in the hands of a more gentle fate. It is devoutly to be wished that this new setting and different kind of enthusiasm will not degrade the superb working animal it has been, and turn it into a *whimpy* dog. ¶The Portuguese Water Dog is here to stay, of that there is no doubt. There will be styling changes over the years but hopefully the inside of the dog can stay the way it is. It has taken a long time to get there, time and human needs and also a lot of care and faith.

Rottweiler

Land of origin: ANCIENT ROME, then GERMANY

Original purpose: Driving livestock, pulling carts, guard and police work

Recent popularity ranking by A.K.C. registration: 6th

American Rottweiler Club
Kay Peltier, Secretary
1012 Franklin Lane
Billings, MT 59101

HEIGHT: Dogs to 27 inches   Bitches to 25³/₄ inches

WEIGHT: Dogs to 90 pounds   Bitches to 85 pounds

COAT
Short, coarse, flat. Undercoat does not show through.

COLOR
Black with tan to mahogany markings on cheeks, muzzle, chest, legs, and over both eyes.
Small white spot on chest or belly is allowed but not desired.

Amount of care coat requires: 1 2 3 4 5 6 7 8 9 10

Amount of exercise required: 1 2 3 4 5 6 7 8 9 10

Suitability for urban/apartment life: 1 2 3 4 5 6 7 8 9 10
UNSUITED

The Rottweiler has a noble and fascinating history. The ancestral form was carried through Alpine passes by Roman legions invading the center of Europe. The dogs were used to drive the cattle needed to feed the troops in countries where raiding was not profitable. Some of these dogs were left behind in Rottweil in Württemberg in southern Germany. The breed hung on there into modern times, although it was virtually extinct around the turn of the century. The rebuilding of the breed began about 1910. ¶ The Rottweiler has been used with great success as a drover, guard, beast of burden, and police dog. He is highly intelligent and very willing, and he accepts virtually any training. Despite the hard usage to which the breed has been put throughout history, the Rottweiler today is affectionate, alert, and very good with his family. He is a natural watchdog and will be very cautious with strangers; with members of his family he tends to be a gentle, easygoing animal not given to temper or hysteria. He will tolerate other animals if they are raised with him and if he is made to understand that they are his master's property. ¶ The Rottweiler is a rugged dog with stamina and a very purposeful approach to life. He is a serious animal and goes about things in an intelligent, deliberate manner. Training should start early and continue, for the breed's capacity to learn is apparently without limit. ¶ Some people do keep Rottweilers in small suburban houses, and they will do well enough under those conditions if close to their family and if given plenty of exercise. They are better on a farm or large estate, though, for they are hard, outdoor animals. Exercise, wherever they live, is necessary for their good health. Too much confinement can make them tense and alter their disposition. ¶ Some storefront "trainers" have been turning out so-called guard and attack-trained dogs, using the Rottweiler along with other large working breeds. These animals are to be avoided as potentially extremely dangerous.

The Saint Bernard, America's most popular giant breed, has a long and romantic history. Sometime after 1550, large working dogs were brought up to a monastery in the high Saint Bernard Pass in the Swiss Alps from the towns and villages below. They may have been obtained by the monks as companions or as watchdogs. The records have been lost that might reveal dates and reasons. We do not know the history of the breed before that, although it is often suggested that they were descended from the great Molossian dog from ancient Epirus (Greece), which in turn may have been descended from giant Asian breeds of the mastiff type. The dog imported by the monks, or rather brought up into the mountains, may have been the Talhund. All of this will probably forever remain theory and conjecture. ¶ In time the dogs (not named Saint Bernard until the 1880s, a long time after Saint Bernard's death in 1153) came to do patrol work with the monks. They were used for testing trails and are said to have been able to predict storms and avalanches. They eventually

Saint Bernard

Land of origin: SWITZERLAND

Original purpose: Unknown—later, patrol and rescue work

Recent popularity ranking by A.K.C. registration: 44th

Saint Bernard Club of America, Inc.
Ms. Charlotte J. Miller, Corres. Secretary
1499 W. 83rd Street
Hialeah, FL 33014

HEIGHT: Dogs to 29 inches   Bitches to 27 inches

WEIGHT: Dogs to 170 pounds   Bitches to 160 pounds

COAT
Shorthaired version—very dense, close lying, smooth, tough, but not rough to touch.
Longhaired version—medium length, can be slightly wavy, not rolled, curled, or shaggy.

COLOR
White with red or red with white, various shades; brindle with white markings. Brown-yellow equal value to shades of red. Faces desirable dark. Never without white; solid and other colors faulty.

Amount of care coat requires:

Shorthaired: 1 2 3 4 5 6 7 8 9 10

Longhaired: 1 2 3 4 5 6 7 8 9 10

Amount of exercise required: 1 2 3 4 5 6 7 8 9 10

Suitability for urban/apartment life: 1 2 3 4 5 6 7 8 9 10
UNSUITED

---

were used to sniff out lost travelers. So much romantic literature was built on these stories that truth and fiction are difficult, if not impossible, to separate. ¶The Saint Bernard is a massive dog of enormous strength. He is traditionally calm and sensible and a fine pet in home situations where there is plenty of room. But he is too large for confined quarters; this is not a breed for the city apartment. He should get a great deal of exercise if his condition is to be maintained. Typical of large dogs, he is not very long-lived, and he appears far too often with hip deformities due to the careless breeding and mass-production engendered by his great popularity. ¶In recent years the press has reported Saint Bernards turning sour and attacking people. This is so contrary to the character of this breed that it must again be laid at the feet of bad breeding and greed. Some of the worst puppy factories ever raided by humane groups have turned out to be farms on which Saint Bernard puppies were being turned out by the crateful. The breed has been subjected to great cruelty, and there are very bad and even dangerous examples around. ¶Only the very finest specialty breeders should be trusted to supply a dog who can truly reflect the intelligent, quiet, sensible, and affectionate nature of this superior breed. And potential owners should not allow themselves to be mesmerized by the "cuteness" of a Saint Bernard puppy. That puppy very quickly becomes an absolute giant of a dog.

The magnificent Samoyed is an extremely ancient dog whose true origins are lost in the mists of the Arctic. Apparently for thousands of years he has been the companion of the Samoyed peoples, who have roamed the northern reaches of Asian Russia. A dog of the tundra, he is hardy and durable and extremely useful in many ways. ¶No one is sure how the Samoyed was first used. He was utilized variously to herd reindeer and to guard the flocks and herds against wolves, bears, perhaps even tigers. He was used to guard the wandering nomads, too, and later the villages and other permanent settlements. He has been used right up to the present time

Samoyed

Land of origin: ARCTIC RUSSIA

Original purpose: Protection, herding reindeer, pulling sleds

Recent popularity ranking by A.K.C. registration: 34th

Samoyed Club of America, Inc.
Mrs. Marilyn Gitelson, Secretary
3311 Concord Blvd.
Concord CA 94519

HEIGHT: Dogs to 23½ inches   Bitches to 21 inches

WEIGHT: Dogs to 65 pounds   Bitches to 50 pounds

COAT
Double. Undercoat soft, short, thick, and very dense. Outer coat long, harsh, straight from body without curl. Should glisten.

COLOR
Pure white, white and biscuit, cream, and all biscuit. No other colors allowed at all.

Amount of care coat requires: 1 2 3 4 5 6 7 8 9 10
                                  • • • • • • • • • • •

Amount of exercise required: 1 2 3 4 5 6 7 8 9 10
                                 • • • • • • • • • • • • • • • • •

*Suitability for urban/apartment life:**   1 2 3 4 5 6 7 8 9 10
                                           • • •

*Provided adequate exercise is given on a regular basis.

for pulling sleds, and indeed there has not been a major Arctic or Antarctic expedition utilizing sled dogs that hasn't had the Samoyed out front with the best of them. The Samoyed, naturally a jolly animal, puts himself into the sled game as readily as he does any other. More than anything else he wants to be part of the action whatever the cost in exertion or even danger to himself. ¶Several characteristics distinguish this truly splendid breed. He is an extremely intelligent dog, perhaps the most intelligent of all sled dogs. He is beautiful—some people say the single most beautiful of all dogs, although we would have to view that as subjective. No one, though, can deny the pure splendor of a Samoyed in fine coat. ¶The great Samoyed by his very nature gets along well with people and other animals. He is a natural with children and is rarely mean or nasty. The standard called for in the American Kennel Club breed guide seems to say it all. Under disposition it says: "Intelligent, gentle, loyal, adaptable, alert, full of action, eager to serve, friendly but conservative, not distrustful or shy, not overly aggressive. Unprovoked aggressiveness to be severely penalized." ¶Despite the fact that the Samoyed is a northern dog and is happiest in cold climates, and even though he is a very active dog, he can survive in an apartment with a properly loving family. He should be exercised a great deal and especially when the weather is harsh. It is never too cold for a Samoyed, and there is never enough running and plowing through snow. The coat, of course, is the breed's crowning glory and must be seen to. Brushing, dry cleaning, and only occasional bathing are the techniques whereby a Samoyed maintains his position at the top level of canine splendor.

The Husky is a striking dog—handsome and solid—and a devoted pet. He is naturally friendly and usually does not make the best watchdog despite his fine size and "wolflike" appearance. ¶The Husky is seldom quarrelsome with people and is usually very good with other animals in the family. He can return to being a hunter, and some will take to molesting stock. This can be a difficult habit to break. It is obviously most undesirable. ¶The Husky is not the easiest dog in the world to train, and anyone contemplating this active, outdoor breed should plan on intensive obedience training. It is particularly important that a Husky be taught to come when called. They are often tramps at heart and will look at their owner beguilingly and then take off tail held high while the owner fumes and rages helplessly. It is not wise to allow Huskies to roam, anymore than it is any other dog, for it is then that

Siberian Husky

Land of origin: SIBERIA

Original purpose: Pulling sleds

Recent popularity ranking by A.K.C. registration: 19th

Siberian Husky Club of America, Inc.
Ms. Carol Nash, Corres. Secretary
54 Newton Road
Plaistow, NH 03865

HEIGHT: Dogs to 23½ inches   Bitches to 22 inches

WEIGHT: Dogs to 60 pounds   Bitches to 50 pounds

COAT
Double, and medium in length. Generally smooth lying and not harsh to the touch. Not to be trimmed or clipped. Undercoat sheds out in summer.

COLOR
All colors are allowed, from black to white. Interesting and very handsome face markings are usual. Eyes may be brown or blue or even one of each.

Amount of care coat requires: 1 2 3 4 5 6 7 8 9 10
                                   •••••••••••

Amount of exercise required: 1 2 3 4 5 6 7 8 9 10
                                 •••••••••••••••

*Suitability for urban/apartment life:**   1 2 3 4 5 6 7 8 9 10
                                           •••

---

*Not really suitable to urban life unless given a great deal of exercise every day with special long weekend and holiday romps.

they get into trouble. ¶ Huskies are so intent on human companionship and so openly affectionate that many people have taken to keeping them in apartments and small, restrictive suburban homes. Locked up alone during the day, a Husky can become destructive. He isn't by nature that kind of dog, and although human relationships are more important to a Husky than anything else, he is better off in cooler climates and in open country—after he has had intensive obedience training. From the very beginning the Husky will try to test the pecking order, and if an owner is indecisive or unassertive, the Husky will be very pleased to be on top. From there on, it is straight downhill until the dog is a first-rate nuisance to everyone. ¶ Huskies are excellent family dogs and generally fine with children. Most Huskies love snow and harsh weather, but believe it or not, there are individual animals who hate to get their feet wet or spend much time in the snow (it is not hard to tell how many generations *that* strain has been out of Siberia). But for the typical Husky there is no temperature that is too low. He can tolerate anything from the Arctic to the Antarctic. ¶ In the spring it is wise to have as much of the Husky's undercoat pulled as possible. It will come away by the handful. The shedding is constant until that coat is gone. ¶ The Husky is only to be recommended to the owner or family that will work with their dog, teach and maintain his manners, and keep the animal from wandering too far afield. A Husky is more than a casual pet. He may be enchanting, but he can also be a destructive pest. The difference lies more with the owner than with the dog.

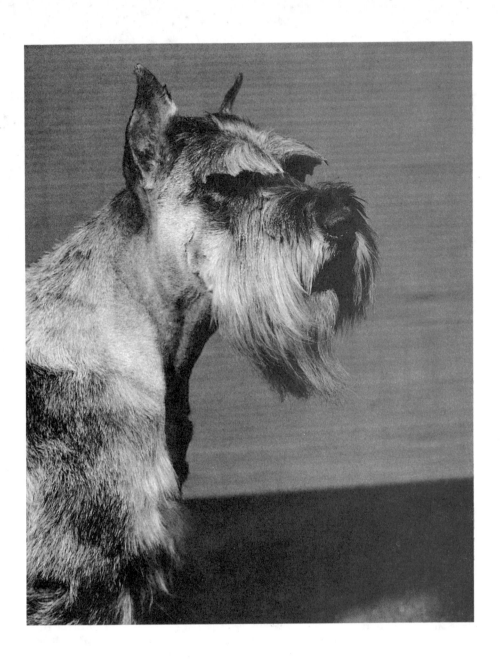

The Schnauzer is known in this country in three sizes—the Giant, the Standard, and the Miniature—and each is considered a separate breed. They are not all shown in the same group. Of the three breeds, the Miniature is by far the most popular, ranking ninth in the country, compared with the Standard's position as seventy-third and the Giant's as eighty-fourth ¶The Schnauzer has long been known in Germany and was painted by Dürer, Cranach, Reynolds, and many other artists, usually as part of a noble portrait. They were companion animals as well as ratters, hunters, guards, retrievers—almost anything a dog could be called upon

Standard Schnauzer

Land of origin: GERMANY

Original purpose: As companion, ratter, hunter, guard, and retriev

Recent popularity ranking by A.K.C. registration: 84th

Standard Schnauzer Club of America
Mrs. Karen Benson, Corres. Secretary
5120 Fino Drive
San Diego, CA 92124

HEIGHT: Dogs to 19½ inches   Bitches to 18½ inches

WEIGHT: Dogs to 37 pounds   Bitches to 35 pounds

COAT
Tight, hard, wiry, and thick. Soft, close undercoat and harsh outer coat.

COLOR
Pepper and salt or pure black. Many shades of pepper and salt from dark iron to silvery highlights. Black as strong as possible. Black rarer in this country.

Amount of care coat requires: 1 2 3 4 5 6 7 8 9 10
                • • • • • • • • • • • •

Amount of exercise required: 1 2 3 4 5 6 7 8 9 10
                • • • • • • • • • • • • • • •

*Suitability for urban/apartment life:**   1 2 3 4 5 6 7 8 9 10
                        • • • • • • •

*But only if properly exercised on a regular basis.

to do. They are among the most intelligent of all dogs, and this has apparently always been the case. In America the Miniature is classed as a terrier, while the Standard and Giant are shown as working dogs, of which the Germans undoubtedly approve. ¶ It is believed that the Schnauzer originated from crosses of a black German Poodle and a gray spitz-type dog. The original stock may have been *pinscher* with these other types crossed in. The breed is old enough that these facts cannot be determined. ¶ Standard Schnauzers are solid, square, highly active animals with great affinity for human beings and human activities. As house pets they are participators and niche fitters. They make the best of all possible worlds out of every situation and have the ability to endear themselves and attract attention. They love to play and they love to work, and they enter into every situation with boundless enthusiasm. They are rugged and tough and will take on all comers. They are excellent watchdogs although not overly suspicious. ¶ Their fine form must be seen to at least twice a year by someone with professional grooming skills, but their day-to-day care is not oppressive. They are, as they say in the horse world, easy keepers. ¶ Standard Schnauzers are fine house dogs and can be kept in an apartment if given plenty of exercise. They are so fast and so quickly caught up by an idea that care must be taken to keep them on a lead anywhere near traffic. They are, nonetheless, eminently trainable in all things appropriate to the companion dog. Early and intensive obedience training is necessary.

[Group 4]

The Herding Dogs

Australian Cattle Dog
Bearded Collie
Belgian Malinois
Belgian Sheepdog
Belgian Tervuren
Bouvier des Flandres
Briard

Collie
German Shepherd
Old English Sheepdog
Puli
Shetland Sheepdog
Cardigan Welsh Corgi
Pembroke Welsh Corgi

The Australian Cattle Dog was developed very deliberately by stockmen in that country beginning about 1830. The records show an original cross between a dog called the Smithfield with the feral dog of Australia, the dingo. The Smithfield was too much of a barker to be of much use with cattle and the idea was to get the bark out of the dog. That worked well enough but it also put a bite in, an unfortunate characteristic. The cross was then bred with smooth blue-merle collies brought over from Scotland. That pretty much got the bite out, but put the bark back in. Dalmatian and Kelpie were added and then a native herding dog. The Queensland heeler emerged as a quiet, controlable, non-biting herding dog that was companionable and about as smart as you could want a dog to be. The name was eventually changed and that is the dog we call the Australian Cattle Dog today. ¶This masterpiece of genetic engineering was not perfected along lines of beauty but pure function. The Australian Cattle Dog is compact, robust and has seemingly un-

Australian Cattle Dog

Land of origin: AUSTRALIA

Australian Cattle Dog Club of America
Nina Schroder, Corres. Secretary
3388 Hwy 99W
Corning, CA 96021

HEIGHT: Dogs 18 to 20 inches   Bitches 17 to 19 inches

WEIGHT: Range of 33 to 50 pounds.

COAT
Moderately short, straight outer coat of medium texture with a short, dense undercoat. A good brushy tail.

COLOR
Blue: Blue or blue-mottled with or without markings of blue or tan.
Red: Red speckle all over with or without dark red markings on head. Even head markings a plus.

Amount of care coat requires: 1 2 3 4 5 6 7 8 9 10

Amount of exercise required: 1 2 3 4 5 6 7 8 9 10

Suitability for urban/apartment life: 1 2 3 4 5 6 7 8 9 10

limited stamina. It is always able, always willing and terribly serious about its assignments. It is generally very slow about accepting strangers but it is incredibly loyal to its master, its family, its stock and its turf. It is a dog that takes well to obedience training and should be offered a lot of training from its early months on. It is too smart and inventive to be left to its own resources. Its work program is better as an assignment than as a solution to its own boredom. ¶The Australian Cattle Dog is not remarkable for its elegance and indeed that has never been the intent of its breeders and fanciers. It will be interesting and perhaps a little sad to see what happens to this breed over the next quarter of a century. The Australian Cattle Dog can be kept in an apartment but out of fairness to the genes that have been built into it the dog should be exercised regularly and often. It is simply not the dog to lock away like a toy. In its present form it is a young breed still close to its origins and those origins meant work. The play the non-stock owning owner may substitute for work had best seem like work, things the dog can feel it is expected to do. An Australian Cattle Dog that is not allowed to feel as if it is fulfilling a role will be a sad dog. ¶There is an undeniable sense of adventure in getting involved with a newly recognized breed just beginning to grow in popularity. It is, though, really a challenge for an experienced dog person. The Australian cattle dog, tough, loyal, resilient and possessive is not an ideal first dog. It is a doggy dog and requires more than feeding and petting. It needs managing. That is a plus when the owner is up to the task.

This very recent addition to the roster of breeds recognized by the American Kennel Club is a British sheepdog. American registration became effective October 1, 1976, but the breed itself may be the oldest of English droving dogs. Certainly it is much older than the Old English Sheepdog. ¶ The "Beardie," as his fanciers refer to him, is a herding dog first, a pet second. He is a natural herder and drover. Children, especially small tots, must expect to be directed, guided, and nudged to where the family Beardie thinks they should be. He is generally excellent with children and ultimately friendly with strangers the family accepts. ¶ The Bearded Collie makes a perfectly awful guard dog. That is not part of his makeup,

Bearded Collie

Land of origin: SCOTLAND and ENGLAND

Original purpose: Drover

Recent popularity ranking by A.K.C. registration: 79th

Bearded Collie Club of America, Inc.
Ms. Patti Carmejoole, Corres. Secretary
80 Union Avenue
Sudbury, MA 01776

HEIGHT: Dogs to 22 inches   Bitches to 21 inches

WEIGHT: Dogs to 55 pounds   Bitches to 45 pounds

COAT
Double—undercoat soft, furry, and close; outer coat harsh, strong, flat, *not* woolly, *not* curly.

COLOR
Slate gray, reddish fawn, black, all shades of gray, brown, and sandy. May or may not have typical white Collie markings on head, chest, neck, legs, feet, and tail tip.

*Amount of care coat requires:** 1 2 3 4 5 6 7 8 9 10

Amount of exercise required: 1 2 3 4 5 6 7 8 9 10

Suitability for urban/apartment life:† 1 2 3 4 5 6 7 8 9 10

*Slightly more during first two years.
†If properly exercised *every* day.

although he is a satisfactory watchdog. He will bark at a strange sound in the night, but don't expect a Beardie to go for a stranger's throat, even an unwelcome stranger. Tail wagging is more likely. ¶The breed is slow to mature, and a Beardie's coat for the first two years requires about forty-five minutes of vigorous brushing a week. After two years, about twenty minutes a week will do. In the breed's favor is the fact that Beardies shed very little. ¶This dog is active; he has a long, lean body and he does not normally run to fat. He has an easy, free movement and does require exercise. Any Beardie maintained in the suburbs or city should get an absolute minimum of a half an hour to an hour of real exercise every day. That double coat means the Beardie can take any weather, certainly more than his mas-

ter is likely to appreciate. A run in an open field is really what a Bearded Collie needs and wants, and for that reason I prefer to see this breed in the country. Still, the dog is not so large that he is a handicap in an apartment, and he is flexible enough to manage the situation as long as he is loved and is walked—a lot. Running is better than walking, when possible. ¶It was predictable that the Bearded Collie would be recognized by the A.K.C., and he is surely a dog destined for stardom. The breed club has been so meticulous that the A.K.C. was able to adopt its studbook outright when the decision was made to give the breed full recognition. One hopes those standards will be maintained and that popularity will not harm this fine, old herding dog from the British Isles.

The Belgian Malinois is one of three virtually identical Belgian sheepherding dogs that differ only in color and to some degree in coat (see also the Belgian Sheepdog and the Belgian Tervuren). All three breeds evolved from the basic shepherd stock of Holland, Belgium, and France that was known as *Chien de Berger*, an animal bred for loyalty, endurance, and intelligence. The livelihood and therefore the lives of the sheepherding people depended in no small part upon the quality of their dogs. Dog owning was not a luxury. You fed an animal who earned its keep, and the herding dogs of Europe, in the Middle Ages, earned their keep and more. Bandits,

Belgian Malinois

Land of origin: BELGIUM

Original purpose: Sheepherding

Recent popularity ranking by A.K.C. registration: 111st

HEIGHT: Dogs to 26 inches   Bitches to 24 inches

WEIGHT: Dogs to 60 pounds   Bitches to 55 pounds

COAT
Short and straight with a dense, protective undercoat. Somewhat longer around neck and on tail and back of thighs.

COLOR
Fawn to mahogany with black overlay; black muzzle and ears. Lighter underneath but not washed out. White on toe tips and *small* white spot on chest permitted.

Amount of care coat requires: 1 2 **3 4** 5 6 7 8 9 10

Amount of exercise required: 1 2 3 **4 5 6 7 8 9 10**

Suitability for urban/apartment life:*   1 2 **3 4** 5 6 7 8 9 10

*But must be exercised regularly and seriously.

stock thieves, and wolves prowled the countryside, and it took no small amount of canine courage to protect flocks and families against intrusion and ruin. ¶ The Belgian Malinois, like the other two breeds, is obviously related at some point to the German Shepherd. The earlier shepherd dogs of western Europe were not bred for color and style but for performance, and it is only in relatively modern times that an effort has been made to standardize them. The Malinois is a short-haired mahogany dog, the Belgian Sheepdog a black breed, and the Belgian Tervuren a longer-haired, mahogany-russet breed. ¶ The overall impression the Belgian Malinois gives is of a square and well-balanced dog. The male is masculine looking, and the bitch unmistakably feminine. The expression is alert, sure, and inquiring. The Belgian Malinois wants to know what you want, whether you are a friend or a stranger. If you are a stranger, the dog certainly wants to know that you are not a threat to the household he was born to protect. ¶ Because they are natural watchdogs and at times openly suspicious of people they do not know, these dogs should be trained early and well. They were used to drive wolves and feral dogs away from the flocks, so they had fear bred out of them. They can be quick to fight, and when they do, there is no stopping them. They will fight to the death. ¶ The Belgian Malinois is a fine, intelligent, and affectionate dog. The least known of the three Belgian breeds in this country, it is still close to its original form. Anyone looking for a breed that has not been watered down by mass-production might well turn to this fine herding dog. As a herding dog, however, it is a breed more suited for open country than for city life, and it should be given a great deal of exercise every day.

Until 1959 all three breeds of Belgian sheepherding dogs were known in this country as Belgian Sheepdogs. The breed we know today as the Belgian Sheepdog (properly also called the Groenendael) had been here since 1907, when the first five specimens were imported. The dog we today know as the Belgian Malinois arrived here in the late 1940s, the Belgian Tervuren in 1954. By 1959 the American Kennel Club had separated the three into distinct breeds, and only the black (with occasionally a very little bit of white), medium-to-long-haired dog is today called and shown as the Belgian Sheepdog. ¶These intelligent dogs have been used extensively for police work in Europe and other parts of the world, in-

Belgian Sheepdog

Land of origin: BELGIUM

Original purpose: Sheepherding

Recent popularity ranking by A.K.C. registration: 82nd

Belgian Sheepdog Club of America, Inc.
Mrs. Geraldine B. Kimball, Corres. Secretary
211 W. Elm Street
Pembroke, MA 02359

HEIGHT: Dogs to 26 inches   Bitches to 24 inches

WEIGHT: Dogs to 60 pounds   Bitches to 55 pounds

COAT
Guard hairs long, straight, and very abundant, particularly around neck, back of front legs; long trimming on hindquarters and on tail. Dense undercoat very protective.

COLOR
All black, or black with restricted amounts of white: moderate strip or patch on chest, between pads of feet, on tips of rear toes only, and gray or white on chin and muzzle. White on tips of front toes a fault.

Amount of care coat requires: 1 2 3 4 5 6 7 8 9 10
                                     • • • • •

Amount of exercise required: 1 2 3 4 5 6 7 8 9 10
                                   • • • • • • • • • • • • • • • • • •

*Suitability for urban/apartment life:** 1 2 3 4 5 6 7 8 9 10
                                        • • •

---

*But must be exercised regularly and seriously.

cluding the United States, and indeed may have been the first breed in Europe to be trained for such work. They are loyal and willing animals who want to please their masters; they are affectionate with people they know but are suspicious of strangers. They were used as patrol and courier dogs in World War I, and hundreds gave their lives in battle. They are without fear and will attack anything they feel threatens their family and their holdings. They are possessive and territorial, as goes with being an outstanding guardian of home and flock. The Belgian Sheepdog is not at all casual about his responsibilities. ¶When one considers that the German Shepherd ranks third in this country in popularity (by 1978 A.K.C. registrations) and the Belgian Sheepdog seventy-eighth, one realizes how unspoiled and still true to purpose and form this dog probably is. Anyone who finds that distinction appealing and who wants to work toward maintaining such early and original perfection might well consider this intelligent breed. ¶The Belgian Sheepdog requires a lot of exercise. He is a rough, tough outdoor animal designed to handle any weather and any assignment. To coop him up and deny him an opportunity to move, to protect, and to participate in an active, outdoor life is to start the breed on the road to disintegration. Training of the Belgian Sheepdog should start early and continue long, and his distrust of strangers should be carefully supervised. He is far too intelligent an animal to be allowed to get the upper hand. Once you surrender it, you might never be able to get it back.

This is the breed known in France and Belgium as the *Chien de Berger Belge*. It is a stunningly handsome version of the black Belgian Sheepdog, different only in color. Before the 1880s, when dog shows became popular and tended to direct attention to a dog's appearance, European shepherds were not concerned with conforma-tion. They were looking for dependability and durability, and they had that in their *Chiens de Berger* no matter what they looked like. But by the 1880s fencing and corralling were commonplace, and the wolves were gone. It was time to start dressing up the working breeds in dependable finery. ¶The Belgian Tervuren, like his

Belgian Tervuren

Land of origin: BELGIUM

Original purpose: Sheepherding

Recent popularity ranking by A.K.C. registration: 90th

American Belgian Tervuren Club, Inc.
Ms. Eileen Hudak, Corres. Secretary
1905 W. Carriage Drive
Santa Ana, CA 92704

HEIGHT: Dogs to 26 inches   Bitches to 24 inches

WEIGHT: Dogs to 60 pounds   Bitches to 55 pounds

COAT
Guard hairs long, straight, and very abundant, particularly around neck, back of front legs; long trimming on hindquarters and on tail. Dense undercoat very protective.

COLOR
Attained at 18 months: rich fawn to russet mahogany with black overlay. Hairs two-colored (black tipped). In males, pronounced on shoulders, back, and rib section. Chest mixture of black and gray. Mask and ears largely black. Tail with darker tip. Lighter underbody but not washed out.

Amount of care coat requires: 1 2 3 4 5 6 7 8 9 10

Amount of exercise required: 1 2 3 4 5 6 7 8 9 10

Suitability for urban/apartment life:*   1 2 3 4 5 6 7 8 9 10

*But must be exercised regularly and seriously.

very close cousins, the Belgian Malinois and the Belgian Sheepdog, is an elegant-looking animal with a lively and graceful gait. His whole attitude is one of willingness, even eagerness to work, to please, to belong. He is obedient when trained well and early and has a long memory for friends and foes. He can be a fighter, because he was made to drive off or kill the feral dogs that ranged across Europe spreading rabies and terror, but his possessiveness and fearlessness must be held in check. Although they are fine base-line qualities, they are not needed the way they once were. ¶Once again, we find in the Belgian Tervuren an animal still close to some original ideal pragmatically arrived at a long time ago in a very rough world, but a breed little known in this country. Only the fine points of appearance have been modified or clarified in modern times—in the last century—and the rest is still probably pretty close to original design. This has great appeal for many people, and so does the fact that the spoilers have not yet chosen this breed for their quick-dollar machinations. ¶The Belgian Tervuren, like his first cousins, needs a great deal of exercise and is of limited appeal in the city. By nature a watchdog, he is best in the suburbs or country, where he still should be controlled and not allowed to fight with other dogs, as some specimens are likely to do. Early and careful obedience training are in order for this herding dog of western Europe.

The cattle-herding people of the northern French hill country and southwestern Flanders needed a really tough dog to guard, herd, and drive their animals. The Bouvier des Flandres emerged as that animal. He is a rough and intelligent dog who was of help to the small farmer and the butcher alike. The itinerant strangers and packs of feral dogs who wandered those hills all needed to be watched, and occasionally attacked, and the Bouvier was the right dog for the job. Afraid of nothing, undeterred by any kind of weather or terrain, and boundless in his devotion to his master, the Bouvier set about his task with particular skill and energy. ¶The seventy-

Bouvier des Flandres

Land of origin: FLANDERS and NORTHERN FRANCE

Original purpose: Cattle herding, driving, and guarding

Recent popularity ranking by A.K.C. registration: 56th

American Bouvier des Flanders Club, Inc.
Ms. Ellen Raper, Secretary
1718 Trinity Road
Raleigh, NC 27607

HEIGHT: Dogs to 27½ inches   Bitches to 26½ inches

WEIGHT: Dogs to 70 pounds   Bitches to 65 pounds

COAT
Rough and tousled. Able to tolerate any weather. Outer coat harsh, rough, and wiry; very, very thick. Undercoat fine and soft.

COLOR
Fawn to black, salt and pepper, gray, and brindle. White star on chest permitted. Chocolate brown with white spotting not desired.

Amount of care coat requires: 1 2 3 4 5 6 7 8 9 10
                                 • • • • • •

Amount of exercise required: 1 2 3 4 5 6 7 8 9 10
                               • • • • • • • • • • • • • • • • • •

*Suitability for urban/apartment life:** 1 2 3 4 5 6 7 8 9 10
                                          •

---

*But exercise is a serious matter and must be regular.

pound Bouvier des Flandres served faithfully in World War I as well. He was an ambulance dog and a messenger. That war, however, nearly did the breed in. The areas where he was best loved and where most of the significant breeding was going on were devastated by the battles that raged back and forth. Most of the stock was lost, and many examples were carried off to Germany. A few good specimens survived, though, and one who belonged to a U.S. army veterinarian was special. Ch. Nic de Sottegem appears as a forebear in perhaps most of the pedigrees seen here today. ¶The Bouvier can be a family dog and is usually good with children. He is loyal and obedient when trained and is a watchdog. But he is also rough-and-tumble and hard to maintain in close quarters. He really is a dog for the countryside, although a suburban neighborhood will do as long as the dog is well trained and well controlled. It must be remembered that the Bouvier des Flandres was used to drive away whole packs of stray dogs, and he is not likely to back down from a fight. Like many herding and driving breeds, the Bouvier des Flandres is protective and territorial, and that can lead to fights, even though the strange dog's intentions are inoffensive. This must be watched, for the Bouvier is far too powerful to be allowed to perform his ancient responsibilities unchecked. ¶A good household pet if there is an opportunity for plenty of exercise, the Bouvier is an interesting large dog with a long and noble tradition of service to man.

The Briard is probably the oldest of the true French sheepherding dogs. These animals originally were used to protect flocks against thieves and feral dog packs. They have exceptional hearing, are extremely agile, and are loyal. They are still the top-rated sheep dog in France and are in use all over the country. Although often known as *Chiens Berger de Brie*, they are popular well beyond Brie. They have had their place of eminence for over seven hundred years, which speaks well for their qualities. ¶The Briard does not learn as quickly as some of the other herding dogs, but once he has been trained, he is trained for life. Further, nothing will deter him. He

Briard

Land of origin: FRANCE

Original purpose: Sheepherding

Recent popularity ranking by A.K.C. registration: 106th

Briard Club of America
Ms. Sue Erickson, Corres. Secretary
P.O. Box 3373
Mankato, MN 56002-3373

HEIGHT: Dogs to 27 inches   Bitches to 25½ inches

WEIGHT: Dogs to 80 pounds   Bitches to 74 pounds

COAT
Long, stiff, and slightly wavy.

COLOR
All solid colors allowed with the exception of white. Dark preferred—black, black with some white hairs, dark and light gray shades, tawny. Or two of these in combination but with no spots—transition between colors to be gradual and symmetrical.

Amount of care coat requires: 1 2 3 4 5 6 7 8 9 10

Amount of exercise required: 1 2 3 4 5 6 7 8 9 10

Suitability for urban/apartment life: 1 2 3 4 5 6 7 8 9 10
                                          UNSUITED

can stand any terrain and any weather, and he has enormous endurance. He is so willing a worker that his short career as a cart dog proved undistinguished, as he tended to overdo and hurt himself. The Briard served well in World War I, carrying supplies and munitions to the front. ¶The Briard is a quick mover—he turns fast, as suits a sheepherder. These dogs are definitely not keen on strangers and tend to remain suspicious even after some time has passed. They are not yappy and silly about newcomers, but they will watch quietly for some sign that they are needed. As natural watchdogs, they can be quite protective. ¶Because they have been bred through so many centuries as active field dogs, they do need exercise to remain happy and in good shape. They cannot be kept easily in an apartment. In any circumstances there must be active members of the family to take them on long walks and runs, and more than once a day. In general the Briard is a well-mannered dog, stoic and reserved. He is a good breed with children that he knows. He does not tend to stray, preferring to stay near the property of his master so that he can protect it. ¶The Briard is not the most elegant of breeds, but he does have a nice square, solid appearance. He looks as purposeful as he is, and in the right setting he makes a good family pet and household guardian. Training has to start early and last long. Once you have brought your Briard to the right point of training, though, you have an exceptionally well-mannered canine friend.

Rough-Coated Collie

Smooth-Coated Collie

The Collie dates back several hundred years to the Scottish Highlands, and given the antiquity of sheepherding, the breed undoubtedly had much earlier origins on the Continent. No one will ever sort out the early history of the Collie, for no records were kept by breeders of herding dogs. These animals were essential to their masters' livelihood rather than to their sense of aesthetics. ¶There are two varieties of Collie, the rough and the smooth, with the former being the more popular. Records indicate that as late as the end of the last century the two varieties might appear in the same litter, but some authorities believe that the two had different origins. Today, though, they are considered varieties of the same breed, and all the rest must remain conjecture. ¶The standards for the two forms are the same except for the coat, and therein lies a world of difference. The Rough-Coated Collie requires a great deal of care if he is to look as he should. His coat is long and dense and

Collie

Land of origin: SCOTLAND

Original purpose: Herding, farm work

Recent popularity ranking by A.K.C. registration: 23rd

Collie Club of America, Inc.
Mr. John Honig, Secretary
72 Flagg Street
Worcester, MA 01602

HEIGHT: Dogs to 26 inches   Bitches to 24 inches

WEIGHT: Dogs to 75 pounds   Bitches to 65 pounds

COAT
Well-fitting, straight, and harsh outer coat with very dense soft, furry undercoat. Very abundant and the dog's "crowning glory" in the rough-coated variety. The smooth variety has a hard, dense, and smooth coat.

COLOR
Four varieties: sable and white (sable running from light gold to dark mahogany), tricolor (predominantly black with white and tan markings), blue merle, and white. The latter is really predominantly white with sable or tricolor markings. Colors are the same for both coat styles.

Amount of care coat requires:
Rough: 1 2 3 4 5 6 7 8 9 10
             ●●●●●●●●●●●●●●●●●●
Smooth: 1 2 3 4 5 6 7 8 9 10
             ●

Amount of exercise required: 1 2 3 4 5 6 7 8 9 10
                    ●●●●●●●●●●●●●●●●●●●

*Suitability for urban/apartment life:**   1 2 3 4 5 6 7 8 9 10
                     ●●●●

*Provided that enough exercise is given every day.

soon will become a hopeless tangle unless brushed out regularly. The Smooth-Coated variety requires virtually no care, but he is not at all popular with American fanciers of the breed. ¶The Collie is a herding dog designed for living in the open. He requires a lot of exercise on a regular basis, for working dogs are creatures of habit. No one should think of owning a Collie unless he plans to exercise him and care for him properly. ¶By nature the Collie is careful with strangers—not hostile, just cautious. He is very affectionate with family and with people he knows well. He is loyal, a good watchdog, and sensible in all things. Like many other breeds, the Collie has suffered from extreme popularity. As a result of books, films, and television series starring Collies, the breed consistently has been one of the most popular in America. Many breeders far more interested in dollars than in the welfare of their breed have capitalized on the demand, and there are many substandard specimens around. They can be unreliable and nervous, the last things one should expect of a fine Collie. ¶Perhaps as much as with any breed in America today, great care should be taken when buying a Collie. Only the most responsible breeders should be considered. Collies are shown in two varieties, rough and smooth, but aside from their coats, the same standards prevail.

The highly popular German Shepherd was derived over a period of several hundred years of native herding and from general farm dogs in Germany and surrounding areas. From the beginning of this century his worldwide popularity has grown steadily. He is the fifth most popular purebred dog in America. ¶The German Shepherd is first, last, and always a working dog designed to serve man in any way needed. A herding dog, a guard dog for livestock, a police dog, a military dog, a dog to lead the blind and pull carts—this sturdy, intelligent animal has never been outclassed by any task or any other breed. He is the preeminent herding dog, and his popularity clearly reflects that fact. ¶A shy or nervous German Shepherd is not to be

German Shepherd

Land of origin: GERMANY

Original purpose: Farm work, herding, guard work

Recent popularity ranking by A.K.C. registration: 5th

German Shepherd Dog Club of America, Inc.
Miss Blanche Beisswenger, Corres. Secretary
17 West Ivy Lane
Englewood, NJ 07631

HEIGHT: Dogs to 26 inches   Bitches to 24 inches

WEIGHT: Dogs to 85 pounds   Bitches to 70 pounds

COAT
Double and of medium length. Outer coat should be dense, straight, harsh, and close lying. Never silky, soft, woolly, or open.

COLOR
Most are permissible, but not white. Black and tan, gray, or black are common.

Amount of care coat requires: 1 2 3 4 5 6 7 8 9 10

Amount of exercise required: 1 2 3 4 5 6 7 8 9 10

*Suitability for urban/apartment life:**   1 2 3 4 5 6 7 8 9 10

---

*But only if properly exercised.

---

forgiven, for the standards clearly state that such personality faults are to be severely penalized. A really nervous German Shepherd is a dangerous animal and should not have access to innocent bystanders. ¶ It is true that 80 percent or more of reported purebred dog bites are caused by German Shepherds. That is because bites by large dogs are more apt to be reported than nips by small dogs, and because the German Shepherd is so very popular. It is also unfortunately true that many inexpert people keep these animals as deterrent dogs. Too many accidents obviously happen as a result. ¶ The German Shepherd can be taught just about anything, and one thing often taught this animal, most unfortunately, is to attack. Private citizens have no more right to an attack-trained German Shepherd than they have to a Luger in a shoulder holster. Laws are going to have to be enacted to regulate the rental and sale of

attack dogs. ¶ A German Shepherd raised as a pet and well trained is as fine a canine companion as anyone could possibly want. Intelligent, alert, a perfect watchdog, careful with strangers but not petty or mean—he is loyal unto death to his family and will do anything to protect family children. That does not have to be built in, it is already there. ¶ The German Shepherd requires a lot of exercise to maintain condition, and his coat should be brushed regularly to keep its sheen. The breed is very susceptible to hip dysplasia, with about a 65 percent heritability factor. ¶ It is not easy nor is it inexpensive to locate a fine example of this breed. When you succeed, you have a superb dog. When you fail (and the exploiters win), you have a mess! Only the very best breeders should be consulted, and no German Shepherd should ever be purchased from a puppy mill.

The Old English Sheepdog is English, without doubt, but not quite as old as his name might imply. The breed probably emerged in the latter half of the eighteenth century, although the groundwork was laid somewhat earlier. The ancestry of the breed is not known. Many people insist on Collie as the foundation stock, while others opt for a Russian dog known as the *Owtchar*. If it was Collie, it was probably what we now know as the Bearded Collie. ¶The dog was a sheepdog, again as the name implies, but not so much a herding animal as a drover. The dog's task was to help drive sheep and probably other livestock to market. The peculiar ursine gait, a

Old English Sheepdog

Land of origin: ENGLAND

Original purpose: Driving livestock

Recent popularity ranking by A.K.C. registration: 45th

Old English Sheepdog Club of America, Inc.
Ms. Frances D. Methelis, Corres. Secretary
185 Coriell Avenue
Fanwood, NJ 07023

HEIGHT: Dogs to 25 inches   Bitches to 24 inches

WEIGHT: Dogs to 65 pounds   Bitches to 60 pounds

COAT
Profuse but not excessive; hard textured, not straight, but shaggy and never curly. Not soft or flat. Undercoat forms waterproof pile.

COLOR
Shades of gray, grizzle, blue, or blue merle with or without white markings. No brown or fawn allowed.

Amount of care coat requires: 1 2 3 4 5 6 7 8 9 10

Amount of exercise required: 1 2 3 4 5 6 7 8 9 10

Suitability for urban/apartment life: 1 2 3 4 5 6 7 8 9 10
UNSUITED

---

wonderful ambling shuffle, speaks of great stamina. The Old English Sheepdog lives inside a protective shield of a coat and should not be stripped of that coat unless it becomes hopelessly matted. Unfortunately, this is a common occurrence. So the Old English Sheepdog's coat does require maximum care. It should be brushed every day to help keep it clean and free from mats. ¶ The Old English Sheepdog is not at his best in confinement, though he is a house dog. Ideal on a farm, he will do well in a suburban home but not in an apartment. He must get plenty of exercise in all kinds of weather. A dog that is closely confined and not exercised can become lame and may be very "flaky" to deal with. Such a bumptious pest is cute for only a very short time. Naturally obedient and decidedly pleasant, the Old English Sheepdog will reflect the care and consideration with which he has been raised. Not meant to be chained or left alone in close quarters, he will be destructive and uncontrollable only if driven to it by conditions he could be expected to tolerate poorly. ¶ The Old English Sheepdog has skyrocketed in popularity in recent years, and there are an inevitable number of poor examples of the breed on the market. Get to know the parents of the dog you are considering. Only puppies from solid, pleasant, and even-tempered stock should be considered. It is a shame to become disenchanted once your puppy has started to grow. And no one should consider the breed unless they have studied it well. This is a large, demanding, working dog who requires extensive obedience training. Only then will he keep his promise as a pet. He is not an ideal first dog.

The Puli is another of the superior shepherd's dogs from Hungary, where they have been in use for at least a thousand years. No one knows where they came from or what their ancestral stock might be. There is a strong argument for the Tibetan Terrier, since the two breeds bear a resemblance, and the Hungarian dogs generally are believed to have come from the East. Arguments that the breed arose from stock from Lapland and Iceland are less convincing. It is a problem that will not be solved, for no records were kept, and the movement of dog breeds and groups of breeds apparently was constant over thousands of years. ¶ The Puli is an agile, active

Puli

Land of origin: HUNGARY

Original purpose: Sheepherding

Recent popularity ranking by A.K.C. registration: 104th

Puli Club of America, Inc.
Mrs. Carolyn Nusbickel, Secretary
8078 Goshen Road, RD 2
Malvern, PA 19355

HEIGHT: Dogs to 19 inches   Bitches to 18 inches

WEIGHT: Dogs to 35 pounds   Bitches to 32 pounds

COAT
Unique. Dense, weather resisting, double. Outer coat long, never silky. May be straight, wavy, or somewhat curly. Undercoat soft, woolly, dense; mats into cords. Seen either combed or uncombed with hair hanging in neat even cords.

COLOR
Solid colors only, dark preferred. Black, shades of gray, and white. Blacks are rust or weathered. Some mixing in grays but overall effect must be of solid-colored dog.

Amount of care coat requires: 1 2 3 4 5 6 7 8 9 10

Amount of exercise required: 1 2 3 4 5 6 7 8 9 10

Suitability for urban/apartment life:*   1 2 3 4 5 6 7 8 9 10

*Must be exercised a great deal.

outdoor dog who is as much a herder today as he ever was in history. A Puli shows his best qualities when being worked. Tough, extremely intelligent, and readily trained by anyone who knows what he is doing, this breed is not for the casual or indifferent owner. A Puli is more than just careful with strangers; he tends to be openly suspicious. He makes, therefore, a first-rate watchdog. He must be regulated, though, lest watchfulness becomes aggressiveness. Although not large, the Puli is like spring steel, probably because the breed is said to have run across the backs of sheep, even to have ridden them. There is no doubt that this is a special breed for special purposes. ¶ The coat of the Puli (the plural form is *Pulik*) is another special characteristic. It tends to cord like that of the Komondor and is protection against all weather. The Puli never has to come inside. They haven't invented weather he cannot thrive in. ¶ If one is to match himself in dog-handling skills to the dog he buys, the first-time owner (or one with very limited patience) should go slow with this breed. Unless managed well and really appreciated for his superior abilities to learn and respond, the Puli will not only be wasted on such an owner but become a nuisance. This breed is headstrong, assertive, and very expert at what it does—handling other animals and guarding the master's territory. It is thought to be one of the most intelligent of all breeds.

The Shetland Sheepdog or "Sheltie" is more than a very small Collie, although the two breeds have some ancestry in common and do resemble each other in conformation. The Sheltie has qualities of his own and very great charm. The ancestral stock carried to the islands from mainland Scotland was the Hill Collie, a smaller animal than the one we know as the Collie today. Various small breeds were crossed in over the years, including some spaniels and a small herding dog from Iceland. Eventually Collies were used again to give the dog a final shape and proper coat. There has been more than a little controversy as to what this breed should look like and how big it should be. ¶The Shetland Sheepdog, despite his diminutive size, is a smart herd-

Shetland Sheepdog

Land of origin: SCOTLAND and SHETLAND ISLANDS

Original purpose: Sheepherding and as watchdog

Recent popularity ranking by A.K.C. registration: 11th

American Shetland Sheepdog Association
Ms. Gloria Cronin, Corres. Secretary
2516 Country Club Drive
Odessa, TX 79762

HEIGHT: Dogs to 16 inches   Bitches to 15 inches

WEIGHT: Dogs to 16 pounds   Bitches to 15 pounds

COAT
Double—outer coat is long, straight, and harsh; undercoat is short, furry, and very dense. Hair on face, feet, and ear tips smooth. Mane and frill abundant and impressive.

COLOR
Black, blue merle, and sable ranging from golden through mahogany. White or tan markings. More than 50 percent white disqualifies. Brindle also not allowed.

Amount of care coat requires: 1 2 3 4 5 6 7 8 9 10

Amount of exercise required: 1 2 3 4 5 6 7 8 9 10

Suitability for urban/apartment life: *   1 2 3 4 5 6 7 8 9 10

*But must be properly exercised.

ing animal and was and would be again fine with sheep. He also works well with hogs and goats. He is fast and alert and responds well to training. He is responsive to human moods and demands and always strives to fit himself in. He was used at the outset as a watchdog, and that is a quality he has not lost. A Shetland today, reserved with strangers but not snappy, is a dog who can be depended upon to give the alarm. He has a loud and insistent bark. Some Shetlands, in fact, tend to overdo it! ¶ The Shetland Sheepdog requires grooming; that resplendent dog we see in the show-ring will not be apparent in the casual owner's living room unless he is brushed regularly and kept in fine trim. It is not a hard job or a long one, since this is a small and obedient dog, but it is a job that should be seen to every day. The Shetland also requires exercise. He is a delightful apartment dog, fine with children, small, neat, and easily trained, but he has descended from working dogs of harsh country and harsh weather, and that part of him must be seen to as well. Long daily walks are in order and, whenever possible, good country romps. ¶ The superior little Shetland Sheepdog can live anywhere as long as he has love and a reasonable amount of attention. He should be trained early and well—something he naturally loves anyway—and taught not to be unnecessarily yappy. A good watchdog is one thing, a noisy nuisance is another. Beware of the mass-production breeders, for the Shetland Sheepdog is one of the most popular breeds in the country, and terrible examples abound. Seek sound advice and do your homework if you intend to add a Shetland Sheepdog to your family. Avoid obviously shy specimens. That can mean poor breeding or bad early handling.

The Cardigan Welsh Corgi is a very ancient breed said to have come to southern Wales as early as 1200 B.C. He is believed to have arrived there in the company of central European Celts and to have had common ancestry with the Dachshund. The breed was used for everything a pastoral people might need—rushing small game, herding, guard work, chasing away neighbors' cattle, ratting, and general vermin work. This dog has enough fire and stamina to handle all these assignments, and he is intelligent enough to take any training required to excel at each task in turn. ¶ The Cardigan Welsh Corgi, "the Corgi with the tail," is a tough little animal

Cardigan Welsh Corgi

Land of origin: WALES

Original purpose: Herding cattle, guarding, flushing small game

Recent popularity ranking by A.K.C. registration: 83rd

Cardigan Welsh Corgi Club of America, Inc.
Mrs. Bonnie Scherer, Secretary
Route 3, Box 271-F5
Sumter, SC 29154

HEIGHT: Dogs to 12 inches   Bitches to 11½ inches

WEIGHT: Dogs to 25 pounds   Bitches to 20 pounds

COAT
Medium length, dense, slightly harsh, but never wiry or silky. Weather resistant.

COLOR
Red, sable, red brindle, black brindle, black, tricolor, blue merle. White markings on neck, chest, face, feet, and tail tip usual. Pure white disqualifies, and predominant white heavily faulted.

Amount of care coat requires: 1 2 3 4 5 6 7 8 9 10

Amount of exercise required: 1 2 3 4 5 6 7 8 9 10

*Suitability for urban/apartment life:**   1 2 3 4 5 6 7 8 9 10

*Proper amount of exercise necessary.

who can raise havoc with other animals. He is utterly fearless and quick and smart in his movements, despite his short legs. He is territorial and protective of his master's property, and that can lead to confrontations. The Cardigan Welsh Corgi should be trained early and well. He is an exceptionally long-lived dog and should be reminded of his training regularly. He has a natural desire to please his master and wants to fit in with everything that is going on around him. He tends to be careful with strangers and even a little too suspicious at times. It is to the owner's advantage to keep that characteristic in check. Being a watchdog, which the Cardigan surely is, is enough. Barking is all that is needed. ¶ The Cardigan Welsh Corgi is above all things intelligent. He watches his master, constantly seeking clues as to what is expected and what will win praise. He responds instantly in his own flashy way, without being hyper and silly. Not quite as soft in nature as the Pembroke Welsh Corgi—there are inevitably many exceptions to that, however—he is a bit one-personish, but the man who has that friendship has a loyalty that cannot be beaten. The love of a Cardigan Welsh Corgi is a special privilege. ¶ The Cardigan Welsh Corgi is not as well known in this country as the Pembroke Welsh Corgi, a very different dog. In 1978 the American Kennel Club reported the registration of 2,349 new Pembrokes and only 339 new Cardigans. Fewer registrations generally mean less interest on the part of the mass-production breeders, but care is still advised so that a satisfying example of the breed may grow up in your home.

The Pembroke Welsh Corgi has a wholly different ancestry from the Cardigan Corgi. He came to the British Isles with the Flemish weavers imported by Henry I in 1107. The weavers settled in Wales, and the little Schipperke-like dog they brought with them evolved into a cattle dog. The Pembroke Welsh Corgi, then, is descended from spitz-type dogs and is not as old as the other Corgi. There was a great deal of interbreeding, but that is not done today. Fanciers of each breed want to keep their favorite distinct, as it should be. Any similarity noted today is a result of interbreeding in Wales up to the last century. ¶ There are easy distinctions to be made be-

Pembroke Welsh Corgi

Land of origin: FRANCE, then WALES from twelfth century on

Original purpose: As general farm dog—cattle herding

Recent popularity ranking by A.K.C. registration: 41st

Pembroke Welsh Corgi Club of America, Inc.
Mr. John Vahaly, Corres. Secretary
1608 Clearview Drive
Louisville, KY 40222

HEIGHT: Dogs to 12 inches   Bitches to 11 inches

WEIGHT: Dogs to 30 pounds   Bitches to 28 pounds

COAT
Short, thick, weather-resistant undercoat with a longer, more coarse outer coat. Wiry, marcelled, or thin coat is very serious fault.

COLOR
Red, sable, fawn, black, or tan, with or without white markings. White allowed on legs, chest, neck, muzzle, underparts, and as blaze on head only. Blue or smoky cast very serious fault.

Amount of care coat requires: 1 2 3 4 5 6 7 8 9 10

Amount of exercise required: 1 2 3 4 5 6 7 8 9 10

Suitability for urban/apartment life:*   1 2 3 4 5 6 7 8 9 10

*Proper amount of exercise necessary.

tween the two Corgis: the Cardigan has rounded ear tips and a good tail, while the Pembroke has pointed ear tips and a very short tail, no more than two inches. The two are quite similar in size and outline, however. ¶ The Pembroke Welsh Corgi is a gentle, sensible, and even-tempered dog. He is a dog for the farm, the suburbs, and the city apartment. He is affectionate, and although he can be a good little watchdog, he is not quarrelsome or foolish and is never mean. It is stated in the standards of the breed that shyness or viciousness are grounds for immediate disqualification, and judges are admonished to dismiss any dog showing these undesirable characteristics. ¶ Corgis travel well and are fine with children. They are, in fact, as close to being ideal pets as can be found. They have spunk and fire and enormous charm. Naturally obedient, they take training well and are very hardy. They are exceptionally long-lived, and specimens approaching twenty years are not unknown; certainly the middle to late teens could be considered normal. They are naturally healthy but should be exercised well to maintain both health and condition. They are so pleasant you can take them anywhere, and it would be the unusual Pembroke Welsh Corgi who could not fit in with other animals. They are very often owned in pairs and are especially pleasant that way. ¶ Be careful in buying a Corgi and rely only on the best breeders to provide you with a satisfactory example of this marvelous companion animal.

[Group 5]

The Terriers

Airedale	Lakeland Terrier
American Staffordshire Terrier	Manchester Terrier
Australian Terrier	Miniature Schnauzer
Bedlington Terrier	Norfolk and Norwich Terriers
Border Terrier	Scottish Terrier
Bull Terrier	Sealyham Terrier
Cairn Terrier	Skye Terrier
Dandie Dinmont Terrier	Soft-Coated Wheaten Terrier
Fox Terrier	Staffordshire Bull Terrier
Irish Terrier	Welsh Terrier
Kerry Blue Terrier	West Highland White Terrier

Once known as the Waterside Terrier, this distinctive animal is today the king of all existing terrier breeds. He is the largest and, in many people's opinion, the most admirable. ¶The Airedale is descended from a cross between a hunting terrier and the Otter Hound; the latter animal helped improve the nose and performance in the water. The resulting terrier was used on fox, badger, weasel, otter, water rat, and other lesser game. It was a breed much beloved and one fostered down to our own time with devotion. ¶As a terrier, the Airedale is by nature courageous and bold. He is also aggressive, but much calmer than most other terriers and never silly or overexcitable. He will attack anything he is sent against and is one of the best all-time

Airedale

Land of origin: ENGLAND

Original purpose: Hunting small- and medium-sized game

Recent popularity ranking by A.K.C. registration: 43rd

Airedale Terrier Club of America
Mrs. Aletta Moore, Secretary
14181 CR40 Epoch Farm
Carver, MN 55315

HEIGHT: Dogs to 23 inches   Bitches to 22 inches

WEIGHT: Dogs to 50 pounds   Bitches to 45 pounds

COAT
Double. Hard, dense, and wiry, lying close to the body. A light, soft undercoat. The outer coat may be slightly wavy.

COLOR
Tan and black or tan and dark grizzle. Some red mixture in black acceptable, as is a small white blaze on the chest.

Amount of care coat requires: 1 2 3 4 5 6 7 8 9 10

Amount of exercise required: 1 2 3 4 5 6 7 8 9 10

*Suitability for urban/apartment life:** 1 2 3 4 5 6 7 8 9 10

---

*With proper exercise.

ratters. ¶ With his master and family the Airedale is an affectionate, gentle, and loyal animal. He is a first-rate watchdog and thrives on rough and tumble play with children. It is unusual for an Airedale to be mean or nasty. He wants to be a part of everything that goes on in the household, and he expects the right to check out strangers. He just likes to be sure, and in security matters he seems to prefer his own judgment to that of a mere human. He easily softens with nonthreatening strangers, though, and is usually too aloof to take exception to a minor insult from a lesser dog. But be careful of an Airedale who has been egged on, for he is a terror when the fight erupts. Fortunately, he generally elects to pass. ¶ Airedale owners resemble religious converts in the intensity of their affection for this breed; they become missionaries. This apparently has been going on for a long time, since the Airedale remains a popular breed, although less so than in the past. ¶ There is the temptation to suggest that because the Airedale is both a dog of considerable substance and active like all terriers, he is not suited to city life. That is not quite true. While probably very happy with a lakeside home in the country, the Airedale will settle down to an urban routine as long as he has his family around him. It remains important, however, that he get a great deal of exercise, and ideally that means several miles every day. Obedience training is highly desirable, for an ill-mannered Airedale would be more than just a nuisance. Given half a chance, this is one dog who will prove himself under any circumstances to be a gentle, loyal, and noble friend. It is more than his size that makes him king of the terrier kind.

The American Staffordshire Terrier (formally known simply as the Staffordshire Terrier) is not to be confused with the Staffordshire Bull Terrier or the Bull Terrier, both recognized as separate breeds. ¶ The American Staffordshire Terrier was derived from the English Bulldog (which in the early nineteenth century looked more like today's American Staffordshire Terrier than today's Bulldog) and a terrier. The exact identity of that terrier is not known although many claims are heard. The cross was originally called the Bull-and-Terrier Dog and then by at least half a dozen other names. It wasn't until 1972 that the name American Staffordshire

American Staffordshire Terrier

Land of origin: ENGLAND

Original purpose: Fighting bulls and other dogs

Recent popularity ranking by A.K.C. registration: 80th

Staffordshire Terrier Club of America
H. Richard Pascoe, Secretary
1501 Woodridge Circle
Euless, TX 76040

HEIGHT: Dogs to 19 inches   Bitches to 18 inches

WEIGHT: Dogs to 50 pounds   Bitches to 45 pounds

COAT
Short, stiff, and glossy. Lies close to the body.

COLOR
Any color, solid or parti. All white, more than 80 percent white, black and tan, and liver are not desired.

Amount of care coat requires: 1 2 3 4 5 6 7 8 9 10

Amount of exercise required: 1 2 3 4 5 6 7 8 9 10

Suitability for urban/apartment life:*   1 2 3 4 5 6 7 8 9 10

*Only if properly exercised.

Terrier was adopted. ¶The early history of this dog and related breeds is a nightmare. They were used for the cruelest of blood sports, and much of that image has come down with these breeds. American Staffordshire Terriers can be good pets, loyal, affectionate, and responsive. They accept training but must always be considered suspect around other animals, for they are terriers, and like all dogs in this group they don't just get into a scrap, they go for the finish. Owners should keep this in mind and not allow their dogs to make a decision as to whether to fight or not. Take it for granted that your dog is probably going to be fine with people but at least questionable with other dogs and with cats. ¶The American Staffordshire Terrier does not require any grooming (an occasional wipe with a harsh cloth will bring out the coat's natural luster) and will be a quiet, sensible apartment dweller if taken on a good walk a couple of times a day. He does make a good watchdog and is an interesting pet for a person able and willing to train and supervise him. He should not be allowed to wander in the suburbs and should not be teased if chained or fenced in. He is a highly questionable choice for an inexperienced dog owner.

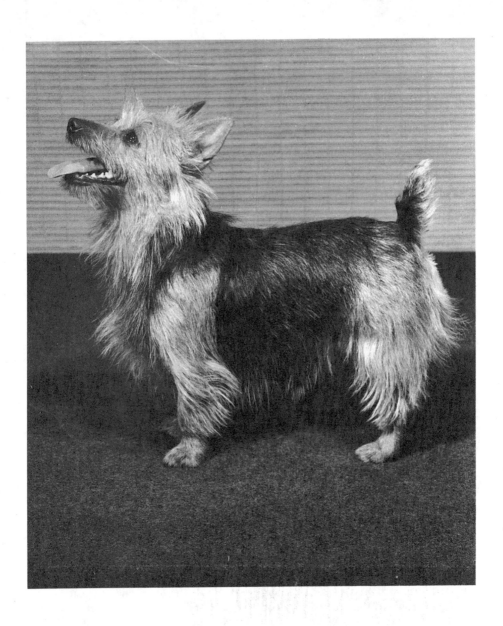

The Australian Terrier (not to be confused, as so often happens, with the Silky Terrier, a toy dog, also from Australia) is a blend of many other terrier lines. It is quite possible that more different breeds were used to create the perky Australian Terrier than went into any other modern purebred dog. At the very least the Scottish, the Cairn, the Dandie Dinmont, the Irish, the Skye, and the Yorkshire Terriers all went into its makeup. The original parent stock was what was known as the Broken-Haired Terrier, sometimes also known as the Rough-Coated. What emerged was a distinctive Australian creation, one of the smallest of the working

Australian Terrier

Land of origin: AUSTRALIA

Original purpose: Companionship and hunting small game

Recent popularity ranking by A.K.C. registration: 81st

Australian Terrier Club of America, Inc.
Miss Carol M. Sazama, Corres. Secretary
3 Pin Oak Trail
Medford, NJ 08055

HEIGHT: Dogs to 10 inches   Bitches to 10 inches

WEIGHT: Dogs to 14 pounds   Bitches to 14 pounds

COAT
Outer coat harsh and straight, about 2½ inches long. Undercoat short and soft. Topknot distinctive feature.

COLOR
Blue black or silver black with rich tan (the deeper the better). Sandy or red markings on head and legs.

Amount of care coat requires: 1 2 3 4 5 6 7 8 9 10
                                    • • • • • • •

Amount of exercise required: 1 2 3 4 5 6 7 8 9 10
                                  • • • • • • •

Suitability for urban/apartment life: 1 2 3 4 5 6 7 8 9 10
                                           • • • • • • • • • • • • • • • • • • •

terriers. ¶ The Australian Terrier is a dog of fire and stamina despite his small size. Barely more than a toy, he can hold his own under any weather and terrain conditions. He has been used on small game in the Australian outback, although the impetus behind his development was undoubtedly the search for a superior companion dog. He was first shown in Melbourne in the middle 1880s and has since attracted attention and devoted followers in a number of countries. ¶ The Australian may be close to the perfect small house and apartment dog. Small enough not to intrude, he is a loyal pet with charm and personality. He isn't a heavy shedder and knows instinctively how to fit in and ingratiate himself. He will hold his own with other animals without being silly and quarrelsome. He makes a good watchdog and will return affection in kind and in depth. Although he is an active little dog by nature, he isn't hyper and doesn't need long walks. He is quite satisfied being a homebody but will participate in any outdoor activities offered him. He is fine on a farm, great in the suburbs, and almost flawless in an apartment. ¶ Although not yet a fad in this country, the Australian Terrier undoubtedly will grow in popularity over the years, and care should be taken to obtain specimens only from the most reliable sources. This is not a breed to be mass-produced, for it would not hold its present fine style. This terrier was evolved so recently and from such a variety of lines that only careful breeding will enable it to solidify all it has gained from the care taken so far.

This spunky little terrier has had a number of names down through the years. He evolved in the north of England from stock that has never really been identified. Known as the Rothbury Terrier and the Northumberland Fox Terrier, he was admired both in England and Wales for his great pluck. He would fight any other dog or any vermin, and was used in pits and demonstrations against his own kind as well as against badgers, rats, foxes, and anything else that would put up a fight. ¶The fire behind that behavior still burns in the Bedlington Terrier, and he generally does better in a one-animal household. He will fight anything that intrudes on his pro-

Bedlington Terrier

Land of origin: ENGLAND

Original purpose: For use on vermin

Recent popularity ranking by A.K.C. registration: 105th

Bedlington Terrier Club of America
Mr. Norman Rappaport, Secretary
25 Delaware Trail
Denville, NJ 07834

HEIGHT: Dogs to 16½ inches   Bitches to 15½ inches

WEIGHT: Dogs to 23 pounds   Bitches to 22 pounds

COAT
Crisp but not wiry—stands out from skin. Not to exceed 1 inch when shown. Has tendency to curl.

COLOR
Blue, sandy, liver, blue and tan, sandy and tan, liver and tan.

Amount of care coat requires: 1 2 3 4 5 6 7 8 9 10
•••••••••••••••

Amount of exercise required: 1 2 3 4 5 6 7 8 9 10
•••••••••••

*Suitability for urban/apartment life:**   1 2 3 4 5 6 7 8 9 10
••••••••••••••••••••

*If properly exercised.

prietorship. A good pet when properly raised, he will be fine with children and is not bad with strangers, if a little cautious. But he doesn't want any other animals around to steal his thunder. In owning a Bedlington, that should be kept in mind. He should not wander where he is likely to encounter other dogs and cats. Away from other animals, he can be quite placid. ¶The Bedlington can make an ideal pet for a couple whose children are grown and who want to share their home with a devoted friend. Because he is a highly spirited terrier, he should be exercised regularly. He needs those long, steady walks on a lead, and he needs a good romp in the country whenever there is an opportunity. He should not be let free near traffic, however, because if he sees another animal, he might take off in pursuit, letting his spirit rather than his good sense guide him. ¶The Bedlington's coat must be seen to if he is to have that appealing if deceptive "little-lamb" look. That does require some instruction to be done well. Many owners prefer to let a professional groomer see to the job. Unique in appearance and full of fire, will, and devotion, the Bedlington Terrier is an interesting pet for the right household.

The Border Terrier is the least-known terrier in the United States. In 1978 the American Kennel Club reported only 136 new specimens registered in this country. And that is a shame. ¶This is a hardy, tough little action terrier from the border country between England and Scotland. For several hundred years this wiry dynamo has been used to drive away and kill foxes and other animals that might tamper with the lambs. Extremely alert and active, this dog can tolerate any weather, any terrain, and will run behind a horse for hours. When a fox is spotted, he will chase it to ground and kill it from above or below, wherever he can catch the quarry. He can

Border Terrier

Land of origin: ENGLAND and SCOTLAND

Original purpose: Killing foxes and vermin

Recent popularity ranking by A.K.C. registration: 88th

Border Terrier Club of America, Inc.
Ms. Jean Clark, Secretary
RD 3, Box 572, Sugar Hill Rd. S,
Weare, NH 03281

HEIGHT: Dogs to 13 inches   Bitches to 12 inches

WEIGHT: Dogs to 15½ pounds   Bitches to 14 pounds

COAT
Short, dense undercoat with very wiry outer coat that is close lying. No curl or wave. Thick, loose hide.

COLOR
Red, grizzle and tan, blue and tan, or wheaten. A small amount of white allowed on chest but not on feet.

Amount of care coat requires: 1 2 3 4 5 6 7 8 9 10
                                                    ● ● ●

Amount of exercise required: 1 2 3 4 5 6 7 8 9 10
                                               ● ● ● ● ● ● ● ● ● ● ● ● ● ●

Suitability for urban/apartment life: *   1 2 3 4 5 6 7 8 9 10
                                                        ● ● ● ● ● ● ● ● ● ● ● ● ● ● ● ● ● ● ●

*But must be properly exercised regularly.

burst through any tangle of wire or brush because his loose skin keeps him from getting trapped. He will climb any wall or overcome any obstacle to get at his enemy. ¶ The tough little Border Terrier is a hardworking field animal and cannot always be expected to double in brass as a pet. He is, though, loyal to his master and anxious to please. If raised in a home, he will respond because he is intelligent and eminently trainable. ¶ It must always be remembered that the Border Terrier has been bred to kill other animals. That is his original calling, and that can lead to trouble unless the dog is held in some kind of check. Border Terriers need early training and a strong-willed master to see to it that deportment is given high priority. The dog is so active and so assertive that if ill-mannered, he could become the neighborhood pest or even menace. That need not be, however, since the breed is so bright and anxious to please. A good trainer can do wonders with this dog, the largest single problem being his penchant to go after other animals, cats included. ¶ This rare dog is attractive and spunky and could enjoy popularity in this country at some future time. Anyone now contemplating the purchase of one should see to it that plenty of exercise is provided. The breed is active enough, and having one go "hyper" for lack of proper exercise is surely unnecessary.

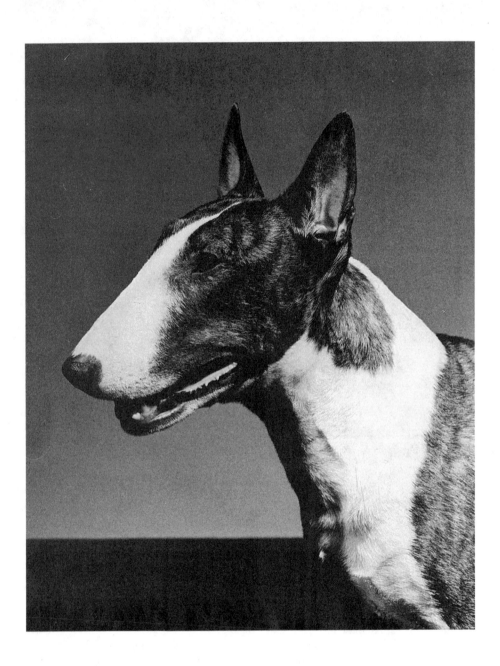

The Bull Terrier is a much maligned dog. It is true that he was originally bred for blood sports, but those were rougher times. There is a kind of nobility to the breed, and he is not a nasty creature at all. But neither is he a wise choice for an inexperienced owner. He should not be one's first dog. ¶The Bull Terrier, a cross between the Bulldog and an extinct variety of white terrier with some Pointer blood thrown in, is a powerful and assertive animal who will answer the ancient call of his kind only if challenged. When that happens, he can kill almost any dog alive. Bull Terriers, because there is always the danger that they will be provoked into a fight,

Bull Terrier

Land of origin: ENGLAND

Original purpose: Fighting

Recent popularity ranking by A.K.C. registration: 62nd

Bull Terrier Club of America
Mrs. Betty Desmond, Corres. Secretary
RD 2, Box 315
Claysville, PA 15323

HEIGHT: Dogs to 22 inches   Bitches to 21 inches

WEIGHT: Dogs to 60 pounds   Bitches to 50 pounds

COAT
Short, hard, flat, and glossy

COLOR
Two varieties. White—all white or white with some markings on head. No other markings allowed. Colored—any color other than white or any color with white markings as long as white does not predominate. Brindle is preferred color.

Amount of care coat requires: 1 2 3 4 5 6 7 8 9 10

Amount of exercise required: 1 2 3 4 5 6 7 8 9 10

Suitability for urban/apartment life:* 1 2 3 4 5 6 7 8 9 10

*If taken on really long walks several times a day.

must at all times be kept under control and never allowed to wander. They don't necessarily look for trouble, but trouble has a way of presenting itself. Unfortunately, Bull Terriers don't just get into fights, they finish them. ¶ With people Bull Terriers can be affectionate, playful, and loyal. They make excellent watchdogs. There is something about them that frightens unwelcome people away. ¶ The Bull Terrier eats a great deal and must be walked often and long. They are not a good breed for inactive people. They require an active, lively family who wants to romp, run, and tussle. Activity is the keynote of this dog's existence. ¶ As for appearance, there are people who detest it and people who love it. That seems to be true of the breed in general—no one just *likes* a Bull Terrier, they either hate or adore him. ¶ Some people insist that there is a greater difference between the disposition of dog and bitch in this breed than in any other. However that may be, the bitch is certainly a softer dog, milder and perhaps easier to train and manage. ¶ The Bull Terrier is a fine old breed of special merit and problems. It is one that should be owned only by people prepared to appreciate the quality, history, and character of the animal and to meet the responsibility of ownership. The Bull Terrier is potentially a first-class companion within the home but a menace as well as a nuisance if not trained and controlled as well as loved and admired. This breed is not to be confused with the American Pit Bull, currently being bred in this country for use in illegal dogfights. Dogfighting has been outlawed in both the United States and England, and the Bull Terrier has not been bred for that purpose, except clandestinely, for a long time.

The Cairn is one of Scotland's super little working terriers, and for hundreds of years he has been used to pursue vermin. He has a game, hunting spirit and is bold and fearless, but he is also a little hardheaded. Some writers insist that the Cairn is the ancestral breed for the Scottie, the West Highland White, and the Skye. He certainly has contributed to all those breeds and to others that we don't even know in this country. ¶The Cairn Terrier has managed to survive fads and quirks and remains, thanks to the determination of his fanciers, much the dog he was hundreds of years ago on the Isle of Skye. He has a broader head than most terriers and a rela-

Cairn Terrier

Land of origin: ISLE OF SKYE, SCOTLAND

Original purpose: Killing vermin

Recent popularity ranking by A.K.C. registration: 38th

Cairn Terrier Club of America
Mrs. Karen C. Wilson, Corres. Secretary
7010 Davis Ford Road
Manassas, VA 22111

HEIGHT: Dogs to 10 inches   Bitches to 9½ inches

WEIGHT: Dogs to 14 pounds   Bitches to 13 pounds

COAT
Hard and weather resistant. Double—outer coat profuse and harsh, undercoat short, soft, and close.

COLOR
Any color except white. Dark ears, muzzle, and tail tip are desirable. Often seen wheaten, grizzle, and tan.

Amount of care coat requires: 1 2 3 4 5 6 7 8 9 10

Amount of exercise required: 1 2 3 4 5 6 7 8 9 10

Suitability for urban/apartment life: 1 2 3 4 5 6 7 8 9 10

tively short, pointed muzzle. He is built close to the ground, but he is not heavy. At least he should not give that impression. The whole feeling should be of an alert, intelligent, active, and assertive dog. And all those things are true. ¶Cairns are perfect house pets and are fine in an apartment. They require only a reasonable amount of exercise, although any time a good romp is available, it should be encouraged. They shed, but not very much, and they are devoted to their master. They can be a little one-personish, but certainly not to the point of being a nuisance or menace. They are generally cheerful, they are always busybodies, and they want to be in on everything going on in their household. Let there be no mistaking the point: The house where a Cairn lives is *his* property. Cairns make good little watchdogs. ¶The Cairn coat is very important to the animal's appearance, but no real clipping is involved. The coat is tidied and brushed; for top show form a little trimming is required. The hair on that broad head is all-important. Although the coat can have a slight wave, any tendency to silkiness or to curl would be a severe fault. ¶The Cairn is hardy and ready to go at all times. Weather doesn't bother him, and he is a very responsive animal, sensing almost magically the moods of his owner. He watches and waits and takes his cues automatically. He is an ideal dog for a single person or a couple without children who want to add a spot of eternal cheerfulness to their life.

The Dandie Dinmont has the distinction of being the only dog named for a fictional character. Dandie Dinmont was a farmer in Sir Walter Scott's novel *Guy Mannering*. The farmer Dinmont kept six rough-coated terriers who had been developed in the border country of England and Scotland, and they became known, because of the great popularity of the novel, as Dandie Dinmont's dogs. ¶ The Dandie Dinmont is a wonderful little character with great purpose and assertiveness. Once a hunting terrier, he is now a companion animal who is characteristically devoted to his master and who is fine with family members. Not mean or petty, the Dandie Dinmont can be reserved and cautious with strangers. ¶ This is not the typical ter-

Dandie Dinmont Terrier

Land of origin: SCOTLAND and ENGLAND

Original purpose: Otter and badger hunting

Recent popularity ranking by A.K.C. registration: 115th

Dandie Dinmont Terrier Club of
America, Inc.
Mrs. Larry Cummins, Secretary
3524 Aquila Avenue N.
Minneapolis, MN 55427-1845

HEIGHT: Dogs to 11 inches   Bitches to 10 inches

WEIGHT: Dogs to 24 pounds   Bitches to 22 pounds

COAT
Double—twice as much crisp outer hair as soft undercoat. Hair on head, including topknot,
silky. Important judging and appearance point.

COLOR
Pepper or mustard—many intermediate shades in both color groups. Pepper from dark
bluish black to light silver gray. Mustards from reddish brown to pale fawn. Head may be
creamy white.

Amount of care coat requires: 1 2 3 4 5 6 7 8 9 10

Amount of exercise required: 1 2 3 4 5 6 7 8 9 10

Suitability for urban/apartment life:* 1 2 3 4 5 6 7 8 9 10

*If properly exercised.

rier; he has none of the terrier's square shape. He is a low-to-the-ground little roughneck with a large head and great, dark appealing eyes. They should be hazel and have deep luster. The Dandie Dinmont's coat requires care on a regular basis, or it will be a mess and have to be stripped. It takes months for a coat to grow back once it has been pulled. The coat is crisp but not really wiry, and the head fur is soft and silky. That topknot is a must. ¶Although a hunting dog, the Dandie Dinmont is very adaptable and will do well in an apartment. The size, of course, is perfect, and he makes a good watchdog, although he is not yappy and foolish. Anyone contemplating this breed should plan on two basic requirements—coat care and exercise. He is fine on a farm, in a suburban household, or in a city apart-

ment, but the Dandie Dinmont does require both of these attentions from his human family if he is to be healthy and happy and keep his appealing good looks. ¶The training of the Dandie Dinmont should start early and continue on a regular basis. The dog can be headstrong and even overly assertive if allowed to go unchecked as a puppy, but this is an intelligent breed that will respond to training by a strong but sensitive owner. A well-behaved Dandie Dinmont is much more pleasant to have around than one who is wild and uncontrolled, but that is true of all breeds. The Dandie Dinmont is not a popular breed yet in this country (that is apt to change at any time), and the breed standards have been well maintained by specialty breeders. It is a good idea to deal directly with them when seeking your puppy.

Wirehaired Fox Terrier

Smooth-Coated Fox Terrier

There are, of course, two Fox Terriers, the Smooth and the Wirehaired. Since June, 1985 they have been considered two separate breeds by the AKC. They probably arose from totally different stocks, and the Wirehaired is undoubtedly the older form, although the Smooth became known first in the show-ring. It was once common practice to cross these two breeds, and although that is no longer done, the dogs are identical except for coat. They do have virtually the same personality; they are the same size and are judged by all the same point standards, again except for coat. ¶The Fox Terriers, Wirehaired and Smooth, are clowns. Play is the thing, night and day without letup. Anyone contemplating these breeds should be prepared to participate, to toss balls, and to have a marvelous little busybody butting into his life at every turn. The Fox Terriers are devoted, loyal, fine watchdogs, and very good with family members. They are apt to be stand-offish with strangers. They seldom walk but go at everything at full gallop. They can be protective, and that has to be controlled. ¶Although once hunting dogs (when the hounds had run the rabbit or fox to ground, the Fox Terriers were sent in for the kill), they are now chiefly companion animals. The instinct to kill is still there, however, and that should be taken into consideration. The Fox Terriers can learn to live in a multianimal household, but the puppy should be introduced carefully and with constant supervision. ¶The Fox

Fox Terriers

Land of origin: WALES and ENGLAND

Original purpose: Fox hunting and companionship

Recent popularity ranking by A.K.C. registration: 49th

American Fox Terrier Club
Mr. William F. Potter, II, Secretary
721 Plantmore
St. Louis, MO 63135

HEIGHT: Dogs to 15½ inches   Bitches to 14½ inches

WEIGHT: Dogs to 18 pounds   Bitches to 16 pounds

COAT
Smooth variety—smooth, flat, hard, dense, and abundant.

Wirehaired variety—broken, hard, and wiry but not silky or woolly. The more wiry
the better.

COLOR
Basically white with black or black and tan markings. Not very important except red, liver,
and brindle are not desirable.

Amount of care coat requires:

Smooth: 1 2 3 4 5 6 7 8 9 10

Wirehaired: 1 2 3 4 5 6 7 8 9 10

Amount of exercise required: 1 2 3 4 5 6 7 8 9 10

*Suitability for urban/apartment life:** 1 2 3 4 5 6 7 8 9 10

---

*If the appropriate amount of exercise is given.

Terriers can live anywhere people can— farm to urban metropolis—and as long as their human families are near, they will be happy. Since these breeds are "hyper" to begin with, it stands to reason that if they are denied proper exercise they will really act up. Improperly worked Fox Terriers become absolutely silly with their spring-steel legs and boundless good humor. That energy *has* to be worked off, and a bouncing rubber ball is one good way of doing it, *if* there is a place to do it. Although eminently trainable, the sytlish Fox Terriers may not always respond as quickly as you want them to when you say, "Come." It is therefore essential to keep them on leads in the city lest a tragedy occur. Many a Fox Terrier has spotted a cat or another dog he was unable to resist, and a Fox Terrier in the middle of a mad dash may not check for cars and buses. ¶The Fox Terriers are long-lived animals and fine with children. There are plenty of bad examples of both breeds around, and care should be taken about source and bloodlines. A good example of either breed is as fine a pet as a dog can be.

The Irish is one of the oldest of the terrier breeds, and his origins are a matter of conjecture. He so strongly resembles the Irish Wolfhound in shape and character that there is a temptation to think of him as the great hound bred down in size—far down to be sure. The Irish Terrier, however, is an authentic terrier type in both appearance and nature. ¶ The energetic, racy red terrier from Ireland is a perfect companion animal. Once he gives his love, it is assigned until death. There is no hardier dog than this and none more adaptable—as long as his master is at hand. A large country estate is fine with an Irish Terrier, but so is an apartment or a small suburban house.

Irish Terrier

Land of origin: IRELAND

Original purpose: Probably sporting

Recent popularity ranking by A.K.C. registration: 100th

Irish Terrier Club of America
Mrs. Marge Andre, Secretary
1534 N. Highway 421
Michigan City IN 46360

HEIGHT: Dogs to 18 inches   Bitches to 18 inches

WEIGHT: Dogs to 27 pounds   Bitches to 25 pounds

COAT
Dense and wiry, rich but not soft or silky. Skin barely shows when hair is parted with fingers. Curly or kinky coats very objectionable.

COLOR
Solid colored; bright red, golden red, red wheaten, or wheaten. *Small* patch of white on chest is allowed but not desirable. Black hair found in puppies should not last into adulthood.

Amount of care coat requires: 1 2 3 4 5 6 7 8 9 10
•••••••

Amount of exercise required: 1 2 3 4 5 6 7 8 9 10
••••••••••••••••••

*Suitability for urban/apartment life:**   1 2 3 4 5 6 7 8 9 10
••••••••••••••••••

*But only if properly exercised every day.

What matters is that the right people live there as well. ¶With the children of the household the Irish Terrier is a perfect playmate, but he is also apt to be protective, and that is something that has to be held in check. Not every kid who comes running into the yard to tackle or wrestle the owner's child is an enemy—but an Irish Terrier may not always be able to make that distinction. This is one breed for whom "no" must mean "NO!" ¶This Irishman has been used as a land and water retriever, and at both jobs he not only excels but thoroughly enjoys himself. He is a born hunter and is death on vermin, but here again the red terrier may not always agree with the neighborhood's definition of vermin. That, too, must be held under some kind of control. What it amounts to is that if you avail yourself of one of these superior terriers, you are going to have to make some of the decisions and pass the news along to your friend. An Irish Terrier should be trained early and well and constantly given refresher courses. ¶During World War I the Irish Terrier was famous as a patrol and courier dog and proved utterly fearless in all situations. No one can reckon how many men survived that holocaust as a direct result of this noble element in the Irish Terrier's character. ¶Show dog, ratter, big-game hunter, war dog, companion, household guard, and playmate—all these things describe the Irish Terrier. The breed is still as good as it is because of the efforts of the fanciers who love it above all others. Turn to them for help if you decide to buy one of these splendid dogs for your own family and home. Be sure to give your Irish Terrier a great deal of exercise; he both needs and deserves it.

The Kerry Blue Terrier is an animal of enormous style and character. He is a substantial dog with temper and temperament. Whether shown "in the rough" as he is in his native Ireland or in a refined shape as he is in the United States, he is handsome and regal. ¶It is sometimes claimed that the Kerry Blue (he came from County Kerry) is descended from the Soft-Coated Wheaten Terrier. Whatever his origin, there is little he has not done in the way of dog's work. He has been used as a water retriever, a trailing dog, a herder, and a general farm utility dog. He has even been trained to a limited extent for police work in the British Isles. ¶The Kerry Blue Ter-

Kerry Blue Terrier

Land of origin: IRELAND

Original purpose: General utility herding, retrieving, and trailing

Recent popularity ranking by A.K.C. registration: 87th

United States Blue Terrier Club, Inc.
Mrs. Jo Ann Custer, Secretary
W. Fernwood Drive
Toronto, OH 43964

HEIGHT: Dogs to 20 inches   Bitches to 19½ inches

WEIGHT: Dogs to 40 pounds   Bitches to 34 pounds

COAT
Soft, dense, and wavy. Never harsh, wiry, or bristly.

COLOR
Important: from deep slate to light blue gray. Quite uniform. Darker areas on muzzle, head, ears, tail, and feet.

Amount of care coat requires: 1 2 3 4 5 6 7 8 9 10

Amount of exercise required: 1 2 3 4 5 6 7 8 9 10

*Suitability for urban/apartment life:** 1 2 3 4 5 6 7 8 9 10

*If properly exercised.

rier is hardy, can tolerate any weather, and is long-lived. At eight years, when some other breeds are nearing the end of their lives, this terrier is still a young animal. ¶ The Kerry Blue is not keen on strangers and can be a little tricky to read at times. He has been known to bite, but this tendency can be offset by early and intense obedience training. Certainly, it is essential that an owner establish at the beginning that there is a chain of command within the household and that the dog is not at the top. The Kerry Blue Terrier would like that position and will try to take it. This is a breed that can explode with other animals, and owners are obligated to keep their pets under firm control—on a leash. If a Kerry Blue Terrier decides he doesn't like another dog he passes in the street, it may take a lot more than a voice command to get the two apart. ¶ The Kerry Blue Terrier is a very devoted friend and can be fine with his owner's family. He will be stubborn if allowed to be, and there again early training is essential. ¶ None of this is to say that the Kerry Blue Terrier isn't a fine pet as well as a watchdog or show dog in the right household, but he is the kind of dog who can prove to be more than the new owner reckoned on. He is so assertive, strong-willed, and loaded with character that inexperienced dog owners should be warned about what they are getting into. The Kerry Blue Terrier is a pushover for a real dog person, but it takes some years of experience to earn that title. ¶ His long life, his high style, his great character and personal power have made the Kerry Blue Terrier something of a cult dog with people well acquainted with the breed. He remains something of an enigma to almost everybody else.

The Lakeland Terrier, a product of the English Lake District, was once known as the Patterdale Terrier. He is one of the oldest of the English working terriers and is typical of that type of dog. He is utterly fearless, impossible to tire, and full of game and fire. He was used to chase foxes and otters to ground and is a deadly adversary. The desire to hunt is as strong in today's dog as it was a century or two ago. ¶The Lakeland is not common in this country, but that is probably due to the fact that he is a working terrier and is not as often reduced to being a plain companion animal as other small terrier breeds. He is more stable than many other terriers,

Lakeland Terrier

Land of origin: ENGLAND

Original purpose: Fox hunting

Recent popularity ranking by A.K.C. registration: 102nd

United States Lakeland Terrier Club
Ms. Phyllis W. Belden, Secretary
P.O. Box 87
Norge, VA 23127-0087

HEIGHT: Dogs to 14½ inches   Bitches to 13½ inches

WEIGHT: Dogs to 17 pounds   Bitches to 16 pounds

COAT
Double—soft undercoat with a hard, wiry outer coat.

COLOR
Blue, black, liver, black and tan, blue and tan, red, red grizzle, grizzle and tan, or wheaten.
Light tans very much preferred over mahoganylike tones.

Amount of care coat requires: 1 2 3 4 5 6 7 8 9 10

Amount of exercise required: 1 2 3 4 5 6 7 8 9 10

Suitability for urban/apartment life:* 1 2 3 4 5 6 7 8 9 10

---

*If properly exercised.

calmer and a good deal more sensible. He is also good-natured and especially good with children whom he knows. He is devoted to his master but slow to take up with strangers. Before entering into an in-depth relationship, the Lakeland wants to *know* that it is a good move. The Lakeland seems to shy away from shallow relationships with people, preferring all or nothing. ¶The Lakeland is strong on land and in the water, probably the strongest of all terriers in his weight class. He works with and therefore generally can live with other dogs; he has been used in England with Otter Hounds and Foxhounds as well as Harriers. ¶Young Lakeland Terriers were highly prized in the Lake District a century or more ago and were kept for breeding purposes. It was some time before examples were really known outside of this small, somewhat secluded region. The tendency to keep the dog at home was strengthened by the fact that the northern districts—counties like Northumberland, Cumberland, and Westmoreland—had their own working terriers and seldom needed to draw upon the outside. Perfecting was done from within, and attention was paid to performance, not to color or conformation. Many of those old working terrier breeds are lost to us today, and, indeed, we don't even know their names. The Patterdale survived, however, to become the powerful and congenial animal we have today. Rare though it may be on this side of the Atlantic, it is a breed to be held in esteem.

Manchester Terrier

Land of origin: ENGLAND

Original purpose: Ratting

Recent popularity ranking by A.K.C. registration: 91st

American Manchester Terrier Club
Ms. Beverly Longuil, Secretary
11165 S.W. 69th Terrace
Miami, FL 33173

HEIGHT:* Dogs to 16 inches   Bitches to 15 inches

WEIGHT: Dogs to 22 pounds   Bitches to 16 pounds

COAT
Short and smooth. Should be thick, dense, close, and glossy. Never soft to the touch.

COLOR
Well-defined jet black and rich mahogany tan. White considered very bad and will disqualify if over ¹/₂ inch in any dimension.

Amount of care coat requires: 1 2 3 4 5 6 7 8 9 10
                                      •

Amount of exercise required: 1 2 3 4 5 6 7 8 9 10
                                  • • • • • •

Suitability for urban/apartment life: 1 2 3 4 5 6 7 8 9 10
                                           • • • • • • • • • • • • • • • •

---

*See also Toy Manchester Terrier (page 231).

The Manchester Terrier is identical (except in size) to the Toy Manchester Terrier. The dimensions given for the two forms are as follows:

	HEIGHT	WEIGHT
Standard	To 16 in.	To 22 lbs.
Toy	To approximately 7 in.	To 12 lbs.

The two are simply size variations of the same breed, although they were once considered two separate breeds. (The ears are cropped in the Standard but not in the Toy.) ¶ The breed probably first emerged in Manchester when a coarse Black and Tan Terrier was crossed with a Whippet to produce a superior gaming dog for the rat pits and for practical use along the waterfront. (Today's Manchester Terrier was also once called the Black and Tan but is, under any name, far more refined than that older parent breed.) ¶ The Manchester in either size is a superior companion animal. He is like a fine racehorse—trim, neat, and with the look of perfection about him. Not only is he affectionate, responsive, and intelligent, but he is also clean, virtually odorless, and fits well into any family situation. He is fine in an apartment and will be satisfied with a limited amount of outdoor exercise. He would still make a good ratter on the farm, but he is almost exclusively a companion animal today. ¶ In an effort to derive the Toy version from the Standard, there was some crossbreeding with the Italian Greyhound, but that practice was abandoned. The smaller version is now well established. ¶ The Manchester Terrier in either size is a good watchdog and a very understanding friend. Only the finest breeders should be trusted, for this is a breed that must not be mass-produced, nor should its standards be abused.

The Miniature Schnauzer was derived in part from the larger forms of Schnauzer by carefully crossing the smallest available specimens with Affenpinschers. It was recognized as a distinct breed by the end of the nineteenth century. ¶The Miniature Schnauzer strongly resembles the larger dogs, but he is the ideal small house or apartment dog. He is long-lived, intelligent, and affectionate. He seems to naturally adore children, and children generally adore him! Whatever is available in the way of space, love, and attention he will take. He loves to play, he seems to be made of springs, and he never tires. Indoors or out he insists on be-

Miniature Schnauzer

Land of origin: GERMANY

Original purpose: Companionship

Recent popularity ranking by A.K.C. registration: 10th

American Miniature Schnauzer Club, Inc.
Mrs. Susan R. Atherton, Secretary
2600 Oakdale Drive
Bartlesville, OK 74003

HEIGHT: Dogs to 14 inches   Bitches to 14 inches

WEIGHT: Dogs to 15 pounds   Bitches to 14 pounds

COAT
Double—hard, wiry outer coat and a close undercoat. Usually plucked—length usually not less than ¾ inch.

COLOR
Salt and pepper, black and silver, or solid black. Tan shading is allowed.

Amount of care coat requires: 1 2 3 4 5 6 7 8 9 10
                                   • • • • • • • • • • • •

Amount of exercise required: 1 2 3 4 5 6 7 8 9 10
                                 • • • • • • • •

Suitability for urban/apartment life: 1 2 3 4 5 6 7 8 9 10
                                          • • • • • • • • • • • • • • • • • •

ing a part of everything that is going on around him. He sulks when omitted. ¶ The Miniature Schnauzer is one of the most popular dogs in America, having ranked in the top ten for years. His popularity is based on his easy keeping qualities and his good disposition. He does like long walks but can survive without them when the weather is bad (he can take the weather, but his master can't always keep up); he is easily trained for any regimen. He is naturally happy and healthy, and if you see more Miniature Schnauzers waiting in the veterinarian's outer office than most other breeds, it is just because there are so many of them around. ¶ The Miniature Schnauzer is perfectly willing to become a first-class food brat if that is what you want him to be. He responds to what is offered and takes advantage of all opportunities. If you want to feed him chopped chicken livers on imported English biscuits, that is fine with him, but so will kibble be if that is what you have to offer. This is a smart little animal, and a lot of owners feel the need to spoil them. ¶ Because the Miniature Schnauzer is so popular, there have been an awful lot of marginal breeders (and that is being kind). Hence, anyone wanting an example of this breed as it was meant to be is going to have to avoid the obvious pitfalls. This is a superlative companion animal, and there are fine breeders all across the country willing to place their puppies in good homes. What the buyer gets is what the buyer is willing to seek out; take the trouble to evaluate and to know what you are getting.

Norfolk Terrier

Norwich Terrier

These Norwich and Norfolk Terriers are among the smallest of terriers in size and among the largest in spirit. The gait, stance, and personality of each reflects true English terrier blood and supports the supposition that both Border Terrier and Irish Terrier blood went into the making of these breeds. The Norwich and Norfolk Terriers are not old breeds, but they do have some special qualities. Developed in England in the 1880s, the original version quickly became a fad dog with undergraduates at Cambridge University. There are still some people who believe the breed (now breeds) should be known as Cantab Terriers in honor of this early support. But actually, at that time their forerunner was known as the Jones Terrier; it wasn't until after World War I that the name *Norwich Terrier* came into use. By 1964 breeders in England had achieved two breeds, Norwich and Norfolk. ¶ Until 1978 the American Kennel Club recognized the Norwich Terrier as the only breed and allowed two ear styles—the prick or upstanding and the drop. In 1979, though, the A.K.C. followed the British example and recognized only the prick-ear variety as the Norwich, calling the drop-ear the Norfolk. They are now two separate breeds for pur-

Norfolk and Norwich Terriers

Land of origin: ENGLAND

Original purpose: As pets, companions, and for some hunting

Recent popularity ranking by A.K.C. registration: 97th (Norwich and Norfolk combined)

Norwich and Norfolk Terrier Club
Mr. Edward M. Resovsky, Corres. Secretary
12 W. Southhampton Avenue
Philadelphia, PA 19118-3909

HEIGHT: Dogs to 11 inches   Bitches to 10 inches

WEIGHT: Dogs to 14 pounds   Bitches to 12 pounds

COAT
Close lying, hard, and wiry. Distinct undercoat, outer coat straight. No curl, and not silky.

COLOR
Shades of red, wheaten, black, tan, and grizzle. Small white markings on chest only allowed.

Amount of care coat requires: 1 2 3 4 5 6 7 8 9 10

Amount of exercise required: 1 2 3 4 5 6 7 8 9 10

Suitability for urban/apartment life: 1 2 3 4 5 6 7 8 9 10

---

poses of registration and showing. The dogs are virtually identical in the United States, except for the ears, but the British standard does call for the Norfolk to have a slightly longer neck. It will be interesting to see if that difference stands here and what other differences, if any, emerge. ¶ The Norwich and Norfolk are incredibly responsive to their environment and their family. They can be exclusively attached to one person if that is what is expected of them, but they can also be family dogs. They are all personality and quickly capture the hearts of anyone who comes to know them. They want to be in on absolutely everything that is going on around them. For the family with or without children, the Norwich or Norfolk can be the almost ideal breed. Each is small and neat and travels well, and is assertive enough to handle himself in almost any situation. Their hard, always straight and wiry coat requires little care. It doesn't retain dirt,

and these dogs are cleaner than most. ¶ Although perfectly fine in an apartment if well exercised, these breeds are best suited for the country or suburbs. They naturally love horses and farm life. Both live with other animals, cats included, but it should be remembered that some of the earliest examples in America were used for hunting. The Norwich and Norfolk love a good chase and will bedevil small wildlife if given an opportunity to do so. Too small to become a real stock killer, they should be trained to guard small farm animals rather than pursue them. This is the kind of training a Norwich or a Norfolk can take, since they are loyal, great little watchdogs, and take to obedience training as if it were the grandest pastime on earth. Some enthusiasts believe that the Norwich has the softer disposition of the two. Now that the breeds are free to go their separate ways, it will be interesting to see how the two develop.

The arguments are endless over the origins of this rather old Scottish breed. Some say the Scottish Terrier is the original Skye Terrier, who is not to be confused with the dog we know by that name today. Other historians have different ideas. In fact, the details of the Scottie's evolution in the Highlands are uncertain, for records were seldom kept. We do know the breed comes from the Highlands; it is respectably old and has long been highly regarded. ¶The Scottish Terrier, or, as it is commonly addressed, the "Scottie," is a game, close-to-the-ground, working terrier who must have been a holy terror on vermin. He is, like all dogs of this line, without a sem-

Scottich Terriers

Land of origin: SCOTLAND

Original purpose: Sporting after small game

Recent popularity ranking by A.K.C. registration: 35th

Scottish Terrier Club of America
Mrs. Diane Zollinger, Corres. Secretary
7521 Interuban Blvd.
Smohomish, WA 98290

HEIGHT: Dogs to 10 inches   Bitches to 10 inches

WEIGHT: Dogs to 22 pounds   Bitches to 21 pounds

COAT
Rather short (about 2 inches)—dense undercoat with very hard outer coat. Should be *very* wiry to the touch.

COLOR
Steel or iron gray, brindled or grizzled, black, wheaten, or sandy. White markings not desired, but *small* amount on chest allowed.

Amount of care coat requires: 1 2 3 4 5 6 7 8 9 10
                                   • • • • • • • • • •

Amount of exercise required: 1 2 3 4 5 6 7 8 9 10
                                 • • • • • • • • •

*Suitability for urban/apartment life:** 1 2 3 4 5 6 7 8 9 10
                                         •

*If properly exercised.

blance of fear. He is also hardy and will take any terrain, any weather, and any number of hours afield. He will back away from nothing as long as he can still draw a breath. ¶ The Scottie is a dour character, as befits his origin, and takes loyalty to his master and mistress seriously. If they have children, he will behave well as long as he is raised with them. He is very slow to accept strangers at all, much less take up with them, and he is never happier than when he is alone with his own family. The rest of the world, man and animal alike, could vanish, and the Scottie wouldn't care a bit. Some people find this aloofness (for that is the best description) one of the Scottish Terrier's most attractive characteristics, and indeed it does make one respect the breed. ¶ The Scottie should be trained early and well. Because he can threaten strangers and can be a scrapper, the Scottie should learn how to obey instantly. Strangers should be advised to give the dog time and let him make the overtures. ¶ Young Scotties are extremely appealing and very demonstrative. Few breeds have cuter youngsters. That jumping and licking display tends to disappear in the adults, and one should not be misled. The adult Scottie is a square, solid, determined, and intelligent dog; he remains reserved except with those he really knows and loves. Because the puppies are so very appealing, prospective buyers should be careful to know the line well. Cute puppies do not always turn out to be splendid dogs.

The Sealyham was developed between 1850 and 1890 in Haverfordwest, Wales. The breed's benefactor—really its designer—was Capt. John Edwardes. The ancestral stock used by Captain Edwardes is not known. After the Sealyham's first show appearance in 1903, it caught on. By 1908 a club had been formed in Wales to further interest in the breed. The breed was recognized in this country in 1911; although it has never been a terribly popular dog, it has been admired, and some fine specimens have appeared. ¶The A.K.C. standards sum up the breed well: "The Sealyham should be the embodiment of power and determination, ever keen and

Sealyham Terrier

Land of origin: WALES

Original purpose: Gaming and hunting vermin

Recent popularity ranking by A.K.C. registration: 118th

American Sealyham Terrier Club
Mrs. Barbara Carmany, Secretary
6160 State Rd. Bx. 76
Sharon Center, OH 44274

HEIGHT: Dogs to 10½ inches   Bitches to 10½ inches

WEIGHT: Dogs to 24 pounds   Bitches to 23 pounds

COAT
Soft, dense undercoat and wiry outer coat. Never silky or curly.

COLOR
All white. Lemon, tan, or pale badger markings allowed on head and ears.

Amount of care coat requires: 1 2 3 4 5 6 7 8 9 10

Amount of exercise required: 1 2 3 4 5 6 7 8 9 10

Suitability for urban/apartment life:*   1 2 3 4 5 6 7 8 9 10

*Provided that enough exercise is given regularly.

alert, of extraordinary substance, yet free from clumsiness." ¶ Like most terriers, perhaps all, the Sealyham is a natural watchdog, and a stranger is unlikely to approach unannounced. Extremely loyal to his family, the Sealyham is likely to be cautious with strangers, animals included. He is fast, tough, determined, and hardy. He needs exercise and loves a good romp. He has a proud carriage and looks just splendid plowing on ahead at the bottom end of a leash. The Sealyham does not shed much and makes an almost ideal house and apartment dog. However, his coat needs care, and the dog looks fine only when properly groomed. The Sealyham is easily trained, although if he detects weakness he will play it and be stubborn. He recognizes a master once his worth is demonstrated. ¶ Other terriers appeared in the United States earlier—dogs like the Scottish Terrier—and that perhaps has held the Sealyham back somewhat. But with our enormous urban population and the desire of people in apartments for watchdogs who are also trouble-free pets, it is predictable that the Sealyham will continue to grow in popularity. His character and qualities are so ideally suited to the urban life-style that he will surely take off and move up on the charts. People thinking seriously of this dog, however, should remember his need for plenty of exercise. The occasional visit to the country will be appreciated.

The terriers generally are not particularly old, but the Skye goes back at least four hundred years, making him one of the oldest. He was the product of the rough, harsh islands off Scotland, particularly the Isle of Skye in the northwest, where he reached the form we know long, long ago. ¶By the middle 1500s the Skye was known in London, where he quickly became a favorite at court and, quite naturally, down through the ranks of nobility until even commoners recognized him as fashionable. For two hundred years at least he ranked as a kind of king among terriers, but then newer breeds began to take over. Perhaps the shorthaired terrier coat of the

Skye Terrier

Land of origin: ISLE OF SKYE, SCOTLAND

Original purpose: Sporting, hunting

Recent popularity ranking by A.K.C. registration: 112nd

Skye Terrier Club of America
Ms. Ann L. Boucher, Secretary
16329 Temple Terrace
Minnetonka, MN 55345

HEIGHT: Dogs to 10 inches   Bitches to 9½ inches

WEIGHT: Dogs to 25 pounds   Bitches to 23 pounds

COAT
Double—undercoat soft, woolly, and short; outer coat hard, straight, flat, and very long.

COLOR
Black, blue, gray (dark or light), silver platinum, cream, or fawn.

Amount of care coat requires: 1 2 3 4 5 6 7 8 9 10

Amount of exercise required: 1 2 3 4 5 6 7 8 9 10

*Suitability for urban/apartment life:** 1 2 3 4 5 6 7 8 9 10

---

*Only if enough exercise is provided on a regular basis.

younger breeds was more attractive because it meant less work. Still, the Skye, less popular now than in the past, has his fanciers, and they are tenacious in their devotion. ¶The Skye Terrier was almost certainly developed to fight tough vermin and run them to ground. How much of that original purpose was based on necessity and how much on sport is hard to say, for man has always claimed much of his sport as necessary. However that may have been, the Skye was a tough roughneck of a go-to-ground dog, and that original terrier fire and determination is still in him. ¶The Skye's coat requires care, and anyone considering this handsome, stylish dog should keep that in mind. They are not self-keep-ers; they need help to look their best. ¶The Skye Terrier is a devoted pet and needs a great deal of attention. Reassurance and the opportunity to interact with human family members must come frequently. An ignored Skye Terrier is an unhappy dog. Because of his devotion to family and his stylish appearance, the Skye is a fine city dog—but only if long walks are provided. That is a commitment the new Skye owner must make and keep. ¶Because he ranks rather far down in popularity, the Skye is generally available from only a few specialty breeders. That is a good thing, too, for this is a dog with a long history and a heritage worth preserving.

Although the Soft-Coated Wheaten
Terrier has been known in Ireland
for centuries, he is new to our shores. Here
is a breed that is just about to catch on. ¶No
one knows the ancestry of this Irish farm
terrier. He has just "always been there." He
may be an ancestral form of the Kerry Blue
Terrier, but that is not known for sure.

Whether it is true that the dogs who swam
ashore from the ill-fated Spanish Armada
are part of this dog's past is not known either. ¶The Soft-Coated Wheaten Terrier
is an all-purpose farm dog, a fine companion for children, and a first-rate watchdog.
He is also adept at herding, hunting, and
chasing any vermin to ground and dis-

Soft-Coated Wheaten Terrier

Land of origin: IRELAND

Original purpose: All-purpose farm work

Recent popularity ranking by A.K.C. registration: 72nd

Soft Coated Wheaten Terrier Club of America
Pamela Donahue, Corres. Secretary
32 Reidwood Ln.
Caledonia, IL 61011

HEIGHT: Dogs to 19 inches   Bitches to 18 inches

WEIGHT: Dogs to 45 pounds   Bitches to 40 pounds

COAT
Abundant, soft, and wavy. Should appear natural and not overtrimmed or styled.

COLOR
Clear wheaten; may be shaded on ears and muzzle.

Amount of care coat requires: 1 2 3 4 5 6 7 8 9 10

Amount of exercise required: 1 2 3 4 5 6 7 8 9 10

Suitability for urban/apartment life:* 1 2 3 4 5 6 7 8 9 10

---

*If properly exercised.

patching them. He is spry, resilient, and intelligent. He will take any training and remember what he has been taught. He is willing, positive in his approach, and extremely responsive to his master and his family. ¶ Although the Soft-Coated Wheaten Terrier is a good working dog, he is a flawless companion animal as well and will settle down in the suburbs and city as long as his family is at hand. Wheatens should be exercised religiously so that they don't become "hyper" from confinement. They love to interact with other living things and should not be left for long periods of time without companionship, or else they will pine. Soft-Coated Wheaten Terriers need to belong and to share. ¶ There should be nothing exaggerated about the Wheaten. His coat is a lovely shade of ripening wheat. It doesn't really settle down until the dog is almost two years old; then coat condition and color are final. Extreme clipping and trimming spoil the look of the dog. ¶ It is likely that the Soft-Coated Wheaten Terrier will become popular in this country. (They weren't even known here until the late 1940s, and by 1961 there were only thirteen reported examples.) When purchasing, care must be taken to find examples that properly represent the fine qualities of this dog; mass-production should not be encouraged.

Staffordshire Bull Terrier

Land of origin: ENGLAND

Original purpose: Sport fighting

Recent popularity ranking by A.K.C. registration: 101st

Staffordshire Bull Terrier Club, Inc.
Judy Keller, Corres. Secretary
1916 Simsbury Ct.
Fort Collins, CO 80524

HEIGHT: Dogs to 16 inches   Bitches to 14 inches

WEIGHT: Dogs to 38 pounds   Bitches to 34 pounds

COAT
Smooth and short; close and not trimmed at all

COLOR
Red, white, fawn, blue, or black, or any of these colors with white. Any shade of brindle with or without white. Black and tan or liver not allowed.

Amount of care coat requires: 1 2 3 4 5 6 7 8 9 10

Amount of exercise required: 1 2 3 4 5 6 7 8 9 10

*Suitability for urban/apartment life:**   1 2 3 4 5 6 7 8 9 10

*If given enough exercise.

In the England of Elizabeth I, bear and bull baiting were major pastimes. Large mastiff-like dogs were developed for these brutal contests, and from them have descended a variety of smaller breeds. One of these is the Staffordshire Bull Terrier, admitted to the American show scene by the American Kennel Club in 1975. He is descended from dogs known variously as Bulldog Terrier and Bull-and-Terrier, and he became known in time as the Old Pit Bull Terrier. He is probably ancestral to the English Bull Terrier we know today. ¶To say that the Staffordshire Bull Terrier has had all of his history bred out of him is wishful thinking. He is still a tough, tenacious, and intelligent dog who will probably continue to be aggressive toward other animals for many generations to come. In fact, aggression may never be bred out of him. ¶The Staffordshire Bull Terrier—he should not be confused with the nineteen-inch American Staffordshire Terrier or the much heavier (sixty-pound) Bull Terrier referred to above—has common ancestry with and was bred for the same purpose as these other fighting dogs, but he has not been used for that purpose for some time. He is now a companion animal who shows great affection toward his human family. He is said by his fanciers to have special fondness for children. ¶Because he is a robust, if not large, and certainly a powerful and athletic dog, he should be exercised regularly and well. He will keep his condition and certainly be less tense if allowed to work off steam every day on a reliable schedule. ¶The Staffordshire Bull Terrier is an easy dog to maintain because he is short-coated and clean. His ferocious background has not made him untrustworthy with people, but he is a potential fighter, and therefore is a dog who should be leashed and controlled at all times.

The Welsh is one of the oldest of terrier breeds and almost certainly figured in the modeling of many of the other terriers we know today. He has had a number of names down through history, including Old English Terrier, Black and Tan Wire-haired Terrier, and various combinations of those names with the designation *Welsh*.

The origin of the breed was undoubtedly old England, but it was in Wales that the Welsh Terrier evolved as a tough sporting dog to hunt foxes, otters, badgers, and anything else that offered a chase and a fight. He was bred to take on all comers and do all the dirty work necessary. He can handle any terrain and just about any tempera-

Welsh Terrier

Land of origin: WALES

Original purpose: Hunting and sporting

Recent popularity ranking by A.K.C. registration: 78th

Welsh Terrier Club of America, Inc.
Ms. Helen Chamides, Secretary
698 Ridge Road
Highland Park, IL 60035

HEIGHT: Dogs to 15 inches   Bitches to 13½ inches

WEIGHT: Dogs to 20 pounds   Bitches to 18 pounds

COAT
Wiry, hard, abundant, and very close.

COLOR
Black and tan or black grizzle and tan. No black marks (penciling) on toes.

Amount of care coat requires: 1 2 3 4 5 6 7 8 9 10

Amount of exercise required: 1 2 3 4 5 6 7 8 9 10

Suitability for urban/apartment life:* 1 2 3 4 5 6 7 8 9 10

*If suitable exercise is provided every day.

---

ture—on land or in the water. Give him something to tackle, and nothing will deter him. ¶ The first Welsh Terrier of record probably came here in 1888, but few were seen for a number of years. Even in 1901, when A.K.C. recognition allowed it to be shown at the Westminster Kennel Club show, only four dogs were presented. ¶ This muscular, well-boned little roughneck needs plenty of exercise. Like all small terriers of his general styling, he has a fire inside, and is like spring steel. He is a dog that needs to run and needs to play and for that reason is great with children. He is good with his family but may be a little slow warming to strangers. He is a natural watchdog and can be relied upon to announce strangers day or night. He isn't yappy or silly, however, and serves well the family with whom he agrees to live. ¶ These tough terriers vary in their adaptability to other animals. Some are just fine and never quarrel unless challenged. Others will be holy terrors wanting to dissect every four-footed creature they meet. One person's experience with the breed may not be a fair indication of what the next owner's will be. You have to watch and wait, and if you do have a scrapper, he must be controlled and trained to behave. ¶ The Welsh Terrier is a first-rate family dog in the country or the city. He is half human most of the time and fun and games all of the time. It helps for you to be young and vigorous at the same time your Welsh Terrier is. He demands that you participate in his high-stepping style of life.

This marvelous little dog shares a common ancestry with the Scottie, the Cairn, and the Dandie Dinmont, as well as with the other rough-haired terriers of southern Scotland. Several of those breeds have never been seen in this country, and some of them, unfortunately, are now extinct. The West Highland White Terrier may have the best of all of them bred into his spirited little body. ¶This is a dog who is both an individual and a lover. He knows exactly who and what he is and never fails to exhibit the true terrier style and temperament. Never shy, he should not be really aggressive—assertive, certainly, but not snappy. He is courageous if a challenge is ever offered, and he is fine with strangers once he has done the usual terrier checkout. ¶West Highland White Terriers like games, toys, their own well-defined posi-

West Highland White Terrier

Land of origin: SCOTLAND

Original purpose: Companionship

Recent popularity ranking by A.K.C. registration: 28th

West Highland White Terrier Club of America
Miss Susan M. Napady, Secretary
5870 US Hwy 6
Portage, IN 46368

HEIGHT: Dogs to 11 inches   Bitches to 10 inches

WEIGHT: Dogs to 19 pounds   Bitches to 17 pounds

COAT
Double. Outer coat straight and hard, to 2 inches, shorter on neck and shoulders. Never silky or curly.

COLOR
Pure white with a jet black nose.

Amount of care coat requires: 1 2 3 4 5 6 7 8 9 10
• • • • • • • • • •

Amount of exercise required: 1 2 3 4 5 6 7 8 9 10
• • • • • • • • •

Suitability for urban/apartment life: 1 2 3 4 5 6 7 8 9 10
• • • • • • • • • • • • • • • • • • • •

---

tion in the house, treats, travel, and the undiluted attention of their master. They like to chase cats but usually for the chase and not with any real intention to do harm (they will live with a cat peacefully). They are adaptable and settle down in new situations as long as their family is with them. I have had friends visit us for weekends with their West Highland White Terrier without any problem, and that required the dog, a mature male, to settle down immediately into a household of six other dogs and ten cats. The Westy managed to check everybody out and get checked out by everybody in the first half hour. Relatively few dogs can handle that kind of situation so well. ¶ Without giving the West Highland human qualities (which one is prone to do), it can be said that this breed has such a strong sense of himself that much of the nonsense some other breeds have to go through in order to establish identity is unnecessary. A West Highland White Terrier walks into a room with self-assurance and an easy grace that seems to put other animals at ease. ¶ West Highlands do shed and their white hair does show, but most owners don't complain. They feel it is worth it. I have known West Highland White Terriers to settle well into a family with children, but once again, if we were to seek a perfect situation, it would be where the West Highland White Terrier could be the child himself. He is certainly ideal for the couple without children or for the couple whose children have grown and left home. ¶ A lot of poor-quality West Highlands are being bred and sold, and a prospective owner should proceed with caution. It is difficult to find an example with a perfect coat, and it is only with a coat at least near perfection that the true style of the West Highland White Terrier really shines through. People seeking this breed should stick with the specialty breeder and hold out for the ideal dog. It is a commitment that they will live with for a long, long time.

[Group 6]

The Toys

Affenpinscher
Brussels Griffon
Chihuahua
English Toy Spaniel
Italian Greyhound
Japanese Chin
Maltese
Toy Manchester Terrier
Miniature Pinscher

Papillon
Pekingese
Pomeranian
Toy Poodle
Pug
Shih Tzu
Silky Terrier
Yorkshire Terrier

No one really knows where the Affenpinscher comes from, although it was somewhere in Europe. The breed dates back to at least the 1600s and probably is much, much older than that. The name translates from the German as "monkey terrier," an appropriate name for this strange, fiery little toy. ¶ It was from the Affenpinscher, some people believe, that the now more popular Brussels Griffon was in part derived. The later breed all but eclipsed the older one, but there is some indication that interest in the Affenpinscher is reviving slightly. ¶ Actually, this little dark dog is an ideal apartment animal. Although in need of some exercise, he adapts

Affenpinscher

Land of origin: EUROPE

Original purpose: Companionship and ratting

Recent popularity ranking by A.K.C. registration: 117th

Affenpinscher Club of America
Bonnie Beskie, Corres. Secretary
248 Hilalary Lane
Penfield, NY 14526

HEIGHT: Dogs to 10¼ inches   Bitches to 9 inches

WEIGHT: Dogs to 8 pounds   Bitches to 7 pounds

COAT
Very important in judging. Hard and wiry and varies from short and dense to shaggy and longer on different parts of body. Longer on face, legs, chest, and underparts.

COLOR
Black is considered best, but also black with tan markings, red, gray, and other mixtures allowed. Very light colors and white markings are faults.

Amount of care coat requires: 1 2 3 4 5 6 7 8 9 10

Amount of exercise required: 1 2 3 4 5 6 7 8 9 10

Suitability for urban/apartment life: 1 2 3 4 5 6 7 8 9 10

easily to life in an apartment. Like a great many of the smaller dogs, the Affenpinscher will wait for an opening and then take over. He needs a firm hand, but he is smart enough to take any training necessary to make him into a suitable canine companion. Heaven help the careless owner; a monkeyish little dog will soon be running the househoud. ¶The Affenpinscher is tough, and he seems to take himself seriously. He is devoted and affectionate and usually quiet. He is, though, capable of real temper and will attack anything if seriously challenged. He can be moody and excitable if not given his own way. Until a real balance has been struck between man and dog, it may be a war of nerves; and it is funny to watch this smart little animal try to work things out to his own advantage.

¶The Affenpinscher requires little care. The coat is best trimmed slightly about every ten weeks, just often enough to maintain the round, wise facial expression. It is ten minutes' work and little more. An occasional brushing is all that is required beyond that. Although a toy, the Affenpinscher is reasonably hardy, but really bad weather and chills should be avoided. ¶It isn't easy to find a good Affenpinscher puppy when you want one. Anyone seriously considering this little character had better start the search early and stay with it until a good pup becomes available. Those people devoted to the breed say it is worth the hunt and the wait. Fewer than one hundred new Affenpinschers are registered with the American Kennel Club in any one year.

The Brussels Griffon has been around since at least the fifteenth century and possibly longer. He was a cross between the Affenpinscher and a Belgian street dog. Later the Pug and a breed known as the Ruby Spaniel were crossed in. At one time he was larger than the dog we know today and was used to control rats and mice around stables. It is believed that the Grif- fon was virtually a household fixture in French and Belgian homes. Long bred for companionship, it is in that capacity we know him today. ¶ The Brussels Griffon is seen in two varieties: the rough and the smooth. The smooth, of course, harks back to the infusion of Pug blood. Both forms are delightful companions, intelligent, out- going, and affectionate. They are not close

Brussels Griffon

Land of origin: BELGIUM

Original purpose: Companionship, and killing of stable vermin

Recent popularity ranking by A.K.C. registration: 96th

American Brussels Griffon Association
Mr. Terry J. Smith, Secretary
221 East Scott, Box 56
Grand Ledge, MI 48837

HEIGHT: Dogs to 8 inches   Bitches to 8 inches

WEIGHT: Dogs to 12 pounds   Bitches to 10 pounds

COAT

Rough style—wiry and dense, the harder the better. Never to look or feel woolly; never silky. Also not shaggy.

Smooth style—like a Boston Terrier, no sign of wiry hair.

COLOR

Reddish brown, black and reddish brown mixed, black and reddish brown markings, or solid black. Often dark mask or whiskers. Black not allowed in smooth form. White a serious fault in either variety except age frosting on muzzle.

Amount of care coat requires:

Rough: 1 2 3 4 5 6 7 8 9 10

Smooth: 1 2 3 4 5 6 7 8 9 10

Amount of exercise required: 1 2 3 4 5 6 7 8 9 10

Suitability for urban/apartment life: 1 2 3 4 5 6 7 8 9 10

---

or mean in their dealings but open and willing. They are neat and take up little space. And they make good watchdogs. ¶ Like many toys, the Brussels Griffon is quite capable of being a little mule, a bully, lording it over everyone in the house. How he behaves depends on how he is handled as a puppy. Without thwarting him or destroying his personality he can be made to behave—especially on a leash, which he generally hates—and his barking can be controlled. He will try tricks to avoid having to be well mannered, and he is smart enough to be challenging to anyone but the owner alert enough to know when he is being duped. ¶ The pert, saucy little Brussels Griffon does well with or without outdoor exercise, although he enjoys a fair romp. Care must be taken around traffic because he cannot be depended upon to have good traffic sense. He travels well, like a great many toys, and prefers to be taken along rather than be left at home. He must not be left in a closed car during warm weather, since he can expire from heat exhaustion in minutes without ventilation. It is a tragic accident that happens more times than one would expect. ¶ The Brussels Griffon is a toy lover's dog in all respects—sassy, assertive, lovingly responsive, and smart as a whip. A dog to admire and, sad to relate, to spoil absolutely rotten. Most owners of this breed do.

The true origin of this smallest of all dogs (he may weigh as little as one pound) is unknown. Apparently the Toltecs had them in Mexico before they were conquered by the Aztecs, who took over the breed. This dog was apparently a status symbol among the ruling class, but there is reason to believe that the common people ate them. There is some tradition to suggest that a hairless or nearly hairless dog reached Mexico from China or some other Asian land in ancient times and that this animal figured in the ancestry of the dog we call the Chihuahua today. The original Toltec dog may have been the Techichi. The name *Chihuahua* comes from the Mexican state of that name, but the dog is no more common there than in any other part of Mexico. Actually, the breed as we know it is more an American creation, its popularity here being great and consistent year after year. ¶ The Chihuahua, in the longhaired or smooth (shorthaired) variety (the latter is much better known), is the ul-

Chihuahua

Land of origin: MEXICO in historical times, but probably ASIA originally

Original purpose: Probably status and companionship

Recent popularity ranking by A.K.C. registration: 16th

Chihuahua Club of America, Inc.
Mrs. Janet M. Mohr, Secretary
4488 Schneider Road
Ann Arbor, MI 48103

HEIGHT: Dogs to 5 inches   Bitches to 5 inches

WEIGHT:* Dogs to 6 pounds   Bitches to 6 pounds

COAT
Smooth style—soft, close, and glossy, should be smooth and well placed over body. Undercoat permissible.

Longhaired style—soft, flat, or slightly curly, with undercoat desirable. Ears fringed; feathering on feet and legs. Large ruff on neck desired. Tail as plume.

COLOR
Any color; may be solid, marked, or splashed. No preferences.

Amount of care coat requires:
Smooth: 1 2 3 4 5 6 7 8 9 10
           •

Longhaired: 1 2 3 4 5 6 7 8 9 10
              • • • • •

Amount of exercise required: 1 2 3 4 5 6 7 8 9 10
                                 •

Suitability for urban/apartment life: 1 2 3 4 5 6 7 8 9 10
                                          • • • • • • • • • • • • • • • • • •

---

*Weight range of 2 to 4 pounds preferred.

timate toy. This is a dog who need never go out, should not be exposed to weather extremes, and who really must be spoiled to be appreciated. He is companionable but highly temperamental, and he despairs if left out of anything that is going on. He does not like other breeds of dogs, and this is often referred to as clannishness. An important factor probably is that all other dogs are bigger than the Chihuahua and may seem challenging and dangerous. ¶The Chihuahua is an ideal dog for middle-aged and elderly people who want to fuss over and be fussed at by a tyrant of a toy. Chihuahuas are no trouble to keep, since they are neat and don't have to be walked. Although small eaters, as might be expected, they are fussy, and that generally pleases the people most interested in the companionship of the world's smallest dog. A bit of white-meat chicken will please the Chihuahua to get and the owner to give. That really is what the Chihuahua is all about. He has a job to do and a niche to fill. He accomplishes his mission with commendable skill. ¶The Chihuahua has long been popular and is variable in quality. Care should be taken in buying one of these fine little characters. The really serious fanciers and breeders are slow to part with a puppy. They want to know the kind of home he is going to get. You must be very reassuring if you want to own a really fine Chihuahua.

The English Toy Spaniel has been known in England for several hundred years and has long been a favorite of royalty. Tradition has it that Mary, Queen of Scots, went to the block with her favorite at her side. The breed is certainly not English in origin, however. It may be an ancient Chinese breed that was exported to Japan and later to Spain and only then to England. That routing must always remain speculative. It is undoubtedly Asian though. ¶The English Toy Spaniel is lovable and good-natured. He gets along with children, better, in fact, than most other toys. He is eminently spoilable, and that is how he is most often encountered—eminent and spoiled absolutely rotten, which is when he is at his best. ¶Because he does not really require outdoor exercise and because he is a pretty little creature when

English Toy Spaniel

Land of origin: Probably CHINA or JAPAN

Original purpose: Companionship

Recent popularity ranking by A.K.C. registration: 114th

English Toy Spaniel Club of America
Susan Jackson, Secretary
21124 Shore Acres Rd.
Cassopolis, MI 49031

HEIGHT: Dogs to 10 inches   Bitches to 9 inches

WEIGHT: Dogs to 12 pounds   Bitches to 11 pounds

COAT
Soft, long, silky, and wavy. Tendency to curl is a fault. Profuse mane down front of chest. Feathering also profuse.

COLOR*

King Charles—rich black and glossy mahogany tan.

Ruby—whole colored, rich chestnut red.

Blenheim—red and white, broken colored.

Prince Charles—tricolor (white, tan, and black).

Amount of care coat requires: 1 2 3 4 5 6 7 8 9 10
• • • • • • • •

Amount of exercise required: 1 2 3 4 5 6 7 8 9 10
•

Suitability for urban/apartment life: 1 2 3 4 5 6 7 8 9 10
• • • • • • • • • • • • • • • • • •

*King Charles and Ruby are shown as the same variety. Blenheim and Prince Charles are shown as the second variety.

properly fussed over and cared for, he is a favorite of a special kind of owner. He is equipped to fulfill many needs. The breed has never been popular in this country, although it is well known in England and on the Continent. None of the push-faced toys have ever really made it in America until recently, with the exception of the Pekingese and the Pug. A refined variety of the English Toy Spaniel, the Cavalier King Charles Spaniel, is gaining in popularity as a separate breed and may soon outstrip any fame this parent breed ever had. ¶ Fine examples of this breed are not easily purchased in this country, and anyone really serious about it may have to use foreign sources. Anyone breeding this dog well here will be extremely careful about whom he sells to. As indicated, the interest being shown in the Cavalier King Charles Spaniel may change that considerably. ¶ A word about spoiling as we use it here: a spoiled Weimaraner or Rhodesian Ridgeback is a crime against society, while a spoiled English Toy Spaniel is quite normal. The difference should be obvious to anyone. Spoiled, of course, refers strictly to the behavior and willfulness of an individual dog and has nothing whatever to do with standards and breeding. Spoiled in the sense of badly bred is intolerable in any breed, large or small.

This lovely little dog, who can be traced back to ancient times, has been the companion of kings and queens for almost as long as there has been written European history. He is nothing more than the ancient Greyhound bred down selectively and then refined. He differs little from the Greyhound except in size and personality.

¶ The stories are legion about the roles this breed played in the lives of royal households. A king knelt weeping in the garden as he dug away the earth with his hands to lay to rest the dog who had sat on the throne with him. More than one king has been said to have gone to war with an Italian Greyhound on the saddle in front of

Italian Greyhound

Land of origin: ITALY, but very ancient

Original purpose: Companionship

Recent popularity ranking by A.K.C. registration: 71st

Italian Greyhound Club of America, Inc.
Mr. Tom Walker, Corres. Secretary
P.O. Box 7050
Richmond, VA 23221

HEIGHT: Dogs to 15 inches   Bitches to 13 inches

WEIGHT: Dogs to 15 pounds   Bitches to 9 pounds

COAT
Short, glossy like satin, soft.

COLOR
Any color and markings, except that dogs with tan markings where they would appear on black and tan dogs of other breeds cannot be shown.

Amount of care coat requires: 1 2 3 4 5 6 7 8 9 10

Amount of exercise required: 1 2 3 4 5 6 7 8 9 10

Suitability for urban/apartment life: 1 2 3 4 5 6 7 8 9 10

---

him. This dog was first seen in England about three hundred years ago and was an immediate favorite in England and Scotland. What lay behind this popularity, particularly among the privileged and superprivileged who could have owned any animal they chose? ¶The Italian Greyhound is one of the most pleasant of all dogs. Mild-mannered, sweet, and affectionate, he is never snappy or nasty, even though his size makes him exceedingly vulnerable. He is fine-boned, and like his relative, the Whippet, he is unable to assume an awkward pose. Often pictured in paintings by the masters and in fine china and porcelain, the Italian Greyhound always looks as if a work of art has suddenly come alive. It probably is the sweetness of his disposition and his beauty that has charmed the artistic and the discerning. ¶Owners of this breed insist that although one no longer has to be of noble blood to own an example, the owner is elevated to nobility, in a sense, by this dog. That is worth thinking about. ¶Italian Greyhounds do not like cold weather and should be protected from it. They are perfect home and apartment pets and are very easy to maintain with their short coats and natural good manners, manners naturally as good as the disposition that goes with them. They can be a little stubborn when it comes to housebreaking, though. ¶Graceful, elegant, refined, beautiful, and exceedingly pleasant, the Italian Greyhound is a dog to admire. His continuing popularity among the discerning is easy to understand.

The Japanese Chin, formerly the Japanese Spaniel, probably originated in China and only reached Japan after being established in his present form. Literally stolen from Japan by visiting sailors, these dogs came to be sold at high prices all over the world. Commodore Perry was presented with some legally, and he in turn presented a pair to Queen Victoria. The avenues of distribution of this breed were not recorded because they were so often contraband. ¶There are actually several different coat styles for these gay little dogs—the profuse coat, the shorter coat, and even a coarser textured coat—but all carry the high style and grand good looks of

Japanese Chin

Land of origin: Presumably CHINA

Original purpose: Probably companionship

Recent popularity ranking by A.K.C. registration: 77th

Japanese Chin Club of America
Ms. Charla Vaughn, Secretary
255 Bolivar SP 149
Salinas, CA 93906

HEIGHT: Dogs to 9 inches   Bitches to 9 inches

WEIGHT:* Dogs to 7 pounds   Bitches to 7 pounds

COAT
Profuse, silky, long, and straight preferred. Totally free from wave or curl. Tendency to stand out. Thick mane or ruff. Profuse feathering; very plumelike tail.

COLOR
Black and white or red and white. Reds range from sable, brindle, and lemon to orange. White to be clear. Good distribution required.

Amount of care coat requires: 1 2 3 4 5 6 7 8 9 10
• • • • • • • • • •

Amount of exercise required: 1 2 3 4 5 6 7 8 9 10
•

Suitability for urban/apartment life: 1 2 3 4 5 6 7 8 9 10
• • • • • • • • • • • • • • • • • •

*There are classes for dogs under and over 7 pounds. Smaller animals very much preferred.

this ancient companion toy. ¶ The Japanese Chin, still a relatively rare breed in this country, is a perfect apartment dog. He does shed, and his coat does require some brushing, but the dog himself is companionable, intelligent, and most affectionate and responsive. He does not require much exercise and is in general easily kept. A lively little animal, he wants very much to be a part of everything his family is involved in, including meals. He wants most of all to be spoiled, and many owners of this breed want them for just that purpose—spoiling. ¶ Often, we must admit, this and other finely bred toys were created and are maintained along such elegant bloodlines expressly for spoiling. They never grow up and are what I refer to as *neotonous*, eternally childlike and perpetually naughty enough to serve their own purpose: to call attention to themselves. ¶ Elderly people, single people, and couples without children may find these characteristics in a dog to be exactly what they have wanted all along, and they often are the ones to favor them. Like most toys, the Japanese Chin travels well and enjoys going along on house visits, to cocktail parties, and on other simple outings. The Japanese Chin is as fragile as most toys are and should not be exposed to extremes. Being locked in a closed car is very often a death sentence and must be avoided at all costs. It is far better to leave your Japanese Chin at home if you know you are going to be making stops where he cannot accompany you.

The Maltese, although often thought of as a terrier, is actually a form of tiny spaniel. He is one of the most ancient of purebred dogs and certainly one of the oldest of the toy breeds. For the romantic dog owner, the Maltese holds special attractions. He was a favorite of the upper classes in ancient Greece and Rome and was the beloved of titled ladies in the time of Elizabeth I. All through history, writers have spoken of this breed with reverence and a little awe. Five hundred years ago fine examples of the breed were selling for what even today would be considered enormous sums—the equivalent of the annual income for an entire village of working-class

Maltese

Land of origin: MALTA

Original purpose: Companionship

Recent popularity ranking by A.K.C. registration: 27th

American Maltese Association, Inc.
Ms. Bonnie Shumard, Corres. Secretary
79 Spauer Rd.
Petaluma, CA 94952

HEIGHT: Dogs to 5 inches   Bitches to 5 inches

WEIGHT: Dogs to 7 pounds   Bitches to 4 pounds

COAT
Long, flat, and silky. No kinkiness, curls, or woolly texture allowed.

COLOR
Pure white. Some tan or lemon on ears allowed but not desirable.

Amount of care coat requires: 1 2 3 4 5 6 7 8 9 10
• • • • • • • • • • • • • • • • • •

Amount of exercise required: 1 2 3 4 5 6 7 8 9 10
• •

Suitability for urban/apartment life: 1 2 3 4 5 6 7 8 9 10
• • • • • • • • • • • • • • • • • •

people. ¶ The Maltese is a child, and no one should entertain the thought of buying this breed without that foremost in mind. The lovely flowing coat needs hours of care and constant attention, and the dog himself never really grows up. He is loving, even adoring, and loaded with personality, but he characteristically is a fussy eater with a tricky digestive system. He can be frail. The Maltese wants (and usually gets) his own way. He wants to be the center of attention and doesn't like sharing his love sources with anybody or anything else. He is, then, a nearly perfect dog for a single person or a couple who will not have children to compete with their dog. Because of his small size he is very appropriate in the apartment, although he is a dog who wants to be exercised a reasonable amount of time each day. Care should be taken in bad weather, though, and paper training as an emergency alternative is to be recommended. The Maltese prefers being warm and dry and makes no pretense of being a retriever or herding dog. This is a dog designed for the lap and the silken pillow almost thirty-five hundred years ago, and he seems to know it in every fiber of his body. ¶ The Maltese generally will not treat strangers or even known outsiders the way he will treat his master. He can even be snappy with people he does not know, although that isn't much of a threat to human safety and well-being. It is, though, a reflection of the spirit and nature of this remarkable little animal with so much of the history of Western culture built into him.

Toy Manchester Terrier

Land of origin: ENGLAND

Original purpose: Ratting

Recent popularity ranking by A.K.C. registration: 91st

HEIGHT: Dogs to 7 inches   Bitches to 6 inches

WEIGHT: Dogs to 12 pounds   Bitches to 10 pounds

COAT
Smooth, thick, short, close, glossy, and dense.

COLOR
Jet black and rich mahogany with clean breaks between the two.

Amount of care coat requires: 1 2 3 4 5 6 7 8 9 10

Amount of exercise required: 1 2 3 4 5 6 7 8 9 10

Suitability for urban/apartment life: 1 2 3 4 5 6 7 8 9 10

The standards for the Manchester Terrier, which is shown as a terrier, and the Toy Manchester Terrier, which is shown as a toy, are the same except for size and for the ears. The ears in the Manchester may be cropped, but they are never cut in the Toy variety. What has been said previously about the Manchester Terrier holds true for the Toy. On the subject of size: the Toy is up to but not exceeding twelve pounds, while the Manchester is from twelve to twenty-two pounds.

Miniature Pinscher

Land of origin: GERMANY

Original purpose: Probably companionship

Recent popularity ranking by A.K.C. registration: 40th

Miniature Pinscher Club of America, Inc.
Mrs. Nancy Mathieu, Secretary
5500 Bentley Avenue
Las Vegas, NV 89122

HEIGHT: Dogs to 11½ inches   Bitches to 10½ inches

WEIGHT: Dogs to 10 pounds   Bitches to 9 pounds

COAT
Smooth, short, hard, straight, and lustrous; uniform over body.

COLOR
Red, lustrous black with sharply defined rust markings, solid brown, or chocolate with rust or yellow markings.

Amount of care coat requires: 1 2 3 4 5 6 7 8 9 10

Amount of exercise required: 1 2 3 4 5 6 7 8 9 10

Suitability for urban/apartment life: 1 2 3 4 5 6 7 8 9 10

Despite many statements to the contrary, the Miniature Pinscher undoubtedly has been around a few centuries longer than the Doberman Pinscher. He is not, as so many people believe, a bred-down version of the latter. ¶ The breed was little known in the United States before 1928. From about 1929 on, the little toy has grown in popularity, and probably will continue to do so. ¶ The Minpin, as he is often called, is a lively little devil with a high-stepping style that marks him everywhere he goes. He is a natural showman and is a favorite in the ring. He is a show-off and an assertive character. ¶ The Miniature Pinscher is best owned by people who are at least as strong-willed as he is. He is affectionate and loyal and a real participator. He is also, given the chance, a bully and a brat. Having one of these handsome little dogs around is like having a gifted child: you have to know how to handle the situation or it quickly will get out of control. But the Minpin does respond well to authority. ¶ Some people feel the Miniature Pinscher is better in a home without children, since he is clearly a child himself. Others have had quite different experiences and claim he is fine with children, indeed with any people as long as he considers them family. He is a perfect watchdog and will never let a stranger come near without giving voice. He is, in fact, a noisy little toy, always quick to express a point of view. ¶ For the individual or family looking for a clean, compact, strong-willed little dog of character and high style, the Miniature Pinscher may be just about the perfect choice. There are more restful breeds, though, and more than a few easier to train and control. Here is a breed that should be matched to a personality need. When that is right, this is an outstanding breed of dog.

The Papillon probably acquired his present form in Spain, for he is, it is believed, truly a dwarf spaniel. These dogs were traded to wealthy fanciers, particularly in Italy and France, and became favorites with members of royalty. They were painted by some of the greatest artists—Rubens, Watteau, Fragonard, Boucher, and other fashionable portrait painters of the court. Madame de Pompadour and Marie Antoinette were fanciers, and in the early 1600s the future queen of Poland was known to own at least one dwarf spaniel. ¶The history of the Papillon is, then, one of elegance, privilege, and a certain élan that belongs only to the truly elite. Al-

Papillion

Land of origin: Probably SPAIN

Original purpose: Companionship

Recent popularity ranking by A.K.C. registration: 64th

Papillon Club of America, Inc.
Ms. Roseann Fucillo, Corres. Secretary
2600 Kennedy Boulevard
Jersey City, NJ 07306

HEIGHT: Dogs to 11 inches   Bitches to 10 inches

WEIGHT: Dogs to 10 pounds   Bitches to 8 pounds

COAT
Abundant, long and fine, silky and flowing, straight and resilient. No undercoat. Ears well fringed. Profuse on chest and tail.

COLOR
White predominates. Patches may be any other color except liver. Also tricolored. Color must cover both ears and extend over both eyes. No solid colors allowed, including white.

Amount of care coat requires: 1 2 3 4 5 6 7 8 9 10
                                 • • • • • • • • • •

Amount of exercise required: 1 2 3 4 5 6 7 8 9 10
                                   • •

Suitability for urban/apartment life: 1 2 3 4 5 6 7 8 9 10
                                        • • • • • • • • • • • • • • • • • •

though he is the only working toy—he is still, they say, a good little ratter—his general use has been to weigh down silk cushions and help dispose of delicacies. He has been used consistently for adornment and rarely fails to make an elegant setting even more elegant, a regal person even more impressive. The little butterfly of dogdom was meant to be spoiled. ¶ The Papillon, although not exactly a Labrador Retriever, is not as delicate as he may appear to some people. He can stand some weather and will do fine in an apartment, in a house, or on the farm. He does prefer to be comfortable, though, and people who fancy this breed will probably feel better themselves if their pet is indoors at night and not out hunting and fending for himself. ¶ Anyone who purchases an example of this breed should make a firm commitment to his coat. It does require care if it is to look its elegant best. This is not something that happens by itself. The dog is small and the task isn't large, just regular and in need of a guarantee. ¶ The Papillon likes exercise because he is an intelligent little busybody, but he does not require a great deal of it. The butterfly dog is affectionate and responsive to his family and is a very good little watchdog. He will not fail to announce strangers.

The Pekingese is second only to the Toy Poodle in popularity among the toy dogs in this country. He has long been a favorite with apartment dwellers who want a splendid little character to fuss over. ¶ The Pekingese, the Little Lion Dog of China, dates back to ancient times, when they say it was a crime punishable by death to steal one. Slave girls were used as wet nurses to suckle these dogs, and special eunuchs were assigned to care for them. Whether they were actually sacred is not known, but they certainly were among the most spoiled dogs who ever lived. Specimens were stolen during the looting of China's imperial court in 1860, and some eventually

Pekingese

Land of origin: CHINA

Original purpose: Ornamental companionship

Recent popularity ranking by A.K.C. registration: 17th

Pekingese Club of America, Inc.
Miss Hetty Orringer, Secretary
3 Carolyn Terrace
Southboro, MA 01772

HEIGHT: Dogs to 9 inches   Bitches to 8 inches

WEIGHT:* Dogs to 14 pounds   Bitches to 10 pounds

COAT
Long, with thick undercoat; straight and flat, not curly or wavy, rather coarse but soft. Profuse ruff; very heavy on tail and legs.

COLOR
All colors allowed: red, fawn, black, black and tan, sable, brindle, white, and parti-colored. Well defined black mask and spectacles with lines to ears desired. White on feet and chest of otherwise solid colored dog is not a parti-color. Good distribution required.

Amount of care coat requires: 1 2 3 4 5 6 7 8 9 10
                                 ●●●●●●●●●●●●●●●●●

Amount of exercise required: 1 2 3 4 5 6 7 8 9 10
                              ●●

Suitability for urban/apartment life: 1 2 3 4 5 6 7 8 9 10
                                  ●●●●●●●●●●●●●●●●●●

---

*The smaller the dog the better; 14 pounds is extreme and anything over that would be disqualified.

reached Europe. But most were slaughtered by the Chinese, who did not want them to fall into the hands of Europeans. Out of all this romantic history comes the top push-faced toy in the world today. ¶Maintaining the coat of the Pekingese, his crowning glory, is a daily task, although not a big one. It must be seen to, however, or the Pekingese will soon look anything but elegant. This is an assertive, headstrong, willful, possessive, positive, brave, and forceful little character. He is not devoted to strangers and will make a good watchdog. Very often children are not adored, although this dog will accept his place in a family and work out all necessary relationships. There will be no problem as long as the Pekingese is where he feels he must be: at the center of the universe. ¶This is, of course, an ideal dog for the couple with limited space everywhere except in their hearts. This is a dog to cherish and share a life-style with. He is not to be left out or denied full recognition as a part of the family. He is the perfect animal to fuss over. He is a "sleeve-sized" dog, and most Pekingese owners like to carry their pets with them. The pets think that is just grand. ¶Owning a Pekingese is like having a human infant with an adult's wiles. It is quite an experience and one that many people simply will not deny themselves.

A very long time ago the diminutive toy we call the Pomeranian was a sled dog, one of the group known as the spitz dogs, essentially northern, full-coated dogs with a curled tail. Later, the breed was used for sheepherding, although its exact history remains uncertain. Somehow the center for breeding the spitz seemed to be in Pomerania on the Baltic Sea, although possibly the ancestral dogs may have come from Iceland and Lapland. It was probably in Pomerania that breeding down started, although it is difficult to understand what may have originally motivated that development. ¶By the time the breed reached England in the middle of the last century, it

Pomeranian

Land of origin: POMERANIA (Baltic Sea)

Original purpose: Pulling sleds, then sheepherding, then companionship

Recent popularity ranking by A.K.C. registration: 14th

American Pomeranian Club, Inc.
Ms. Audrey M. Roberts, Corres. Secretary
1410 S. 10th Street
Leesville, LA 71446

HEIGHT: Dogs to 7 inches   Bitches to 6½ inches

WEIGHT: Dogs to 7 pounds   Bitches to 5 pounds

COAT
Double—short, soft, thick undercoat with a long, coarse, glistening outer coat. Off-standing and profuse. Always straight.

COLOR
Red, orange, cream and sable, black, brown and blue, white, sable, chocolate, plus others.

Amount of care coat requires: 1 2 3 4 5 6 7 8 9 10
•••••••••••

Amount of exercise required: 1 2 3 4 5 6 7 8 9 10
••

Suitability for urban/apartment life: 1 2 3 4 5 6 7 8 9 10
••••••••••••••••••

---

was down considerably in size, although specimens probably weighed five or six times as much as they do now. It is said that some were still in the thirty-pound class. That is a far cry from the four- to five-pound toys we see today. ¶ The Pomeranian now is strictly a companion dog. He is a spirited, brash, proud little strutter with some of that old northern spitz fire still evident. He is a dog who is made to be spoiled, and both owner and dog, apparently, are happiest when that is the situation. The Pomeranian tries to take over; that appears to be his chief motivation in life. Many Pomeranian owners, amused by the brashness of this little charmer, seem pleased to relinquish command. ¶ Some Pomeranians are fine with children, but as a general rule they are best when they are the children of the household. They have a short temper when someone tries roughing them up and are ideal for single people and elderly cou-

ples. They are fiercely loyal and are good little watchdogs. ¶ The Pomeranian is an ideal apartment dog. He requires little exercise, since even a brief walk with his short legs seems like miles to him. He likes to be comfortable and neat and will use a paper in a plastic pan, making walks in bad weather unnecessary. That is particularly important for some people who are limited in their outdoor activities and who do not like to go out in the city at night. ¶ The Pomeranian's coat is glorious. The dog should not be bathed very often because that does soften his coat, which needs some care. Brushing is important to keep the coat off-standing and glistening. ¶ Pretty as a picture, sassy as a bumblebee, the little Pomeranian is just about the perfect dog for the right kind of home. He is demanding but rewarding to own, assertive yet loving and protective.

Toy Poodle

Land of origin: Possibly GERMANY, but not really known

Original purpose: Probably water retrieving

Recent popularity ranking by A.K.C. registration: 3rd

Poodle Club of America, Inc.
Mrs. Richard Kiczek, Corres. Secretary
S. New Boston Rd., P.O. Box 211
Francestown, NH 03043-0211

HEIGHT: Dogs and bitches under 10 inches

WEIGHT: Dogs to 7 pounds   Bitches to 6 pounds

COAT
Naturally harsh in texture, extremely profuse and dense. Seen in a variety of clips.

COLOR
Solid only, never parti-colored. Colors seen include blue, gray, silver, brown, café au lait, apricot, cream, black, and white.

Amount of care coat requires: * 1 2 3 4 5 6 7 8 9 10
•••••••••••••••••

Amount of exercise required: 1 2 3 4 5 6 7 8 9 10
•••••••••

Suitability for urban/apartment life: † 1 2 3 4 5 6 7 8 9 10
••••••••••••••••••••

*Varies somewhat with style of clip and age of dog.
†If appropriate exercise is provided.

The standard, history, and origin of the Toy Poodle is the same in all respects as that of the Standard and Miniature Poodles. ¶The Toy Poodle is to be ten inches or under and should weigh between five and seven pounds. There is a much smaller Toy now called the Teacup Poodle, who is the size of a small Yorkshire Terrier, probably not much over two pounds. ¶All poodles combined (Standard, Miniature, and Toy) rank third in popularity among purebred dogs in America. The Toy is the most popular of the three and makes a splendid apartment pet because of his size. His coat, of course, requires a great deal of care if he is to look his best. All in all, the Toy Poodle is a companion or "sleeve dog" without peer.

We assume several things when we take up the Pug. First, we assume the breed originated in China a long time ago. This animal has the pushed-face and curled-tail look of a Chinese dog. We also assume the Pug was never intended for any task except loving, for that is where the Pug fits into human society. The Pug is a child who never grows up. ¶The Pug doesn't have a particularly strong odor, although like all push-faced dogs he does tend to gulp air, and that has predictable results in a closed room. He doesn't shed much, and he doesn't drool. This is altogether a pleasant little dog to have around. He is another of those dogs who make absolute prisoners

Pug

Land of origin: CHINA

Original purpose: Companionship

Recent popularity ranking by A.K.C. registration: 29th

Pug Dog Club of America, Inc.
Mrs. Ann R. White, Secretary
Route 13, Box 45A
Lincoln, NE 68527

HEIGHT: Dogs to 11 inches   Bitches to 10 or 11 inches

WEIGHT: Dogs to 18 pounds   Bitches to 17 pounds

COAT
Fine, smooth, short, glossy, and soft to the touch. Neither hard nor woolly.

COLOR
Black, silver, or apricot fawn. The light-colored dogs have black masks and ears and a dark line or trace on back.

Amount of care coat requires: 1 2 3 4 5 6 7 8 9 10

Amount of exercise required: 1 2 3 4 5 6 7 8 9 10

Suitability for urban/apartment life: 1 2 3 4 5 6 7 8 9 10

of their owner. Pug owners tend to be Pug owners all their lives once they have tried the breed. ¶ A Pug is good with children, although a small child might seem something of a challenge to him. Children, when they get a little older, from five or six on, seem to do better with this breed than in their earlier years. The Pug is jealous of other dogs, and small children seem to get lumped in there. A disgruntled Pug may decide to punish his owner by neglecting previously well understood rules about toilet habits. Pugs, in fact, train well and easily and, once they catch on to the idea of reward at the far end, are not difficult. This dog, however, is always looking for an opening and will quickly take over and run the show if indecision and lack of assertiveness become apparent. For example, a Pug is not a picky eater as a rule, but let an owner start with the diced chicken breast and bonbon routine, and he will have a first-rate food

brat on his hands. In brief, some Pugs, like some children, are a lot smarter than some parents, and it really isn't reaching too far out to suggest that people who avail themselves of a Pug come closer to parenthood than dog ownership. ¶ The character of the Pug—smart, tidy, willing, and loving—should be viewed in light of the breed's development. He does exactly what he was designed to do perhaps a thousand or more years ago. He is only playing the role for which he was cast. ¶ The Pug owner of today is joining a long line of famous and royal men and women who have preferred this breed. Many Pugs have sat beside the throne, and the trick with the Pug is to convince him that he doesn't belong *on* the throne. If you want to love with the absolute certainty of being loved back, you might want to think about the Pug, this dog of ancient China.

The Shih Tzu (pronounced *sheed-zoo*) is a legendary creature who also just happens to exist as a flesh-and-blood companion animal in our own time. We do not know where he came from originally, although the Byzantine Empire, Tibet, and other areas of Asia and the Middle East have been proposed. What we do know is that by the seventh century A. D. the breed was the rage in the royal courts of China. The breed does have the typical Asian-dog pushed face and curled tail, but it is clear his true origins will never be known, so the legends do nicely and add to the character of the beast. ¶ The Shih Tzu probably always was bred for exactly what he is used

Shih Tzu

Land of origin: CHINA since the seventh century; unknown before that

Original purpose: Companionship

Recent popularity ranking by A.K.C. registration: 13th

American Shih Tzu Club, Inc.
Ms. Barbara A. Flaharty, Corres. Secretary
RD 24, Box 929
York, PA 17406-9685

HEIGHT: Dogs to 10½ inches   Bitches to 10 inches

WEIGHT: Dogs to 18 pounds   Bitches to 16 pounds

COAT
Luxurious, long, and dense. May be slightly wavy but never curly. Woolly undercoat.

COLOR
All colors allowed.

Amount of care coat requires: 1 2 3 4 5 6 7 8 9 10

Amount of exercise required: 1 2 3 4 5 6 7 8 9 10

Suitability for urban/apartment life: 1 2 3 4 5 6 7 8 9 10

---

for today: companionship. It is unlikely that he was ever a guard dog or a hunting animal, although he most likely was once a little larger than his present nine to eighteen pounds. His popularity as a companion of kings and queens a thousand years ago is easy to understand when you get to know a few good examples of the breed today. ¶The Shih Tzu, whose name means "lion" in Chinese, is a perfect companion animal for the city dweller who enjoys having something to fuss over. A sprightly little character with great charm and personality, the little chrysanthemum-faced dog prefers the quiet dignity of a well-appointed apartment to the longest dog run in the world. If you gave an adult Shih Tzu an entire national park for a playground, he wouldn't use an acre. For the Shih Tzu, home is where his human family is and where the goodies, the comfort, and the security he demands are. ¶Enormously appealing to fanciers of the toy breeds, the Shih Tzu stands twenty-fourth in popularity of all breeds in America, although he has been known here only since the end of World War II. Although not even accepted by the A.K.C. stud registry until 1969, the breed is already among the top five toys in popularity. ¶The Shih Tzu, needless to say, has a coat that demands attention. This is a dog to cherish and fuss over and enjoy for his great charm, his unfaltering loyalty, his beauty, and his exotic and romantic past.

The Silky Terrier is apparently a cross between the Australian Terrier and the Yorkshire Terrier. Like the latter, he is shown as a toy today, although he is clearly terrier all the way through. ¶ The lovely little eight- to ten-pound Silky is more active than some of the other toy breeds and should get plenty of exercise. He can be an exhausting little creature with his endless demands for attention and action, but most people who have known the breed have felt it was worth the effort. ¶ There are stories of Silky Terriers being used in Australia as ratters and snakers on poultry farms, but knowing something of the character of Australian snakes, I tend to doubt most of

Silky Terrier

Land of origin: AUSTRALIA

Original purpose: Companionship, and to some extent ratting

Recent popularity ranking by A.K.C. registration: 48th

Silky Terrier Club of America, Inc.
Mrs. Florence A. Males, Corres. Secretary
11 Swansea Lane

HEIGHT: Dogs to 10 inches   Bitches to 10 inches

WEIGHT: Dogs to 10 pounds   Bitches to 9 pounds

COAT
Flat, very fine in texture, glossy; decidedly silky; 5 to 6 inches long on mature dog.
Pronounced topknot.

COLOR
Various blues and tan.

Amount of care coat requires: 1 2 3 4 5 6 7 8 9 10
•••••••••••••••••••

Amount of exercise required: 1 2 3 4 5 6 7 8 9 10
•••••••••

Suitability for urban/apartment life: 1 2 3 4 5 6 7 8 9 10
••••••••••••••••••••

those tales. The Silky Terrier is essentially a companion animal, like all toys, and at that task he excels. He is bright to a fault, responsive, demanding, and even, at times, aggressive. Apparently no one has bothered to tell the Silky just how small he is. He makes a great little watchdog, for he does tend to be vocal. In fact, when you add up all of the Silky Terrier's qualities, what you have is a perpetual-motion machine. He is seldom still. ¶A great many people live fairly active lives, even though they are essentially city dwellers. The space available to them may necessitate a small dog, while they may crave an active animal of forceful character. The Silky Terrier is the answer for those people, for he is really the largest dog in the world pushed down into a very small body. ¶The Silky Terrier is one of those breeds with a crowning-glory-type coat, and it does require care. That lovely silky look will last *only* as long as the dog is bathed and brushed and combed and his coat kept from getting stringy and matted looking. It does take all that and some judicious trimming to have a Silky Terrier look like a Silky Terrier is supposed to look. It is important to keep that in mind when considering this breed. ¶There are signs of rising favor for this breed in the United States, and it will be wise to be wary of poorly bred or mass-produced puppies. Some are passed off as Yorkshire Terriers and vice versa. It is wise to stick with an established specialty breeder and avoid all risk.

The Yorkshire Terrier is a fantastic bundle of assertiveness. This cross of perhaps several different terriers with a few toys is a creature of dignity and character. In our household we have a Bloodhound that weighs well over a hundred pounds, a large male Golden Retriever, an English Bulldog bitch, a bitch Siberian Husky, a random-bred shepherd bitch, a Yorkshire Terrier, and several cats. The Yorkie is without question not only the dominant male but the dominant animal. None of the other dogs challenges him or fails to back off when he gives warning of temper. ¶ The Yorkie is a delightful little animal, ideally suited for an apartment and unstinting in

Yorkshire Terrier

Land of origin: ENGLAND

Original purpose: Companionship

Recent popularity ranking by A.K.C. registration: 12th

Yorkshire Terrier Club of America, Inc.
Mrs. Betty R. Dullinger, Secretary
RFD 2, Box 542
Kezar Falls, ME 04047

HEIGHT: Dogs to 9 inches   Bitches to 9 inches

WEIGHT: Dogs to 7 pounds   Bitches to 6 pounds

COAT
Very important—glossy, fine, silky, and long; straight, highly styled.

COLOR
Steel blue and golden tan.

Amount of care coat requires: 1 2 3 4 5 6 7 8 9 10
                       ● ● ● ● ● ● ● ● ● ●

Amount of exercise required: 1 2 3 4 5 6 7 8 9 10
                       ● ●

Suitability for urban/apartment life: 1 2 3 4 5 6 7 8 9 10
                                 ● ● ● ● ● ● ● ● ● ●

his display of affection. He is a participator and expects to be taken along, even if only in a handbag. He couldn't care less about walks and exercise, and many city people simply train him to a cat litter box with fresh newspapers several times a day. ¶What the Yorkshire Terrier saves the owner in long walks in bad weather he makes up in the care his coat demands. It must be seen to, preferably at least once a day. The marvelous little Yorkshire becomes, then, a perfect dog for people who want to fuss. As it happens, many Yorkshire Terrier owners do not brush their pets once a week, much less once or twice a day. Their pets look it. Because his hair does hang to the floor when in its full splendor, the Yorkie quickly is in a first-class mess in the country. Most people keep their Yorkshire Terriers at home. ¶No matter what the owner does, the Yorkshire Terrier is going to run the show. People and animals all get in line, and the little tyrant of the dog world, the marvelously well-organized Yorkshire Terrier, takes over. He spends his every waking hour seeing to the matter of his household. He is a fussbudget, busybody, watchdog, and knockabout dictator. He is among the most lovable and most clever of all dogs. Beware of mass-producers and retailers, for there are *many* poor examples of the breed around. Some are passed off as Silky Terriers, and vice versa. Fine examples of the Yorkshire Terrier are a work of art, and they will both look and act the part.

[Group 7]

The Nonsporting Dogs

Bichon Frise
Boston Terrier
Bulldog
Chow Chow
Dalmation
Finnish Spitz

French Bulldog
Keeshond
Lhasa Apso
Poodle
Schipperke
Tibetan Terrier

The Bichon Frise is a small French toy-like companion dog whose derivation is cloaked in mystery. The breed has been known by many names, we think, and among them may be Tenerife Dog, Curly-coated Poodle, and Bichon à Poil Frise. In all likelihood any number of old French toy breeds went into the makeup of this little white bundle of charm. ¶ The Bichon Frise was bred to be a companion animal. If he fails at that, he fails at everything. He should be gay, playful, affectionate, and lively. The whole attitude should be one of involvement, participation, and willingness. Shy, snappy, or overly moody specimens were probably poorly bred or badly

Bichon Frise

Land of origin: FRANCE

Original purpose: Companionship

Recent popularity ranking by A.K.C. registration: 30th

Bichon Frise Club of America, Inc.
Mrs. Bernice D. Richardson, Corres. Secretary
Route 2, Gulch Lane
Twin Falls, ID 83301

HEIGHT: Dogs to 12 inches   Bitches to 12 inches

WEIGHT: Not specified in breed standards

COAT
Double—outer coat is profuse, silky, loosely curled; 2 inches or longer.

COLOR
Pure white; sometimes with cream, apricot, or gray on ears.

Amount of care coat requires: 1 2 3 4 5 6 7 8 9 10
●●●●●●●●●●●●●●●●●●●

Amount of exercise required: 1 2 3 4 5 6 7 8 9 10
●●●

Suitability for urban/apartment life: 1 2 3 4 5 6 7 8 9 10
●●●●●●●●●●●●●●●●●●●●●

raised. The Bichon Frise should give the impression that he is smiling. When he is serious, he is even more endearing. He is an ideal apartment dog and requires little exercise, although a chase around the coffee table after a rubber toy will be appreciated, perhaps more for the pleasure of interacting with a human being than for the exercise obtained. ¶ Anyone contemplating this breed should keep that coat in mind. It does require care, and the dog you so admire in the show-ring or in photographs will not be the dog you have at home unless you are prepared to give it some time each day. A Bichon Frise can be a matted, ropy mess or a picture-book white muff of a dog. The difference is the time spent allowing the one or achieving the other. ¶ The Bichon Frise is one of the most recent breeds to gain recognition in the United States, and it is attracting a great deal of attention because of the continual demand for ideal urban pets. Its small size and predictable popularity are going to bring a great many unscrupulous backyard breeders into the field. Bichon Frises should be purchased with care. They are enough like other European toys and nonsporting dogs to tempt less-than-honest breeders to use what they can find—the Maltese and other breeds as well. Stick with the professional breeder who is devoted to perfecting and perpetuating this delightful breed. Any would-be owner of this new breed to America's shores may well be in the vanguard with what could be one of the most popular dogs in the country ten to fifteen years from now.

The Boston Terrier, the descendant of the crossing of an English Bulldog and a white English terrier, is an American breed, one of the few. He is also one of the most delightful of canine companions. Naturally bright and high-spirited, this is a consummate pet dog for any setting; farm, suburban home, and city apartment are all equally his natural turf. ¶The Boston has only one use: love. He is certainly not a hunting dog and not a working or herding animal, and although he will bark when strangers approach, he isn't much of a guard dog either. He was bred for loving, and that is what he does best, first, and always. ¶There is great need for city dogs,

Boston Terrier

Land of origin: UNITED STATES

Original purpose: Companionship

Recent popularity ranking by A.K.C. registration: 25th

Boston Terrier Club of America, Inc.
Mrs. Beverly Staley, Corres. Secretary
766 Woodview Drive
Edgewood, KY 41017

HEIGHT: Dogs to 17 inches   Bitches to 16 inches

WEIGHT: Dogs to 25 pounds   Bitches to 19 pounds

COAT
Short, smooth, bright, and fine. Must be shiny and alive.

COLOR
Brindle and white or black and white. Brindle and white with nicely balanced distribution considered best.

Amount of care coat requires: 1 2 3 4 5 6 7 8 9 10

Amount of exercise required: 1 2 3 4 5 6 7 8 9 10

Suitability for urban/apartment life: 1 2 3 4 5 6 7 8 9 10

---

dogs that, although they like exercise and should get their share, are not demanding and do not require long walks in foul weather. The Boston Terrier may fit the bill of the perfect city dog. Any Boston will be grateful for the chance to chase a ball (the breed seems addicted to this sport), but he is content to sit and be quiet or fuss with a rubber toy on the kitchen floor. He wants to be in on everything in the family, but he gives as good as he gets. This is one of the most affectionate of all breeds. The Boston is also intelligent and takes to training with enthusiasm. To a Boston it is all part of the lovely game of living. Fortunately, he tends to be very long-lived, often making it into the upper teens. ¶Bostons hardly shed at all, and they do not have a "doggy" odor. They seldom need bathing, and a minute or two a week with a brush does it all. They are shiny, clean little animals. ¶Like the other short-nosed dogs, Bostons snort and gulp enough air to make them gassy. They

may vomit when upset, but none of these things are bad enough to be a problem. Counter them with the fact that you can housebreak a Boston Terrier in a matter of hours or days. ¶Fortunately or unfortunately, depending on how you view it, the Boston Terrier has long been one of the most popular dogs in America. Examples are registered now at the rate of ten to twelve thousand a year, and so many Bostons are bred for the pet trade that at least as many are not even registered. So be careful when you buy a Boston and avoid the buck-rakers. If you buy from the wrong line, you may not get a superb companion but an idiotic, neurotic, snappy monster. Buy *only* from a recognized specialty breeder and when you have a chance to meet your puppy's parents and see what manner of dogs they are. When you set out to buy this super little dog, you have every right to expect the best in performance and character.

The Bulldog was designed to fight bulls, and that, simply, is how he got his name. He probably also was used to fight bears and other pit animals in a much more cruel era of England's history. Despite all of that nasty background, the English Bulldog of today is a gentle, companionable animal. ¶ The Bulldog is adoring and wants to be adored back. He can do well with other animals as long as they will recognize who is at the top of the order. Bulldogs do not like being challenged or insulted. When a fight does start, all hell breaks loose, and the other dog may be dead before anything effective can be done. Bulldogs should definitely be on leashes when they are apt to encounter strange dogs. ¶ Curiously, bulldogs and cats get along

Bulldog

Land of origin: ENGLAND

Original purpose: Bullbaiting

Recent popularity ranking by A.K.C. registration: 31st

Bulldog Club of America
Ms. Karley Patterson, Secretary
6816 Roswell
Houston, TX 77022

HEIGHT: Dogs to 15 inches   Bitches to 14½ inches

WEIGHT: Dogs to 50 pounds   Bitches to 40 pounds

COAT
Straight, short, flat, close lying, fine, smooth, and glossy.

COLOR
Brindle or red brindle, solid white, solid red or fawn, piebald; colors should be bright and clearly defined.

Amount of care coat requires: 1 2 3 4 5 6 7 8 9 10

Amount of exercise required: 1 2 3 4 5 6 7 8 9 10

Suitability for urban/apartment life: 1 2 3 4 5 6 7 8 9 10

---

very well together as long as the cats understand the position Bulldogs take over a food dish—total possessiveness. There can be unfortunate accidents involving otherwise extremely sweet Bulldogs if this fact is overlooked. If the household contains other animals, Bulldogs are best fed by themselves, and food dishes should not be left around. ¶ With children Bulldogs are another story. They seem to have a built-in sense of manners, and even the smallest child is unlikely to be knocked over. Bulldogs approach babies as if they really did understand their own weight and power. They are flawless pets, giving and getting love endlessly and never tiring of the opportunity to interact with human beings. ¶ There has to be a debit side, and in that column can go snoring. Bulldogs seem to sleep more contentedly than almost any other breed, and they certainly let you know it. The variety of snorts, wheezes, grunts, huffs, and snores that can come from a sleeping Bulldog is nothing less than astounding. ¶ Bulldogs are immensely appealing with their marvelous shoulders-out attitude, and they tend to enslave their owners. They are like superpowered tanks when faced with a challenge, charging forward even when in doubt because of their poor eyesight. Much of that is bluff, however, and a harsh word will turn most Bulldogs off. ¶ Bulldogs like a walk and can be downright frisky pups, but as they mature, they need little strenuous activity. They are fine on the farm, in the suburbs, or in an apartment. They are not long-lived dogs, and ten years would be an old and perhaps even unusual Bulldog. They should *never* be locked in a car, for they mind the heat terribly. More than one Bulldog standing in the sun at a dog show has ended up with an oxygen mask over his face. Their health generally requires careful watching under all circumstances.

This dog of China is at least two thousand years old. There are endless suggestions as to what animals were ancestor to this breed and to which breeds it in turn gave rise. No one knows, and the mystery is compounded by the fact that the Chow Chow is the only breed of dog left on earth with a black mouth. Because the polar bear also has a black mouth, there are absurd stories about a direct line of descent from the great white bear of the North. It may in fact be the ancestral breed to many of the sled and spitz-type dogs we know today— for example, the Akita. It is generally agreed that it did not come from any familiar Western breeds. ¶ The Chow Chow

Chow Chow

Land of origin: CHINA

Original purpose: Probably hunting and some guard work

Recent popularity ranking by A.K.C. registration: 7th

Chow Chow Club, Inc.
Ms. Jill C. Stillwell, Corres. Secretary
Route 3, Box 306-B
Dallas, NC 28034

HEIGHT: Dogs to 20 inches   Bitches to 19 inches

WEIGHT: Dogs to 60 pounds   Bitches to 55 pounds

COAT
Dense, abundant, straight, and off-standing. It is rather coarse in texture, and there is a woolly, much softer undercoat.

COLOR
Any clear color, solid throughout. There are generally lighter shadings on ruff, tail, and breechings.

Amount of care coat requires: 1 2 3 4 5 6 7 8 9 10
• • • • • • • • • • • • • • • •

Amount of exercise required: 1 2 3 4 5 6 7 8 9 10
• • • • • • • • • • • •

Suitability for urban/apartment life:* 1 2 3 4 5 6 7 8 9 10
• • • •

*If properly exercised.

(very often just referred to simply as the Chow) is an aloof and dignified dog. He was used extensively for hunting in China and also, apparently, for guard work. He is not at all demonstrative and can be very hardheaded. He is a massive-looking animal, handsome and powerful, and to some people he appears to be ferocious. The heavy head and ruff and the thick muzzle may give that impression. In fact this dog is not ferocious; he is just very self-contained. He should not be expected to act like a romping hound or a terrier looking for a game; that is not his style. He is loyal, may be affectionate toward his owner, and can be an excellent watchdog. Because he can be a little on the tough side, he should be watched around other animals. This is not always the best breed for a household with children. The Chow Chow may be fine with an owner's kids, but friends of the kids are another matter. ¶That magnificent Chow Chow coat does require a lot of care. Bathing tends to soften it, so it is not recommended any more often than necessary. Constant brushing is essential if mats are to be avoided. There is considerable shedding in the summertime. ¶People looking for a cuddly pet should not look to a Chow Chow. This is an animal of high style; he is both decorative to the discerning and formidable to the uninvited. He is a stunning dog in the show-ring and should be obedience-trained simply because he is powerful and is a bit on the stubborn side. Strangers should not expect much in the way of a greeting. In fact, they should expect to be ignored as long as they do not appear to be threatening toward the household.

The Dalmatian, wherever he came from (the point has been argued in print for more than a century), is a charmer with more ways to please an owner than we can probably record. In their long and varied careers these dogs have been shepherds, guard dogs on border patrol, war dogs as couriers and sentinels, ratters, bird dogs, retrievers, draft dogs, coach dogs, general farm dogs, and household pets. You ask it, and a Dalmatian will do it with élan. We know he was very popular in Dalmatia, part of former Austria-Hungary, in the last century, and hence the name. ¶The Dalmatian is an active animal—a spirited and willing animal who takes train-

Dalmatian

Land of origin: Ancient and unknown, but later AUSTRIA

Original purpose: Hunting, ratting, guard patrol, war, draft dog, shepherd, and coach dog

Recent popularity ranking by A.K.C. registration: 24th

Dalmatian Club of America, Inc.
Mrs. Irvin D. Fleming, Secretary
4390 Chickasaw Road
Memphis, TN 38117

HEIGHT: Dogs to 23 inches   Bitches to 23 inches

WEIGHT: Not specified in breed standards

COAT
Short, hard, dense, fine, sleek, and glossy. Never woolly or silky.

COLOR
Very important in standards. Ground color pure white. Black or liver spots as near uniform in size as possible. Patches a fault. Puppies born pure white.

Amount of care coat requires: 1 2 3 4 5 6 7 8 9 10

Amount of exercise required: 1 2 3 4 5 6 7 8 9 10

Suitability for urban/apartment life: * 1 2 3 4 5 6 7 8 9 10

*But not at all unless given a great deal of exercise.

ing more readily than many other breeds. He loves to run with horses (and horses seem to love being with Dalmatians), and he is a historical necessity in the firehouse. ¶ Wherever the action is, there the Dalmatian wants to be. He isn't yappy, but he will bark with excitement as he runs back and forth along the ladders of fire apparatus rushing into action. He is a good watchdog and is fine with children. ¶ The Dalmatian is devoted to his master above all else and is good within the family circle. While not a particularly suspicious and certainly not a shy dog, he does like to get his facts straight when it comes to strangers. He takes his time and then generally makes a wise decision. ¶ This is a clean dog, easily house-trained and requiring little care. He is hardy and solid, and he loves to be in motion. For that reason he is a questionable choice for city life. Of course, there are city dwellers who lead active lives, taking long walks in the streets and heading out to a country place on weekends and holidays. A Dalmatian can enjoy that kind of life as long as he gets his workouts on schedule. People leading a sedentary life should resist the perfectly understandable temptation to own one of these splendid animals and should look elsewhere for a pet to share their quiet life-style. ¶ There is an inherited tendency for deafness among Dalmatians, and the prospective owner should be cautious before confirming a purchase. The spots are extremely important in judging this breed and in the ideal those on the body should not be smaller than a dime or larger than a half-dollar. The spots on the head and face should be smaller than on the body and should be separate and distinct with as little running together as possible. A well-put-together Dalmatian is a beautiful animal. People have apparently thought so since ancient times.

This active, spry busy-body is the national dog of Finland where it is known by the virtually unpronounceable name of *Suomenpystykorva*. Very little was done to establish standards for the breed until the end of the 19th Century, when a few enthusiasts travelled through northern Lapland looking for outstanding examples of a dog that had been known in the region for several thousand years. It was already the most popular and frequently encountered dog in both cities and on farms. It was known as an absolutely fierce hunter despite is relatively small size. ¶The origins of the Finnish Spitz remain a mystery in part because of its antiquity. It is said to have derived from the ubiquitous pariah dog that is found near human settlements around the world yet it is a typical northern spitz-type dog, a group that includes the Norwegian Elkhound, the Keeshond and all of the sled dogs including the Samoyed and Husky from Siberia and the Malamute from Alaska. In any case, there is surely a good deal of wolf in the genes of this breed as there is in the genes of all of the northern dogs. That means more than the genes of their original wolf ances-

Finnish Spitz

Land of origin: Ancient and not really known. Reportedly in Finland and Lapland for thousands of years.

Original Purpose: Hunting—everything from squirrel to bear.

Recent popularity ranking by A.K.C. registration: Too soon to tell. Standard not accepted until June, 1987.

Finnish Spitz Club of American
Bette Isacoff
4000 Houcks Road
Monkton, MD 21111

HEIGHT: Dogs to 20 inches   Bitches to 18 inches

WEIGHT: Not in published standards

COAT
Double. Short, soft, dense undercoat (which sheds out in warm weather) and long, harsh straight guard hairs measuring one to two inches on the body. Coat very imnportant in judging. No trimming except for feet is allowed.

COLOR
Bright and clear, pale honey to deep auburn. Undercoat paler. Only white allowed is on tips of toes and quarter-sized spot or half inch wide white stripe on chest. Sparse, individual black hairs on tail and back allowed, the fewer the better.

Amount of care coat requires: 1 2 3 4 5 6 7 8 9 10

Amount of exercise required: 1 2 3 4 5 6 7 8 9 10

Suitability for urban/apartment life: 1 2 3 4 5 6 7 8 9 10

tor, but includes input along the way as the breed evolved in high northern latitudes. ¶It wasn't until 1927 that the first pair of the reconstructed Finnish Spitz was brought to Great Britain and seven years later that the Kennel Club accorded the breed recognition. By the early 1970's the breed began showing up in Canada and by 1974 it was recognized by the Canadian Kennel Club. It made its way south and is now recognized in the United States. It was well known here well before the time recognition came. It has been a long trip for a breed dearly beloved by all who own them. ¶The overall look of the Finnish Spitz is best described as foxy and very alert. It is a compact, solid little dog that should never be either coarse or snipey. It is a dog of balance and style. ¶On the first encounter with a stranger, a Finnish Spitz is likely to be cautious, but that should not mean shy. Shyness is a fault. When the ice has been broken the Finnish Spitz is typically friendly, active, very lively and willing to engage in any game or activity. It is a brave little dog and faithfulness is to be expected and that means a good watch dog with a sharp alarm bark. ¶The Finnish Spitz makes a fine house pet as long as it gets a reasonable amount of exercise. Owners who are willing to give some care to that glorious reddish coat with the handsome neck and tail display, and who are able to attend a basic obedience course with their dog are certain to have a first class pet that is at once very well mannered and a splendid display piece. The affection part of the contract comes naturally to any health dog that is treated well.

If there is such a thing as a perfect apartment dog, the French Bulldog could be it. He certainly would be in the finals when the choice was made. This is a neat, clean, compact dog who sheds hardly at all, is easily trained, has nice manageable habits, and doesn't need or really want too much exercise. ¶The French Bulldog has nearly caused international incidents: the English laugh at the name, recognizing in the breed a miniature of the English Bulldog that didn't suit the English fancy and was exported to France; the French, in a kind of desperate thrashing around, claim him as an original. The English are undoubtedly right, but that's history, and it doesn't

French Bulldog

Land of origin: ENGLAND and FRANCE

Original purpose: Companionship

Recent popularity ranking by A.K.C. registration: 89th

French Bulldog Club of America
Mr. David F. Kruger, Secretary
816 Fairfax Drive
Gretna, LA 70056

HEIGHT: Dogs to 12 inches   Bitches to 12 inches

WEIGHT: Dogs to 28 pounds   Bitches to 22 pounds

COAT
Moderately fine, short, and smooth. Skin soft and loose.

COLOR
Solid brindle, fawn, white, brindle and white, and any colors *except* black and white, black and tan, liver, mouse, or solid black.

Amount of care coat requires: 1 2 3 4 5 6 7 8 9 10

Amount of exercise required: 1 2 3 4 5 6 7 8 9 10

Suitability for urban/apartment life: 1 2 3 4 5 6 7 8 9 10

much matter. What does matter is that the French Bulldog is an outstanding companion animal under the right circumstances. ¶The ideal situation for this breed is an apartment or house with a single person. The French Bulldog does not like to share and is not keen on strangers. This breed is also less than perfect with children. That is not to say that a French Bulldog would not settle down and become a good family dog—the family including a parcel of youngsters—because a great many have. It is just that if one were to seek the ideal setting, it would be with one person in need of getting and giving boundless affection and one French Bulldog in the same situation. ¶The overall impression one gets from one of these little companions is of a muscular, alert animal of good substance and intelligence. And all of that

is true. Size is important, and dogs over twenty-eight pounds in weight are disqualified from showing. ¶If a person wants to show a dog, this is a good breed to consider. There aren't too many of them around, so the competition is not overwhelming, and the dog is easy to transport because of his small size. His coat requires virtually no care, so there is not a lot of get-ready time. Pick up your dog and walk into the ring ready to go. ¶A single person seeking both love and involvement might find owning and showing a French Bulldog just about a perfect outlet. None of this should discourage other categories of owners, though, for this dog also will be happy on a farm. He may not do a heck of a lot of work, but he will be happy as long as he has access to his special person. And there is always a special person in the life of a French Bulldog.

The Keeshond (the plural form is *Kees-honden*) has a complex and colorful history. In the period just before the French Revolution, the followers of the Prince of Orange, known as the Partisans, were vying with a group known as the Patriots to become the dominant political force in Holland. The leader of the Patriots was a man called Kees de Gyselaer of Dordrecht. He owned a dog, also called Kees, an example of a breed we know today as the Kees-hond. The dog became the symbol of the Patriots, a party of working-class people. ¶ In time the Prince of Orange prevailed, and a lot of people apparently felt it best not to have living symbols of the opposition around the house. The Keeshond did not so much fall from favor as vanish for safety reasons. Once seen on all the small barges moving along the canals and in almost every farmhouse, the Keeshond soon became something of a rarity. About 1920 the Bar-

Keeshond

Land of origin: HOLLAND

Original purpose: Companionship and as watchdog

Recent popularity ranking by A.K.C. registration: 36th

Keeshond Club of America
Ms. Jeanne Buente-Young, Secretary
Kiousville-Palestine Rd.
Mt. Sterling, OH 43143

HEIGHT: Dogs to 18 inches   Bitches to 17 inches

WEIGHT: Dogs to 40 pounds   Bitches to 36 pounds

COAT
Abundant, long, straight, harsh, and off-standing. Thick downy undercoat. On legs, smooth and short except for feathering. On tail, profuse and plumelike. Never silky, wavy, or curly and not parting on back.

COLOR
Mixture of gray and black. Undercoat pale gray or cream. Outer-coat hairs black tipped. White markings not allowed. Dark spectacle markings on face typical and desirable.

Amount of care coat requires: 1 2 3 4 5 6 7 8 9 10

Amount of exercise required: 1 2 3 4 5 6 7 8 9 10

*Suitability for urban/apartment life:**   1 2 3 4 5 6 7 8 9 10

*As long as proper exercise is provided.

oness van Hardenbroek took an interest in the breed and found enough good examples still left to re-establish it in Holland and, since then, around the world. ¶The Keeshond is another perfect house dog. Handsome, small, and companionable, he is generally quieter and perhaps more sensible than the other spitzlike breeds to which he is related. All the relationships have not been worked out, but it is likely the Keeshond has common ancestry with the Pomeranian, Samoyed, Norwegian Elkhound, and Finnish Spitz. ¶The splendid little Hollander depends a great deal on his handsome coat for his high style, and there is daily work involved in keeping it in good condition. The hair is brushed against the grain to keep it off-standing. Since washing tends to soften hair and make it floppy, the Keeshond is seldom, if ever, bathed. ¶The Keeshond is a loyal, loving family dog and a good watchdog, and he is easygoing with other animals. He does not take immediately to strangers but will accept those who do not appear to be threatening to his home and family. He should be walked regularly, of course, but the Keeshond does well in the suburban home and the apartment. This dog has an engaging personality and a lot of style. Mass-producers and retailers have tended to make something of a mess of this breed, producing outsized and unpleasant-looking specimens, so the prospective Keeshond owner should head for the specialty breeder. The Keeshond seldom disappoints the new owner who has taken the time and trouble to learn about the breed and to seek a fine specimen. Charming in the show-ring and never failing to attract attention, they are equally desirable as family pets.

The Lhasa Apso, one of the four breeds that we know came from the mountains of Tibet, was the small companion animal kept inside the house to warn of intruders. Outside was the fierce Tibetan Mastiff. The Lhasa Apso, because he was the inside dog, naturally became a pet. He is bred for that role today and is rapidly increasing in popularity. Aiding his rise in favor is the fact that he is a perfect city companion and has high style and charm. ¶ Lhasa Apsos are devoted to their masters and mistresses and to their families. They are forever suspicious of strangers, a characteristic that harks back to their early role as watchdogs. Strangers coming into the

Lhasa Apso

Land of origin: TIBET

Original purpose: Companionship and as inside watchdog

Recent popularity ranking by A.K.C. registration: 15th

American Lhasa Apso Club, Inc.
Mr. Stephen G.C. Campbell, Secretary
37 Greenwood Dr.
Freehold, NJ 07728

HEIGHT: Dogs to 11 inches   Bitches to 10½ inches

WEIGHT: Dogs to 15 pounds   Bitches to 14 pounds

COAT
Heavy, straight, hard, and dense. Not woolly or silky. Long.

COLOR
Golden, sandy, honey, dark grizzle, slate, smoke, parti-color, black, white, or brown. Golden or lionlike colors are considered best. Dark tips to ears and beard very good.

Amount of care coat requires: 1 2 3 4 5 6 7 8 9 10

Amount of exercise required: 1 2 3 4 5 6 7 8 9 10

Suitability for urban/apartment life: 1 2 3 4 5 6 7 8 9 10

---

home should let them be, and allow them to make any overtures. Pushing yourself on a strange Lhasa Apso is one way of forcing an issue and making him snappy. ¶ Because the Lhasa Apso is such a demanding pet, this is not always the best breed to have around young children. He will be in direct competition for the role of baby of the house and will tend to be jealous and resentful. This is a strong-minded, purposeful little animal, not a pushover in any category. The owner should establish at the start who is to be master of the house. The Lhasa Apso is perfectly willing to take over and become a splendid despot, and if that happens only the owner is to blame. ¶ The coat of the Lhasa Apso, one of his shining highlights, does require care, considerable care, and enough time should be left each

day to bring it up to full glory and keep it there. The Lhasa Apso will compensate for the time you spend on his coat by not demanding long walks in nasty weather. Although his typical Tibetan coat (all Tibetan dogs apparently have that heavy coat and the upcurled tail seen in this breed) will enable him to withstand any weather you are likely to encounter, the dog does not crave long walks and is happy around the house. ¶ The Lhasa will take training readily and will always strive to please family members. He is playful and affectionate and loyal. He has risen so suddenly in popularity in the last few years that it is wise to be careful when making a purchase. Make sure you are getting a really good puppy from a truly good line or you will inherit a bundle of bad manners and disappointing conformation.

No one really knows where the Poodle originally came from. It almost
certainly is not France, despite the fact
that he is so often referred to as the French
Poodle. It may have been Germany, although even that is doubtful. The breed is
probably of great antiquity. ¶ Almost everywhere in the world that the breed is known
it is at the top of the popularity chart. In the
United States it is consistently in first
place. Many reasons are put forward for

this phenomenon, but the answer probably
lies in intelligence. The Poodle is one of
the most intelligent of all dogs. He seems
able to learn anything, he makes a fine
watchdog, and he is an excellent water retriever. We are told that the exaggerated
clips we see today are outgrowths of clips
that facilitated the retrieving Poodle in water. The name *Poodle* is derived from the
German slang word *pudeln*, which means,
roughly, to splash around in the water.

Poodle

Land of origin: Possibly GERMANY but not really known

Original purpose: Probably water retrieving

Recent popularity ranking by A.K.C. registration: 3rd

Poodle Club of America, Inc.
Mrs. Richard Kiczek, Corres. Secretary
S. New Boston Rd., P.O. Box 211
Francestown, NH 03043-0211

HEIGHT
Standard—dogs and bitches over 15 inches

Miniature—dogs and bitches between 10 and 15 inches

WEIGHT
Standard—Dogs to 55 pounds   Bitches to 50 pounds

Miniature—*Dogs to 16 pounds   Bitches to 15 pounds

COAT
Naturally harsh in texture, extremely profuse and dense. Seen in a variety of clips.

COLOR
Solid only, never parti-colored. Colors seen include blue, gray, silver, brown, café au lait, apricot, cream, black, and white.

Amount of care coat requires:† 1 2 3 4 5 6 7 8 9 10
•••••••••••••••••••

Amount of exercise required:‡ 1 2 3 4 5 6 7 8 9 10
•••••••••••••

Suitability for urban/apartment life:§ 1 2 3 4 5 6 7 8 9 10
••••••••••••••••••••

---

*See Toy Poodle for specifications of that variety.
†Varies somewhat with style of clip and age of dog.
‡Larger varieties require more.
§If appropriate exercise is provided.

¶The Poodle in his magnificent show clip is the brunt of many jokes, and the uninformed sometimes see it as an effete kind of status symbol. Were they to know! The Poodle in any clip is a superb dog—assertive, extremely responsive, loyal, and intelligent beyond belief. ¶Because Poodles come in such a variety of colors and can be clipped in so many ways, they serve any taste. That, too, no doubt, has added to their popularity. They do not shed, although their hair is fast growing and has no apparent maximum length. It keeps right on growing as long as you let it. It does need regular clipping and styling—every four to six weeks—and that is a chore many people prefer to leave to the experts. It is not inexpensive, but the Poodle, owners feel, are worth the investment. ¶Poodles get along well with children, and with other dogs and cats. They fit in and respond to the people around them in an almost uncanny way. A Poodle in the family is truly like having an extra person on hand. There is nothing Poodles do not seem to understand. They are, as a result, immensely popular and probably will be for a long time to come.

The Schipperke, a dog from the Flemish areas of Belgium and to some extent northern France, is not of spitz derivation, although this has been suggested. He is bred down from the Belgian Sheepdog and is a version of the sheepdog known as the Leauvenaar. The name *Schipperke* (pronounced *skip-er-key*) is Flemish for "little captain" and refers to his use as a watchdog on barges that plied the rivers and canals of northern Europe. ¶Generally an outstanding pet, the Schipperke is a born watchdog. Though not argumentative or snappy, he is very curious about everything that is going on around him. He checks out things and people and will be

Schipperke

Land of origin: FLEMISH BELGIUM

Original purpose: House companionship and as watchdog

Recent popularity ranking by A.K.C. registration: 50th

Schipperke Club of America, Inc.
Mrs. Lee Ann Stusnick, Secretary
101 Eight Avenue
Plattsmouth, NE 68048

HEIGHT: Dogs to 13 inches   Bitches to 12 inches

WEIGHT: Dogs to 18 pounds   Bitches to 16 pounds

COAT
Abundant, longer on neck, forming ruff or cape. Undercoat short and dense. Outer coat somewhat harsh to touch.

COLOR
Solid black only.

Amount of care coat requires: 1 2 3 4 5 6 7 8 9 10

Amount of exercise required: 1 2 3 4 5 6 7 8 9 10

*Suitability for urban/apartment life:**   1 2 3 4 5 6 7 8 9 10

---

*If properly exercised.

---

quick to let you know if he finds anything amiss. He is a vivacious dog, intelligent, loyal, and very responsive to his own family and their likes and needs. He has one outstanding specialty, though: children. He is naturally drawn to them and watches them constantly. He is not only their companion but also their guardian. His small size makes him an ideal house pet. ¶The bobbed tail and foxy face of this lively little outdoor dog is most distinctive, and the breed just can't be confused with any other. He does well on the farm, where he makes a good ratter, and he has been used to hunt small game; he will be equally fine in the suburbs and the city. In an apartment there is an obligation to provide exercise. The Schipperke needs walks several times a day, and in the country a good romp is deeply appreciated. ¶The Schipperke's coat is deep and sheds water. It will take any weather and does shed out in the summer. It is easy to care for, and a good brushing a couple of times a week will keep it in order. ¶The Schipperke, while never a fad dog in this country, has a devoted following. People who get to know the many fine qualities of this breed tend to stick with it. It is a long-lived breed, and more than a few individual dogs have been known to reach seventeen or eighteen years. Schipperkes are strong, durable, healthy, and easy to keep.

The *exact* origin of this ancient breed cannot be established. It was almost certainly somewhere in or near Tibet or China, however. This gay little sprite is related to the Pekingese, Pug and Japanese Chin but is distinctly not a spaniel anymore than the Tibetan Terrier is a terrier. ¶It is believed that the breed did finally evolve in closely-guarded kennels in Tibetan monasteries. It has been called the Tibetan prayer dog because one of its duties is said to have been to turn the prayer wheels. It was probably more heavily relied upon as a companion, good luck charm and watch dog. It is still doing those jobs today although the good luck part is really a matter of personal faith. ¶The first Tibetan Terriers in the U.K. arrived in 1920. In the mid-60's they began appearing in North America. The breed is now recognized in

Tibetan Spaniel

Land of origin: Tibet/China

Recent popularity ranking by A.K.C. registration: 107th

Tibetan Spaniel Club of America
Herb Rosen, Secretary
11404 Lhasa Lane
Lutherville, MD 21093

HEIGHT: About 10 inches

WEIGHT: 9 to 15 pounds

COAT
Double, silky, smooth on face and front of legs, moderate on body but lies rather flat. Ears and back of legs well feathered.

COLOR
All colors and mixture of colors allowed.

Amount of care coat requires: 1 2 3 4 5 6 7 8 9 10

Amount of exercise required: 1 2 3 4 5 6 7 8 9 10

Suitability for urban/apartment life: 1 2 3 4 5 6 7 8 9 10

the United States and Canada. ¶This little dog is typically gay and very assertive. It is active and alert and is extremely intelligent, enough so to be overtly manipulative. Although it tends to be aloof with strangers it is deeply involved in everything that goes on within its family circle. It likes to initiate as much of that activity as possible but will be happy playing by your game plan as long as it is in the thick of things. It is not a passive animal. You can't be when you believe the world was invented for your personal enjoyment. ¶Despite its obvious antiquity the Tibetan Spaniel is a "new breed" to the West and therefore offers an opportunity to get in on the formation years where the Western version of the breed is developed. It will probably become one of those very popular breeds, well suited to relatively small living quarters. It has a quality badly needed by millions of people; it gives humans the sense of being needed. A great many people do need to be needed and that kind of situation suits the Tibetan Spaniel just fine. ¶This breed requires enough coat care to keep the owner-pet interaction regular and ideally routine. That is good for both man and beast. It is a pretty little dog and that provides a sense of pride. Tibetan Spaniels take very readily to being spoiled and that works well in the relationship between dog and owner, too. For many kinds of people the Tibetan Spaniel is a breed made in heaven. It is supposed by many that that is where the monasteries of the Himalayas are. ¶When a dog so perfectly fits so many human personality types and needs it must reckoned a welcome addition to our national canine picture. One thing is certain, the Tibetan Spaniel, vain little commander that he is, is sure that that is the case.

Tibetan Terrier

Land of origin: TIBET

Original purpose: As mascot and watchdog; was held sacred

Recent popularity ranking by A.K.C. registration: 86th

Tibetan Terrier Club of America, Inc.
Ms. Marteen Nolan, Secretary
100 West US Highway 6
Valperaiso, IN 46383

HEIGHT: Dogs to 16 inches   Bitches to 16 inches

WEIGHT: Dogs to 23 pounds   Bitches to 22 pounds

COAT
Double—undercoat is a fine wool; outer coat profuse and fine but not silky or woolly. Long and either straight or waved.

COLOR
Any color, including white, or any combination of colors. Nose must be black.

Amount of care coat requires: 1 2 3 4 5 6 7 8 9 10

Amount of exercise required: 1 2 3 4 5 6 7 8 9 10

Suitability for urban/apartment life:* 1 2 3 4 5 6 7 8 9 10

*If properly exercised.

The Tibetan Terrier is another of those Asian breeds that comes down to us from ancient times loaded with legend, romance, and tradition. The Tibetan Terrier was said to have been bred exclusively by monks in a hidden valley and only given as gifts to honored friends (usually visiting monks), never sold. Only males were ever given, and these sometimes were crossed with the so-called Tibetan Spaniels. The dog was slow in reaching the outside world and is now attracting a great deal of attention. ¶The Tibetan Terrier is distinctly *not* a terrier. He was named that years ago when all large dogs were called *guard dogs*, all medium-sized dogs *hunting dogs*, and all small breeds *terriers*. It is doubtful that there is a trace of terrier in the breed; a more likely choice would be a spaniel-like dog and some small form of mastiff. Misnamed or not, the Tibetan Terrier is a fine, solid little character and one treasured by those lucky enough to own examples. They are good watchdogs, being slow to take up with strangers. They are busybodies and participators. In the city they can tolerate limited exercise, but they love a good romp, particularly in the country. ¶The look of the Tibetan Terrier is solid and square. He moves well, and although not "hyper" and silly, he is active and playful. He is fetching as a puppy and should become popular fairly quickly now that he is here and has American Kennel Club recognition (approved in 1973). Tibetan Terriers still vary in size, and no doubt a preference will be shown in the years ahead and the standards altered accordingly. ¶There is a studied ragamuffin look about the Tibetan Terrier, but the coat does require some attention every day or it can become tangled. ¶This breed is bound to become a super niche fitter. The real popularity days of the Tibetan Terrier may be just ahead.

Afterword

If you have this book, it is reasonable to assume you have an interest in dogs, or at least *a* dog. There are some matters that transcend breed, however, and have a great deal to do with all dog owners.

Don't breed your own pet, except in truly exceptional cases. The individual dogs photographed by Alton Anderson for this book are outstanding representatives of their kind. Many of them are the best examples in the United States today, or at least they have won more Best-of-Breed, Group l's, and Best-in-Show ribbons than nearly all other members of their breed now alive. The chances are your pet will not look quite as much like the idealized dog as these specimens do. Unless you pay a considerable amount of money for your pet, and then are very lucky, your dog will be a lovable example of what we call *pet quality*. No pet-quality dog should ever be bred, for the following simple reason: There are already far too many puppies. The shelters, pounds, and humane societies in this country destroy between thirteen and fifteen million puppies and kittens every year—many of which are pure-bred (not that it matters if a homeless puppy is pure-bred or random-bred). Or perhaps there are far too few suitable homes. Either way, the tragedy can be reduced in dimensions only if fewer puppies are born.

What dogs should be bred? Only those that are such outstanding examples of their breed that their individual genetic potential is really needed for the continuation and even the improvement of the breed. These finest dogs will produce more than enough pet-quality puppies in time to fulfill most people's desire to own an example of one breed or another.

So, again, unless you have invested heavily in a dog and have shown it all the way through to champion status, do not allow it to produce puppies that will add to that already tragic surplus. Even if you find homes, good homes, for each of the puppies you allow to come into this world, you will be killing another puppy. For each one you place, another will sit unadopted in a cage until its time runs out. You will have used up a home. *One puppy placed is another puppy killed.* Sad, but it is the truth.

What about random-bred dogs, so called mutts or mongrels? All dog breeds were mixed at some stage in their development. The histories of those breeds that came into being in recent enough times for records to survive show a blending of several and sometimes many breeds to achieve a desired result. With the mixed-breed dog found today by the millions in shelters, the mix is admittedly random and the result that will be produced—what the puppy will look like when it matures, for example—is not easily predictable. But an interest in pure-bred dogs should not be an exercise in snobbery. Random-bred dogs can make magnificent pets and fit in very well in a multi-dog household. Nevertheless, all random-bred animals, males as well as females, should be neutered as soon as your veterinarian says it is safe to do so. No random-bred animal should ever be bred, again because of the staggering surplus.

I have stressed time and again in the breed descriptions that certain dogs should be obedience trained professionally, or that the dog in question will make a much better pet if a professional guides you in your training regimen. That advice can be misleading only in that I did not stress it in every breed description. I should have. All dogs are better for obedience training; all kinds of problems with housebreaking, chewing, barking, car chasing, wandering, and a good many more irksome traits, can generally be solved by basic obedience training. Just *Come, Sit, Stay, Down, Heel,* and most especially *No* are usually enough to turn a monster of a dog into a mature and stable friend.

Somewhere near where you live there is a humane society struggling to stay alive and carry out its mission of mercy and humane education. If you care enough about dogs to own one, care enough to help out. Locate the humane society nearest you and pitch in. If you can't spare time, perhaps you can spare dollars. If pet owners don't care to help other pets in trouble, who will? On the national level I think The Humane Society of the United States (1100 L St. N.W., Washington, D.C. 20037) is the one to join. Why not write to them and find out what they are doing to help solve the seemingly endless array of humane problems this country faces.

When you accept the responsibility of a dog you should give careful consideration to your friends and neighbors. Their affection for, even tolerance of dogs may be limited in some cases. Don't let your dog become a nuisance, and never let it become a menace. Your neighbor's shrubs are not for wetting, and no one wants to hear your dog bark and yowl. No one, certainly, wants to have their kid thrown from a bicycle or their car charged by an ill-mannered dog. All of those matters must be under your firm control. Your dogs must fit in and be good citizens.

Man apparently began keeping dogs about twenty thousand years ago. There were pure-bred dogs almost ten thousand years ago. There must be something to it. Of course, there is. It is a fine idea, one of the most durable man has ever had. And since it is such a good idea, it is worth doing right. Congratulations on your decision to get a dog; once that decision has been made, pick wisely and love a lot. You will be rewarded with ten to fifteen years of enormous pleasure.

Roger Caras

Photographer's Note

In photographing the dogs for this book I have often felt I was hobnobbing with royalty—the dog's aristocracy deriving not only from their distinguished ancestry, the result of great breeding, but also from their crowns earned in ring competition. Many of the dogs are at the very top of their breed. Even included is the number one champion of all breeds in the country—the white poodle.

The great ones have usually been the easiest to photograph. Their ring presence carries over into their photographs. Consider the Irish Setter: When I asked the professional handler to have him turn his head "a little bit this way," the dog understood and did it!

Any camera can take good dog pictures. All it requires is some knowledge of the breed you're photographing and, most important, patience and practice. The camera I use is a Mamiya RB67 (Pro S). RB stands for *revolving back*, which gives me a horizontal or vertical negative without taking the camera from the tripod. The negative size is 2¼ inches by 2¾ inches, several times larger than a standard 35mm negative. This permits me to enlarge a portion of a negative and still get sufficient quality without excess film grain. Although I always use an exposure meter, the information sheet included with most film is very accurate when photographing dogs outdoors; the only variation to remember: Close your camera diaphragm at least one half stop for light-colored dogs and open at least one half stop for dark-colored dogs. Try to photograph only in bright sunlight. You need the brilliant light to give the coat sparkle and "aliveness."

A typical exposure outdoors on a sunny day, using Kodacolor 400 film, would be ¹/₂₅₀ of a second at f16. You need fast film to stop action, and also to get sufficient depth of field to have your dog portraits sharp. If you have a short focal length lens, let's say 90mm or less, you will have to worry about distortion. With a longer focal length lens, minimum 127mm (which is what I use), your pictures will be better. If you have a short focal length lens, you should stand farther away from the dog, then enlarge only a portion of the negative. You will lose some print quality, but there will be no distortion.

Although I usually shoot about fifty pictures at a dog sitting, I consider myself fortunate if I end up with one outstanding portrait. On rare occasions almost every exposure results in a good picture, but some breeds, notably terriers, are such bundles of motion that a good picture requires great patience.

In photographing indoors with flash, you can still use Kodacolor 400 since this film is balanced for flash lighting (daylight). However, I prefer incandescent light, in the form of quartz iodide units. Using a light meter, a typical exposure is $1/60$ of a second at f8 or f11, depending on whether the dog is dark- or light-colored. But with incandescent light you must use a proper indoor film, available from Kodak at specialty photo shops in only slow film (ASA 100).

If you are using flash with outdoor film, remember to use the flash off-camera, above or to the right or left, about two to three feet from the camera. This is necessary to prevent "hot spots" in the dog's eyes. If the flash unit is attached to the camera, have the dog face away from the camera.

You may have noticed that the full-dog photos in this book are without a handler holding up a tail or head. What I was trying to do was to portray these champion dogs the way most of us see our dogs: outdoors and around the house, sitting and lying down, in relaxed attitudes.

In photographing the many breeds (some of them very rare), professional handlers were most helpful, and I appreciate their kindness. Among area people I thank Ele (Eleanor) Wilson; Roger Cornell, who owns a fictitious guard dog and has dire warnings posted on his exterior doors; Bob and Sylvia Sherman, color processors who were often baffled by dog coat colors, since they have been conditioned to human flesh tones; and, finally, Allen and Mara Borack conversion (color-to-black-and-white, panalure) experts, whose love of dogs was so evident. What wonderful people!

Alton Anderson

Index